CONTEMPORARY NOVELISTS AND THE

AESTHETICS OF TWENTY-FIRST

CENTURY AMERICAN LIFE

THE NEW AMERICAN CANON:

THE IOWA SERIES IN

CONTEMPORARY

LITERATURE

AND

CULTURE

Samuel Cohen,

series editor

CONTEMPORARY NOVELISTS AND THE AESTHETICS OF TWENTY-FIRST CENTURY AMERICAN LIFE

by Alexandra Kingston-Reese

University of Iowa Press,
Iowa City

University of Iowa Press, Iowa City 52242
Copyright © 2019 by the University of Iowa Press
www.uipress.uiowa.edu
Printed in the United States of America

Design by Ashley Muehlbauer

No part of this book may be reproduced or used in any form or by any means without permission in writing from the publisher. All reasonable steps have been taken to contact copyright holders of material used in this book. The publisher would be pleased to make suitable arrangements with any whom it has not been possible to reach.

Printed on acid-free paper

Library of Congress Cataloging-in-Publication Data

Names: Kingston-Reese, Alexandra, 1989– author.
Title: Contemporary novelists and the aesthetics of twenty-first century American life / Alexandra Kingston-Reese.
Description: Iowa City : University of Iowa Press, 2020. | Series: The new American canon : the Iowa series in contemporary literature and culture | Includes bibliographical references and index.
Identifiers: LCCN 2019010728 (print) | LCCN 2019981283 (ebook) | ISBN 9781609386757 (paperback) | ISBN 9781609386764 (ebook other)
Subjects: LCSH: American fiction—21st century—History and criticism. | Art and literature—United States.56 | Cognitive dissonance in literature. | Affect (Psychology) in literature. | Realism in literature. | Life in literature. | Literature—Psychology. | Experimental literature, American—History and criticism.
Classification: LCC PS374.A76 K56 2020 (print) | LCC PS374.A76 (ebook) | DDC 813/.92093561—dc23
LC record available at https://lccn.loc.gov/2019010728
LC ebook record available at https://lccn.loc.gov/2019981283

For Sam, in whose company time stills

CONTENTS

Acknowledgments ix

Preface xi

INTRODUCTION: The Aesthetics of
Contemporary American Life 1

CHAPTER 1: Enstrangement 31

CHAPTER 2: Slant Rhyme 57

CHAPTER 3: Synesthesia 91

CHAPTER 4: Transcription 109

CHAPTER 5: Suspension 134

AFTERWORD: Politics of Aesthetic
Experience Now 167

Notes 173

Works Cited 179

Index 195

ACKNOWLEDGMENTS

Writing *Contemporary Novelists and the Aesthetics of Twenty-First Century American Life* has been a truly international affair. I have written parts in Aotearoa/New Zealand, Sydney, London, York, Copenhagen, New York, and Austin, on trains and planes, in galleries, and in airports. The intellectual support I have received from my friends and colleagues in the Department of English and Related Literature at the University of York has given it a home. To Nicoletta Asciuto, *grazie mille*; to Katherine Ebury and JT Welsch, for the warmest welcome possible; to Cadence Kinsey, Michael McCluskey, Jane Raisch, and Hannah Roche, for enriching conversation about the book and too many other things to account for; to Derek Attridge, John Bowen, Matt Campbell, Kenneth Clarke, Hugh Haughton, Adam Kelly, Deborah Russell, Freya Sierhuis, Claire Westall, and James Williams, for term-time sympathy, as well as invaluable and entertaining advice; to Victoria Coulson, for the brilliant anecdote about Zadie Smith and Billie Holliday that didn't end up making it into the book but nevertheless shaped my work on Smith in many ways; to Claire Chambers, Emilie Morin, and Gillian Russell, for their unwavering support and intellectual generosity; and to Helen Smith, for helping me make space for writing amid the chaos of teaching. This book has also benefited from the superb conversations emerging from my research strand Creative Dissonance: Writing Now and its reading group. Thank you to the Centre for Modern Studies at the University of York for funding it. I owe my warmest thanks to my colleague and collaborator Bryan Radley, whose work on humor taught me to never take my work on negative feeling too seriously.

Outside of York, special thanks to Alix Beeston for conversations about navigating life in foreign lands and for her thoughtful attention to an early draft; to David Alworth, Kevin Brazil, Catherine Gander, Dorothy Hale, Cara Lewis, and Alys Moody, for being wonderful interlocutors about art and contemporary literature; to Eleanor Catton, for our inspiring conversation about the novel today; and to David James, for his unwavering and generous support of the book from its early stages to the very end.

Though the writing of this book has come to an end in the Northern Hemisphere, it began in the English Department at the University of Sydney. The research ethos of friends and mentors there affected the book's intellectual investments in unshakable ways. Rebecca Johinke played a vital role in shaping my critical sensibilities, inspiring me to read and write with aesthetic attachment in mind.

It has been a pleasure to work with Samuel Cohen ever since our first email exchange—thank you for thinking of the project for the New American Canon series. Thanks also to the editors and staff at the University of Iowa Press for the object this has become. Early versions of material in chapter 2 were published as "Teju Cole and Ralph Ellison's Aesthetics of Invisibility" and "Slant Rhyming"; thank you to the editors of *Mosaic* and Abram Foley at *ASAP/J* for permission to reprint and expand on work that saw the first light of day in their pages. I am particularly indebted to Teju Cole for his generous permission to use his photographs in the book.

Finally, I am immensely grateful for the steadfast encouragement of my friends and family for always listening, questioning, bolstering, comforting, and distracting. *Arohanui*. Sam, this book is dedicated to you; I could not have done it without you.

PREFACE

In an essay for *Frieze* magazine in 2013, Ben Lerner reflected longingly on the ineluctable and "(largely indefensible) distinction between the actuality of visual art and the virtuality of the literary." Envy abounds as he admits to "being jealous of artists who work with something other than words." He tells us that though the jealousy that underpins his "wish" to practice "a more tactile art . . . has various sources," the one that overpowers all others is "the unsophisticated yet unshakable sense that a work of visual art—even a photograph or film installation—is more real, more actual, than a machine made out of words." But his short-lived wistful envy is deceptive: rather than lamenting language's "thingly" deficiencies for too long, he states that its virtuality is something he has "come to embrace." Extolling the aesthetic potential of novelistic form in the mediation of works of visual art, he claims that "one of the powers of literature is precisely how it can describe and stage encounters with works of art that can't or don't exist, or how it can resituate actual works of art in virtual conditions." Artists may make art using "real" materials like "paint or foam or metal or whatever," but "[l]iterature can function as a laboratory in which we test responses to unrealized or unrealizable art works, or in which we embed real works in imagined conditions in order to track their effects." Visual art may *be* art, in other words, but literature can imagine it, invent it, and test it. For Lerner, the novel "is the privileged form" for charting the tenor of our aesthetic experiences through sustained single perspectival visions or split between a kaleidoscope of characterological studies; they have their metaphorical fingers on the pulse of how these experiences are inflected by, or affect, other daily experiences like working, traveling, living, worrying, and loving.

Through a series of negative turns, Lerner arrives at a definition of the novel as a form that operates mostly against: he positions visual art's "thingly" qualities against literary virtuality; the aesthetic potency of the novel emerges through a rejection of the very tactility he opens by envying; the "something other" gestures to an absent alternate; the repeated grammar of "or" oscillates between materials and narrative effects. While the essay detours through affective uncertainty around craft and ends up reinforcing the value of literary representations of art and aesthetic experience, it takes a wrong turn by suggesting that visual art and literature are ruled by mutual exclusion. "Mutual exclusion," as C. Namwali Serpell has argued, "has become a very popular technique for uncertainty in contemporary narratives" (41). Interested in the kind of mutual exclusion that adheres to "duality" (41) and "tends toward . . . dialectical opposition" (42), Serpell details how "a common trick of this kind of narrative to perform a last-minute reversal, to cast doubt on what has taken place" (41). Considering the gestures of against charted here, has Lerner tricked us? Are the twists and turns that lead us from envy to acceptance manufactured? Are we being manipulated to occupy the same dialectical opposition?

What is, on the one hand, a relatively simple argument put forward by a novelist about his aesthetic practice, and affective positioning toward his form, poses on the other hand a range of questions about contemporary aesthetic value, judgment, and experience. Lerner's "unsophisticated yet unshakable sense that a work of visual art—even a photograph or film installation—is more real, more actual, than a machine made out of words" isn't necessarily a new anxiety. When Henry James argued for a kind of novel that could be elevated to the heights of fine art in "The Art of Fiction" (1884), this was in part to distinguish the modernist art novel from its commercial counterparts, but also to reduce the gap that has long been perceived between art and literature.¹ As Mark McGurl noted in *The Novel Art*, by "stak[ing] a visible claim in the discursive field of the fine arts" (2), such art novels "set out after unprecedented heights of artistic prestige" to become "bearer[s] of cultural capital" (29).

Nor is Lerner alone in his fetishization of what Hannah Arendt calls the "thing-world" (178). In an interview with Matthew Hart and Aaron Jaffe, Tom McCarthy argued that the realm of visual art has invented "an operational logic . . . that is basically the *right* one," where artists simultaneously "work . . . at self-consciously negotiating the symbolic structures of their day, and at self-consciously negotiating their relationships with dead ancestors" (677). The "literary world," however, as "the world represented by today's publishing world and its attendant institutions and media, has got the wrong operational manual. It's got a kind of humanistic, idealist one that is just no good. It's not going to produce anything interesting. It's become a branch of the entertainment industry" (677). As a writer indelibly concerned in his novels, essays, and art projects with constructing a radical avant-garde that does not just redirect the "false trail" of "the naturalist route" (675), he nevertheless suggests that "[w]e need to be really suspicious of th[e] schematic" that describes the current "literary landscape" as opposing *both* "middlebrow realism" and "the avant-garde" (680). In an interview in late 2016, Maggie Nelson was even more scathing: "I am often bored by just plain old literary culture."

Such equivocal atmospheres of dissonant feeling among "writer-critics"—Zadie Smith's terms ("Read Better")—reflect the legacy of what Rachel Greenwald Smith has called "compromise aesthetics," "the belief that contemporary art is at its most socially relevant when it forges compromises between strategies traditionally associated with the mainstream on the one hand and those associated with experimental departure from the mainstream on the other" ("Six Propositions" 182). The turn of the millennium marked a demonstrable "aesthetic shift" away from accepting compromises between formal innovation and commercial interest, heralded by a "new generation of writers" who were "frustrated by the limitations of these two positions, and as a result [are] rejecting en masse the notion that formally inventive literature requires intentional opposition to the norms of mainstream writing and the expectations of mainstream audiences" (183).

The tension between popularity and innovation in twenty-first century literature signals a shift away from the return to conventional form during the first decade of the twenty-first century. As Adam Kelly has argued, this "praise of convention" in place of experimentation "had coalesced into a self-conscious ethos among a significant set of American novelists, an ethos that found its aesthetic manifestations in such prominent literary trends as the revival of narrative realism, the enthusiastic adoption by celebrated authors of standard genre forms, and the boom in historical fiction" ("Formally Conventional Fiction" 47). But if the 2000s saw a reinforcement of convention, the 2010s have seen a rise in interartistic, critical play spurred by dissatisfaction with playing it formally straight, marking a return in a sense to the intertextuality and intermediality characteristic of postmodern "American self-conscious metafiction," in Amy J. Elias's terms ("Postmodern Metafiction" 22). Although such metafiction "self-consciously parodies themes and story elements of other texts" (23), recent self-reflexive American novels from the last ten years exhibit a mode of aesthetic sincerity that is less about parody and more about ethical authenticity.[2] Indeed, these formal experimentations aren't themselves marketed or labeled with the tag "experimental" but illuminate a mood that encompasses a restless aesthetic and formal ambition, fueled by the drive for authentic experience, which pushes against a prevailing culture of anxiety about the direction of aesthetic experience in an era of hypercommodification.[3]

This state of aesthetic boredom populates a range of recent interviews and essays by contemporary writers.[4] In her well-known essay "Two Paths for the Novel" from 2008, Zadie Smith likewise lamented the tendency toward a highly wrought lyrical realism; Teju Cole has criticized the overdependence literary culture has on categorizing texts as fiction or nonfiction; and McCarthy was "dishearten[ed]" to hear "[t]ime and again . . . about a new desire for the real, about a realism which is realistic set against an avant-garde which isn't" ("Writing Machines"). Karl Ove Knausgård noted in an interview with James Wood that "I had a feeling that novels tend to obscure the world instead of showing it, because their form is so much alike from novel to novel . . . the same form, the same language, makes everything the same" (76). The contemporary art novel emerges out of this aesthetic boredom and ethical frustration with the formal, affective, and stylistic inauthenticity.

There isn't a lot of uniformity in what contemporary art novels look like. Some art novels include images; some don't. Some employ experimental typographical techniques; some don't. But all are intimately concerned with comprehending how aesthetic experiences have been radically reshaped by the hyperaestheticized, hypercommodified, and hypermediated nature of contemporary life. As this book will show, novels by Cole, Lerner, and Smith as well as Sheila Heti, Siri Hustvedt, Chris Kraus, and Rachel Kushner regularly work against what we historically know aesthetic experience to sound and feel like. By mediating sensory experiences of painting, poetry, photography, installation art, and music, their art novels disturb the way we perceive, talk, and reflect on aesthetic experience now. Sitting alongside the recent work by cultural theorists, these seven major novelist-critics investigate a range of a negative affective states that aesthetic theory is only beginning to accommodate. One of the central questions that this book seeks to examine, therefore, is how aesthetic experience—a previously tired and old-fashioned kind of experience—presents sites for novelists and critics to examine their critical attachments and aesthetic detachments.

What happens when art *disturbs* us, when it jars and vexes our perceptions? What affective distortions do aesthetic experiences produce when solace isn't the ultimate ambition? What scope is there for our aesthetic experiences when art fails to move us? In the relentless aestheticization of contemporary life, we find novelists attempting to square the aesthetic with the ineffability and inexpressibility of personal and communal losses or disasters (from rape to terrorism to global warming to infidelity). This book argues that such art novels work against the long history of the consecration of aesthetic experience in aesthetic theory, offering a new vision of contemporary aesthetic experience no longer bound to the sublime and the beautiful. And in the interrogation of the aesthetic experience, both novel and theory together can come to redefine the aesthetics of twenty-first century life.

CONTEMPORARY NOVELISTS AND THE AESTHETICS OF TWENTY-FIRST CENTURY AMERICAN LIFE

INTRODUCTION
The Aesthetics of Contemporary American Life

"The place in which I'll fit will not exist until I make it."
—JAMES BALDWIN, *Native Sons*

"Internal time stretched and stilled, inattentive to the minutes and hours outside of itself. Five minutes! He says it irritably whether thirty have gone by or a hundred or two hundred. Pornography does that too. Art, too, so they say."
—ZADIE SMITH, *NW*

Contemporary life is relentlessly aestheticized. Take for example Beyoncé and Jay-Z's luscious "Apeshit" music video (2018). A revised art history of sorts, the video uses as its backdrop the empty galleries of the Louvre, in which black bodies of various shades dance in front of the art that erased such faces from Western histories of colonialization and subjugation. A shot of *The Raft of the Medusa* references both the long history of slavery and the ongoing refugee crisis as Jay-Z sings "I can't believe we made it." In front of the *Portrait of Madame Récamier*, two nearly nude black dancers wearing trailing white headscarves echo the form of the daybed that the nineteenth century French socialite reclines on, alluding to the invisible labor erased from the painting. As we listen on and pick up the repeated refrain "I can't believe we made it (this is what we made, made) / This is what we're thankful for," we can't escape the sumptuousness of the video. Because Beyoncé and Jay-Z refuse to look at any of the artworks until the final shot, aesthetic attention is drawn specifically to them as aesthetic objects: dressed in "expensive fabrics," "we livin' lavish, lavish." When rewriting art history, it seems, you must also possess a certain degree of aesthetic extravagance.

Everything from Instagram's grids to Marie Kondo's mantra "spark joy" contributes to what Jacques Rancière has called the "aestheticization of common life" (*Dissensus* 129). What all these examples have in common is their emphasis on curation, a method of consciously organizing images and things in order to invent the effect of a gestalt aesthetic. Though Fredric Jameson didn't mean The Carters, or Instagrammers, when he claimed that the "emblematic figure of the curator" has come to rival the conductor of the nineteenth century, becoming for the twenty-first century "the demiurge of those floating and dissolving constellations of strange objects we still call art" ("Aesthetics" 110), he has ended up being inadvertently right. In the "ontology of the present," curation has transformed dramatically, evolving from its museum origins to kitsch and now meaning anything from a styled social media presence to a minimalist wardrobe to thematically organized stock market portfolios.[1] In popular culture, to be a curator is to be the epitome of the late-capitalist subject. We can make our lives conform to what Hal Foster calls "total design and Internet plenitude" (25), in which the "aesthetic and utilitarian are not only conflated but all but subsumed in the commercial, and everything—not only architectural projects and art exhibitions but everything from jeans to genes—seems to be regarded as so much *design*" (17; original emphasis).

Though these examples are faddish ones, they are useful for delineating the paradox between the aesthetics of contemporary life and the claims aesthetic theory makes about it. Though the phrase "aesthetics of contemporary life" is tantalizingly vague, it is imprecise because its plural form implicitly insists upon the multiplicity of aesthetic experience today. As Sianne Ngai has argued in her compelling study *Our Aesthetic Categories* (2012), although "recent efforts to 'rescue' beauty or 'recover' the aesthetic might confuse us into thinking" that the aesthetic is "imperilled" in contemporary life, "aesthetic experience has come to saturate virtually every nook and cranny of the world that postmodern subjects inhabit" (241). To borrow Ngai's phrasing, "[i]t is the hypertrophy of the 'aesthetic function,' not its atrophy, that makes the art and culture of the present moment so distinctive" (242). They are also useful because they represent a starkly different attitude toward the aesthetic than Enlightenment and post-Enlightenment aesthetic theory, against which we still index much of our understanding of the aesthetic today. In Ngai's formulation, unlike "the eighteenth and nineteenth centuries," which "in response to the loss of the sacred under conditions of secular, industrial modernity" brought about "a resacralization of the aesthetic, the contemporary moment seems defined by a desacralization of the aesthetic . . . caused precisely by the aesthetic's hyperbolic expansion" (242). The reorientation of the aesthetic experience away from sacralization to a secular, hypertrophic mode reconditions "neither art nor beautiful/sublime nature [as] the obvious go-to model for reflecting on aesthetic experience as a whole, or for reflecting on art in its newly displaced relation to aesthetic experience as a whole" (20). Acknowledging this genealogy, this study's aim is tracing how contemporary novels stage and critique aesthetic experience, while also seeking to grapple with a particular kind of ethics for the contemporary aesthetic subject in an era Tom McCarthy has called, in his recent novel *Satin Island*, the "Present-Tense" (127).

In this hyperaestheticized world, however, the category of the aesthetic toggles precariously between saturation and "exhaustion," to borrow a term from Hans Ulrich Gumbrecht (315). As soon as a certain aesthetic is pushed to near ubiquity, like the glossy, pink, "candytopia" aesthetic popularized by Instagram, the sooner that aesthetic burns out (the *Atlantic* declared in 2019 that, despite the platform's intense commodification of this aesthetic during the second decade of the twenty-first century, the cultural influence of "pretty" has now been depleted [Lorenz]). This also holds true for the limited number of objects, genres, and forms of art the

Western canon has deemed an appropriate source of aesthetic experience, like the *Mona Lisa*. Has there ever been an object more infamous for its shortage of aesthetic power? We expect the *Mona Lisa* to hold aesthetic power for many reasons—not least because of the mythology of the painting—but ultimately because of the "aura," to use a Benjaminian term, of the work of art. But although Walter Benjamin advocated for the dissipation of this aura, conventional aesthetic theory still maintains that what constitutes an aesthetic experience essentially boils down to some realization of the beautiful/sublime index. The failure of the *Mona Lisa* to elicit any feelings remotely related to the beautiful/sublime lies in its utter exhaustion: as Gumbrecht notes, "nothing that would not have fit into the established frames of aesthetic experience two hundred years ago is ever allowed to be enjoyed as beautiful or as sublime today" (315). Spaces of aesthetic experience, such as museums, fail to transport viewers into a state of appreciation too (although the assassin Villanelle, from the HBO show *Killing Eve*, is a psychopath who is unable to access a normal range of human feeling, she nevertheless touches a nerve when she yells "This is boring!" at a wall of masterpieces while in a museum in Amsterdam).[2]

For viewers, then, Beyoncé and Jay-Z turning to look at the *Mona Lisa* might be a more affecting aesthetic experience than simply looking at the painting itself, precisely because this removes the power to create aesthetic experiences from the object, and instead positions the aesthetic subject at the center of the experience. As David Hume put it in "Of the Standard of Taste," "[b]eauty is no quality in the things themselves: it exists merely in the mind which contemplates them; and each mind perceives a different beauty" (234–35). Or, in Rancière's terms, "the property of being art refers back not to a distinction between the modes of doing, but to a distinction between modes of being" (*Aesthetics and Its Discontents* 29).

This particularity of aesthetic subjectivity is at the heart of Kondo's "spark joy," a feeling that relies on the individual subject's specific relationship to their own objects. As I come back to in chapter 1, even the feelings of disappointment and boredom felt by the viewing public in front of the *Mona Lisa* can be classed as aesthetic today—as Ngai has shown, even deeming a work of art "interesting" requires aesthetic judgment (*Our Aesthetic Categories*). Because it tends to revolve around repeated actions to the point of saturation, contemporary exhaustion is mostly traceable in experiences of things we know to be familiar, whether famous works of art or everyday objects. In place of the beautiful/sublime, however, a broader spectrum of familiar feelings is allowed to take their place to the extent that "aesthetic experience no longer seems definable by the presence of a single exceptional feeling (say, 'disinterested pleasure') than through a set of aesthetic categories based on complicated intersections of ordinary affects" (*Our Aesthetic Categories* 23). Although Kondo's "spark joy" recalls what Hannah Arendt termed the "modern enchantment with 'small things,'" in her case "preached by early twentieth-century poetry in almost all European tongues" as a form of minor sublimity, it is gratitude and satisfaction that governs the reorientation of the self toward everyday objects (52). Arendt's "art of being happy . . . between dog and cat and flowerpot" is a much less sublime ambition than being carried away by a transformative performance of music.

The aestheticization of the present shows quite how much the formulation of aesthetic experience has moved away from traditional definitions of aesthetic experience. Its negative and ordinary affective modes shift the focus from the pleasurable experiences of beauty of the kind John Dewey pointed to in *Art as Experience* (1934)—as simply "appreciative, perceiving, and enjoying" (50)—to negative ones like anxiety and frustration. It also deviates from Peter de Bolla's claim that they are often "distinguishe[d]" from everyday affective experiences by "the fact that they are occasioned by encounters with artworks" (9). It also shows how our understanding needs to move away from the belief that "aesthetic experience in everyday worlds" adopts, in Gumbrecht's words, "the structure of an oxymoron": one that suggests that at the level of terminology, *aesthetic* experience "impl[ies] that its content . . . is something that, invariably and metahistorically, will not be available in everyday situations" (299). My aim is to not create a strict equivalence between the everyday and the aesthetic. As I will return to in chapter 5, although reading prose or poetry, writing, viewing art works, and listening to music take place in everyday life, they are not necessarily constrained by the temporal patterns of the everyday. Just as the everyday is a specifically "temporal term," as Rita Felski suggests, the aesthetic is also informed by a certain and peculiar tempo. It is precisely in the ordinary world that aesthetic experiences arise, and it is with everyday affects that we experience things aesthetically. Once it is detached from the concept of

INTRODUCTION 5

aesthetic autonomy as the distinguishing and organizing principle of such experience, it becomes clear, as Felski argues, that "aesthetic experience need not be severed from everyday life" ("Invention" 17). If "it makes more sense to think of the everyday as a way of experiencing the world rather than a circumscribed set of activities within the world," it also makes sense to understand the aesthetic in the same terms (31).

As Janet Wolff and Zygmunt Bauman have argued, we are living in an age of uncertainty and anxiety, moods that are often touted as the predominant tone of twenty-first century arts. Even the emphasis on the pursuit of happiness and beauty in recent wellness movements draws stark attention to the dissonant feelings involved in living and working today. And if aesthetic experiences now refer to a much wider combination of affective responses to both art and ordinary life—spurred on by this mood of uncertainty and anxiety—then aesthetic theory has some catching up to do. I agree with Ngai that there is a manner of intransigence about this field in the fact that "it is . . . aesthetic theory that needs resuscitation in our contemporary moment, not the aesthetic" per se (*Our Aesthetic Categories* 242). This is a challenge that bears repeating precisely because of how slowly this field moves. Writing at the turn of the millennium in *The Radical Aesthetic* (2000), Isobel Armstrong challenged the anti-aesthetic discourse of the last two decades of twentieth century cultural thought. She argued that "the concept of the aesthetic has been steadily emptied of content" because "the politics of the anti-aesthetic" (primarily constructed through hermeneutics of suspicion) "rely on deconstructive gestures of exposure that fail to address the democratic and radical potential of aesthetic discourse" (2). Incorporating dissonance into aesthetic experience is in part an attempt to replenish the disciplinary "resuscitation of aesthetics" Frederic Jameson celebrated in the early 2000s with the unexpected ways writers have interrogated—at turns celebrating and diminishing—the beautiful, the profound, and the transcendent with the political complications of everyday living (*Singular Modernity* 3).

Because the re-turn to the aesthetic and the turn to affect both accelerated around the turn of the millennium, I see them as deeply intertwined in their ambition to illuminate negative or discordant states of feeling.[3] As Eugenie Brinkema writes, affect has even become "the negative ontology of the humanities" (31). As something that was *turned to*, a detour from the norm, the very language we use to document the effects of affect on the field is structured by repulsion—"as signaling principally a rejection: not semiosis, not meaning, not structure, not apparatus, but the felt visceral, immediate, sensed, embodied, excessive" (30). Even denoting affective effects employs negative terminology, to

> disrupt, interrupt, reinsert, demand, provoke, insist on, remind of, agitate for: the body, sensation, movement, flesh and skin and nerves, the visceral, stressing pains, feral frenzies, always rubbing against: what undoes, what unsettles, that thing I cannot name, what remains resistant, far away (haunting, and ever so beautiful); indefinable, it is said to be what cannot be written, what thaws the critical cold, messing all systems and subjects up. (xii)

Specific affective modes exhibit this negativity too. As Heather Love has explored, the "tradition of backwardness"—delineating affects of "shyness, ambivalence, failure, melancholia, loneliness, regression, victimhood, heartbreak, antimodernism, immaturity, self-hatred, despair, shame"—works on a system of "refusal" (*Feeling Backward* 146).

Relying on the dialectic of phobia/philia, minor "aesthetic emotions" that are "weaker and nastier," Ngai argues,

> can be described as "semantically" negative, in the sense that they are saturated with socially stigmatizing meanings and values (such as the "pettiness" one traditionally associates with envy); and as "syntactically" negative, in the sense that they are organized by trajectories of repulsion rather than attraction, by phobic strivings "away from" rather than philic strivings "toward." (*Ugly Feelings* 11)

Unlike more recent work on negative affect, Ngai approaches "the negativity at stake" as "algorithmic or operational, rather than value- or meaning-based, involving processes of aversion, exclusion, and of course negation" (12).

By considering a range of fraught affective states today, this book theorizes *against* as the unifying structure of contemporary aesthetic experience. As a mood that encompasses a push-pull across formal ambition, novel style, and affective experiences of art, *against* refers to the proximal sense of "to be against"—next to, to run up against—as well as opposition—between the literary and the real, intense and weak feelings, excitement and boredom.

INTRODUCTION 7

What this book considers then is not a resurgence, but a recalibration of aesthetic experience to embody moments of affective disquiet to newly productive ends for aesthetic theory, critical practice, and the contemporary novel. It is my contention that contemporary novels mobilize aesthetic theory away from aesthetic norms to negative aesthetic categories better tied to contemporary living, without replicating the same theoretical structures that reduce the aesthetic back to these same categories. For David James, this realignment seems "to affirm how the novel, after an era of being subjected to self-reflexive deconstruction and epistemological doubt, still has the capacity to simulate and thereby intensify our attention to the aesthetic dimensions of ordinary experience, while probing the political and ethical implications of inhabiting those dimensions anew" ("Renaissance" 857). Just as Jacques Rancière reminds us, "in the aesthetic regime of art, the property of being art is no longer given by the criteria of technical perfection but is ascribed to a specific form of sensory apprehension" (*Aesthetics* 29), so, too, reading, writing, thinking, traveling, wandering, and even eating cornflakes are described in minute perceptual detail and attended to at the level of art. After all, as Michael Wood notes, when not ostensibly concerning the work of art, the novel nevertheless represents "a form of lived experience" (9).

NOVEL EXPERIENCE

Despite occupying anxious, negative aesthetic states, despite showing aesthetic experience to be fraught, despite approaching the aesthetic experience with ethical trepidation, and despite acknowledging the weakened states of aesthetic experience due to contemporary life's hyperaestheticization, contemporary art novels do still portray sublime experiences of art. Partway through Chris Kraus's second novel, *Aliens and Anorexia* (2000), the narrator feels the effect of music's terrible beauty:

> Everything seemed hopeless. It was a rainy afternoon, early November. Bach's *Partita for Cello in B minor*, performed by Ute Uge, came on the radio. I pulled over to the shoulder of Springs Fireplace Road and wept. My skin became so porous that the tremor of the cello crept into my body like an Alien. . . . Alien encounters are a phenom-

enon of marking—pins on the map of an emotional landscape that
you'd been moving through but didn't realize had a shape. Despair's
a maudlin ecstasy of baroque romanticism. (45–46)

A strange, visceral description, it carries somatic intensity that is particular to the experience of listening. The narrator's persistent feelings of "hopeless[ness]" lead here to an unsentimental yet distinctively sublime revelation; she is moved to tears precisely because the cello resonates with overwhelming internal, ineffable states, capturing the capacity for music to elicit "despair" and "maudlin ecstasy" all at once.

Nevertheless, after this moment of sublime contemplation and emotional collapse, the narrator continues on her journey unaffected. While literary aesthetic experiences are often resistant to or anxious about sublimity, Kraus's narrator embodies Martin Donougho's observation that "the sublime has by now come to form part of the furniture of our common world" (909). Distracted flitting along the surface of things transforms momentarily into true attention. This mode of attention is marked by (often sudden) intensification of feeling, where somatic and emotional undercurrents come sharply into focus—but only briefly.

In the middle of one night in *A Death in the Family* (2009), the first book of his *My Struggle* series, Karl Ove Knausgård, too, is occupied by this hyperaware mode. Taking "one of the art books from the shelf above the sofa," he sits "flicking through it" (185). But rather than falling into deep contemplation, this action of letting his "eyes skim" over the pages containing "[m]ostly oil sketches, studies of clouds, countryside, sea" is enough to move him "to tears." So far, the reaction is not surprising, given that the set of "feelings it aroused" was his "only parameter with art": even the briefest of "impression[s]" grows an atmosphere of uncontrollable emotion. Probing this idea further, Knausgård questions what it is about art that provokes reactions like these:

The feeling of inexhaustibility. The feeling of beauty. The feeling of presence. All compressed into such acute moments that sometimes they could be difficult to endure. And quite inexplicable . . . It was a fantastic picture, it filled me with all the feelings that fantastic pictures do, but when I had to explain why, what constituted the 'fantastic', I was at a loss to do so. The picture made my insides tremble, but for what? The picture filled me with longing, but for what? (185–86)

Pondering Constable's *Cloud Study* (1822), he questions why it was that some works evoked intense surges of emotion while others "by contrast, left [him] cold":

> For if I studied the picture that made the greatest impression, an oil sketch of a cloud formation from 6 September 1822, there was nothing in it that could explain the strength of my feelings. At the top a patch of blue sky. Beneath, whitish mist. Then the rolling clouds. White where the sunlight struck them, pale green in the least shadowy parts, deep green and almost black where they were at their densest and the sun was furthest away. Blue, white, turquoise, greenish-black. That was all. (185)

With its unremarkable description, this passage focuses on the basics of visual analysis: color and, though it only hints at it, form. Again, the reason for this is that "reasoning vanished in the surge of energy and beauty that arose in me" (186). So, as he "kept flicking back to the picture of the greenish clouds," its essence still eluding him, it "was as if two different forms of reflection rose and fell in my consciousness, one with its thoughts and reasoning, the other with its feelings and impressions, which, even though they were juxtaposed, excluded each other's insights." Instead, the work called to him, and suggested something more: "*Yes, yes, yes,* I heard. *That's where it is. That's where I have to go.* But what was it I had said yes to? Where was it I had to go?" (186).

Questioning the affective mysteries of aesthetic experience is characteristic of Knausgård's literary project. In an interview in 2013, he explained that while art history and literary studies have "to do with the intellect" and "a lot of theory," he wanted the *My Struggle* series to specifically examine what these fields deem "unimportant": the "emotion that pictures or books can evoke in you" (Interview with Gale). He asked: "[W]hy should those feelings be important, and in what way? It makes you feel sad, it makes you cry, it makes you laugh, but what's the importance of that?" In *A Death in the Family,* Knausgård echoed this sentiment: "I had studied the history of art and was used to describing and analyzing art. But what

I never wrote about, and this is all that matters, was the experience of it" (185). Why not? "Not just because I couldn't, but also because the feelings the pictures evoked in me went against everything I had learned about what art was and what it was for" (186).

But though compelling, Knausgård is not alone in his ambition to show how "experiences with art or with books have to do with emotions" (Interview with Gale). By engaging the internal subjective experience of art, contemporary art novelists question how encounters with art are, as Peter de Bolla puts it, coterminous with "affective" ones (5). This is not to say that the mental processes enacted to cause these encounters aren't in some way influenced by emotion, but rather that, as in Jesse Prinz's fairly uncontroversial acknowledgment, "when we appreciate a work, the appreciation consists in an emotional response" (71). However art manages to do this, such suppositions tend to be fraught with tension familiar enough in aesthetics between the perspectives that claim "artworks express emotions" themselves and those that suggest they possess the capacity to "evoke emotions" in the viewer. This perspective resonates with Vernon Lee's argument in 1913 that the emotional response to art is different to our normal responses to pleasurable sensory experiences:

> [A]rt can do nothing without the collaboration of the beholder or listener; and that this collaboration, so far from consisting in the passive "being impressed by beauty" which unscientific aestheticians imagined as analogous to "being impressed by sensuous qualities," by hot or cold or sweet or sour, is in reality a combination of higher activities, second in complexity and intensity only to that of the artist himself. (128)

And so, as Knausgård reflects, though he registers that the painting stimulates "the feeling of beauty" that "made [his] insides tremble," "the surge of energy and beauty" didn't originate from the painting itself, but "arose in" him instead.

The tender attention in this scene in *A Death in the Family* gives us an insight into how contemporary literary writers imagine aesthetic experience and what is at stake, motivationally speaking, in literary engagements with art. To begin with, Knausgård thematizes much of what we have in mind when we conceptualize aesthetic experience. We notice the admission that some but not all art provokes intense feeling, but also the insistence that those works of art that do possess "the feeling of inexhaustibility," "the feeling of beauty," and "the feeling of presence" stir an indescribable "longing." Note how when pressed to explain what it is so "fantastic" about the object, Knausgård finds it "quite inexplicable." As we'll see in the mode of the afterimage, despite the novelistic compulsion for ekphrastic description, this inexplicability is a distinctive component of aesthetic experience. But while Knausgård isolates the cloudscape's "feeling of inexhaustibility," and the difficulty of enduring its compression into "acute moments" certainly adheres to the structure of the sublime, it's a quieter, domestic version.

Rather than the awe of the work's unassailability, it might the painting's beauty that, in Elaine Scarry's phrasing, causes Knausgård at once "to gape and suspend all thought" (*On Beauty* 29–30). Experiencing beauty has a quickening effect on mentation, "prompt[ing] the mind to move chronologically back in the search for precedents and parallels, to move forward into new acts of creation, to move conceptually over, to bring things into relation, and does all this with a kind of urgency as though one's life depended on it" (30). But though the flickering of thought between "reasoning" and "impression" echoes this cognitive process, for Knausgård the distinguishing quality of this experience isn't the simultaneous stillness and energy Scarry describes that occurs predominantly in the mind, refracting a conceptual optics of artistic sensibility, but how aesthetic experiences ultimately evade explanation and exert profound consequences on emotion and bodily sensation. So, while representing this kind of experience in novel form draws on acts of the intellect—such as reflection, description, explanation, and narration—it nevertheless occupies a sensorial register rooted firmly in the impressions of the emotions.

Contemporary novels, as Nancy Armstrong notes, not only "make us think about feeling" but also make us consider "how novels make us feel" (444). Since the start of the twentieth century, novel reading has been transformed, as Suzanne Keen notes, "from a morally suspect waste of time to an activity cultivating the role-taking imagination" (3). And yet, though the novels I consider throughout this book move through the interior realms of what Rachel Greenwald Smith terms "the emotional specificity of personal experience" (*Affect* 1), they don't seek to replicate the empathetic structures of literature of her formulation of the "affective hypothesis" (2). Instead, they "emphasize the unpredictability of affective connections" (1)—for contemporary novels, art feeling is multitudinal and dissonant. Indeed, they also set the stage for readerly engagement: Knausgård's experience of Constable, during a period of sleeplessness, is also ours. And later, when he sets out for a walk, frustrated about the questions surrounding the circumstances of his father's death, and remarks that "the various cloud shapes and hues meant nothing, what they looked like at any given juncture was based on chance, so if there was anything the clouds betokened it was meaninglessness in its purest and most perfect form" (346), we remember the conviction Knausgård will attribute all sorts of unattainable meaning to later in life. The novel is doing something tricky with time here: staging aesthetic experiences as personal, intimate experiences draws attention to our own aesthetic experiences during the immediacy of reading. It even seems like the novel is giving us a peek into what Knausgård longs for all those years later in the middle of the night, looking at Constable's *Cloudscape* (though it could hardly be that easy).

Form can help intensify these affective states. When Jennifer Egan's Pulitzer Prize–winning novel *A Visit from the Goon Squad* was published in 2011, some critics greeted the formal shift in the penultimate chapter with some trepidation. The source of the consternation was a series of slides through which the novel leaves behind its relatively linear narrative to force the reader into gleaning textual details through elusive, gestural fragments. But, as one reviewer put it, "[t]hough appealing, even amusing," these slides "leave one uncertain about their artistic merit, much as conceptual painting can" (Mishra).

To be sure, the unapologetic visual twist is perceptually bracing. Reflecting in 2014 on crafting the slides, Egan described how the difficulty of moving from the fluidity of prose to the "totally static form" of the slide—"a pixelated/pointillist form . . . consist[ing] of discrete units with no real continuity between them"—pushed her to think about novel form in a new temporality (Interview with Dinnen). Rather than the action-based movement of plot, for her the slides captured a way of attending to the "moment." Recalling the process of creating the slides, Egan explained:

> With each new slide, I'd ask myself: What is the moment I am describing here? I'd start by creating a series of bullet points on the

slide that seemed like the essential elements of the moment in question. Then I would ask: what is the relationship among these elements? PowerPoint is about diagramming the essential structure of a moment. Is it cycle? Cause and effect? A huge mess? A process? Is it going from A–B in a series of steps? Back and forth?

Casting aside the linearity of narrative prose, Egan wanted the novel to be able to show "elements that just coexisted" without cause and effect; affective experiences that that were "unrelated but [existed] together."

Formally, the slides were a way of "incorporating" Egan's fascination with "the idea of the pause, what it means and how it can function in music"—without boring the reader. Routing this fascination with pauses through Alison's brother, Lincoln, a child on the autism spectrum, she reflects that "the pauses must have been driving my curiosity about PowerPoint without even my knowing it." Intuitively, Egan even unconsciously arranged the slide chapter in the novel "at exactly the same point where pauses often appear in songs: just before the last refrain." Importantly, "the PowerPoint chapter *itself* functions as a pause," not only like a pause in music, but a pause in an argument, the silence of the desert, and the stillness of the night—a moment, in other words, that sits in negative contrast to narrative prose (figs. 1 and 2). As Sasha explains to her husband, Drew, when he asks why pauses matter so much to his son: "The pause makes you think the song will end. And then the song isn't really over, so you're relieved. But then the song *does* actually end, because every song ends, obviously, and THAT. TIME. THE. END. IS. FOR. REAL" (*Goon Squad* 289). With visual pauses created on the page, reading time is slowed and brought to a stop; the form itself alters the rhythm of the final pages and, in so doing, signals the conclusion's collision with the real. A form paused dictates aesthetic time.

Structured in thirteen interlinked stories, *Goon Squad* captures a cast of characters searching for the elusive aesthetic *moment*, of the sublime intensity and existential pleasure that is "rhapsodic joy" or "euphoria" (343). Sasha's incurable kleptomania helps her "assert her toughness, her individuality" (4); the pure music not yet beset by digitization brings on Bennie Salazar's "first erection in months" (31); the rapture at a music concert Alex observes in the final chapter makes the distance between him

Two "pause" slides from "Great Rock and Roll Pauses," from *A Visit from the Goon Squad* (Egan 290, 310).

and his wife and daughter feel "irrevocable, a chasm that would keep him from ever again touching the delicate silk of Rebecca's eyelids, or feeling, through his daughter's ribs, the scramble of her heartbeat" (345). With her slides, twelve-year-old Alison Blake attempts to capture the subtle affective reverberations in interactions between her parents and her brother. In one slide she graphs the "Relationship of Pause-Length to Haunting Power" of songs from Doobie's "Long Train Runnin'" to "Mighty Sword" by the Frames (313). In another, she details "Songs with Lincoln's Comments"—"Foxey Lady" by Jimi Hendrix features a "great early pause: 2 seconds long, coming 2:23 seconds into a 3:19-minute-long song. But this one isn't total silence; we can hear Jimi breathing in the background" (252). In this sense, the visual organization of the slides affirms how the contemporary novel, despite its intermedial investments, hasn't yet shaken the nineteenth century aspiration to embody "a simulacrum of the mind-blowing complexity of human experience filtered through perception" (Interview with Dinnen). This reader is reminded of the sense of relief another character feels several years earlier (but only a few pages before the slides) when he realizes he is not in Naples to search for his missing niece, but "here to look at art ... [t]o look and think about art" (*Goon Squad* 233).

Because intermedial variations mark out permanent changes to the object of the novel, such formal innovation does not foreclose attention to perception. Indeed, that literary forms have the capacity to structure fraught predicaments of perception *in form* advances the contemporary novel's continued investment in ekphrastic methods—a descriptive mode of verbal imagery that allows us to see an object that we aren't looking at. It rings true when Samuel Otter argues that "[t]o attend to form [as] an object of sense and of thought, is to press" upon "the relations of parts to wholes and inside to outside," but more importantly, "to assess the circumstances of perception" (120). Experiential considerations of form in emergent criticism have directed renewed attention toward literary mediations of perception, alongside considerations of how readers experience different aesthetic forms. Art novels that play with form, such as those I will discuss in chapter 5, mobilize affect precisely because it emphasizes perception, the sensorial, and experience. As we will see in the following chapters, etching affect visibly into form directs formal attention toward the immaterial, transitory, and fleeting. With the emphasis on aesthetic experience, intermedial play represents a conscious poetics of the immediacy of the reading experience—what Elaine Scarry terms the "immediate sensory content" encounters with works of art (*Dreaming* 40). Attention to the visual aspects of the texts illuminates the way the rhetoric of visuality in the novels themselves is inextricably interlinked with ethical and aesthetic dilemmas of visibility and negativity, expression and ineffability.

Showing form to be pliant, the intermediality of the kind we see in *Goon Squad* crystallizes, subjectivizes, and subverts perception. Aesthetic experience and image entwine so that how we see and what we see evoke novelistic ethics and aesthetics. Perspectivalism is not restricted to literary style but embodied on the level of readership, where the texture of experience is often prioritized over plot. When recombined in an "artificial environment" like the novel, Lerner notes, our encounters with these artworks are staged in such a way as "to test how one's response is altered" in complex and multitudinous scenarios (Interview with Rogers 228). For Cole, too, it is "the curation of incident" that gives the writer space to mull so extensively on sensorial perception (Interview with Nair). Construed both as an action that organizes narration (through form) and as a subject of these narratives (through aesthetic experiences), perception allows pleasure to reign in the visual vivacity of this artistic form, even if such "incidents" occasion affective discord or formal disturbance.

ETHICAL ENCHANTMENT

At what point, though, does aestheticizing ordinary objects, observations, and encounters cause us ethical disquiet? This study sheds light on how these kinds of experience, as they are constructed and reflected upon in unexpected ways throughout these novels, compel us to wonder about how other exigent factors, like the ethical and the political, might skew the contemporary novel toward the aesthetic. Novelists have the stylistic capacity to craft almost any experience aesthetically. This aestheticization, although largely a matter of style, can nevertheless compromise the ethics of representation, where exigent categories like race and trauma cannot afford to be smoothed away. Indeed, "when carried to an indiscriminate extreme," as Martin Jay cautions, "such an extension could lead to a promiscuous aestheticization of the entire world, reducing it to a mere occasion for disinterested pleasure" (18). Although such a model encourages "reenchantment" of the commonplace "as if any object or event, however mean, were a legitimate occasion for aesthetic experience" (16), the novelists at the center of this book are far from indiscriminate in their efforts to illuminate the moral consequences of aesthetic attention. As we know from Smith's criticism of lyrical realism outlined in her now seminal essay "Two Paths for the Novel," it is a problem that, when "the world is covered in language," "[e]verything must be made literary": in Joseph O'Neill's *Netherland*, one of the two central novels in question, "personal things are so relentlessly aestheticized" not only to "signify" their "importance" but to offer the "possibility of transcendence, this 'translation into another world'" (Smith, "Two Directions" 78). This echoes Joan Didion who, some forty years earlier in an interview for the *Paris Review*, worried that because experience is "largely a matter of language"—the way in which it is discussed, framed, understood, and described—forms such as the novel work within "a *literary* idea of experience" (Interview by Kuehl).

In part this is a study about novelistic description. A problematic site for the writers in this book, language is constantly in the process of being closely analyzed; the novel's descriptive and representative force, its language and forms, its ability to construct an image of experience, dissected. Relegating artifice, they reinvest artistic purpose in democratizing the space of the novel, even the most introspective ones. These efforts, I suggest, are at once interior and exterior, aesthetic and social, and they expose novelistic aesthetic experiences as sources of ethical responsibility and political resistance. This book thus reveals how the mediations of and meditations on aesthetic principles of literary expression by Cole, Heti, Hustvedt, Kraus, Kushner, Lerner, and Smith are enriched by a paradoxical concern with the ineffability and inexpressibility of personal and communal losses or disasters, drawing on the anxious tone of postmillennial artistic production. This speaks to a wider culture of twenty-first century novel writing that obsessively interrogates the aesthetic experiences of thinking, reading, and writing, and which reveals ethical dilemmas of representation and subjectivity even as writers work to console and comfort. As Janet Wolff argues, "[t]he work of art . . . always meets its viewer . . . in the context of a specific social and historical moment in which the aesthetic, the ethical, and the political, as we now know, are never quite separable" (141).

Examining what experiences writers render aesthetically only takes us so far without turning an eye to *how* such novelists mediate aesthetic experience and judgment. Throughout its pages, this book considers not simply the various literary strategies writers employ in their novelistic works, but their reflections on literary and artistic praxis. These critical vocabularies take pride of place in discussions of representation of aesthetic experience in the contemporary novel, particularly as they help us negotiate the ethical considerations that travel in counterpoint to moments of sheer perceptual experience. As Michael Clune points out, "[m]oments of ekphrasis are always useful occasions for reflecting on art's desire—on what art wants to be and do" ("Make It Vanish" 246). And what today's literature wants to do is "discern the direction of our new period's art" itself (246). But rather than revisiting a form of object-oriented ontology, that which Arendt and Andy Warhol believed in, "[t]he world goes inside"—"[t]oday's most vital art, today's most *revolutionary* art, attacks objects," through "the transmission of private vision: absorption, authenticity, intensity" (244). Its dissatisfaction with habitual relations between art, market, reader, and world reflects what Clune refers to as "[t]he new artistic immortality" (244). The "utopia" of such novels is "a community not founded on recognition," but "a world where subjectivity encounters no border, no seam" (244). Novels that turn to aesthetic experience exhibit what Clune calls "radical subjectivity," the "dominant form" of which "is the narrative of private experience" (245), not least because examples such as Cole's *Open City* (2011) or Hustvedt's *The Blazing World* (2014) privilege first-person consciousness, but because the novels transcribe in minute detail intersubjective experiences and feelings that occasionally seem to "enter and colonize" readers' own perceptions (247). These structures of perception take on metacritical significance in the "new art" of the twenty-first century, in which "experience nibbles away at institutions, objects, individuals, old politics, modernism, postmodernism" (247), and even the modes in which we write about aesthetics.

Luxuriating in sensation, even if it is uncomfortable, is essential to this mode. Although inserting actual visual images, poems, or essays is formally curatorial, this mode is not only concerned with the art object, but how aesthetic experience itself makes the character, the narrator, the author, *feel* in time; how it is experienced; how it affects other perceptual experiences; how it seeps into fictionalized consciousness. In other words, narratives move between various forms of aesthetic *response*, where as Charles Altieri notes, "the sensation" of experience becomes "charged with possibility" (237).

What kinds of possibilities does sensation charge in the contemporary novel? The kinds of aesthetic experiences explored throughout these novels represent what Dorothy Hale has described as a broader literary "conception of the novel as a social discourse different from other social discourses, made different by the aesthetic effects and ethical dilemmas particular to it" ("Aesthetics" 904). The "renewed pursuit of ethics" in twenty-first century literary criticism, as Hale notes, "has been accompanied by a new celebration of literature, and it is in the imbrication of these endeavors—the revival of ethics leading to a new defense of literature—that literary theory and moral philosophy find common ground in the twenty-first century" (896). Indeed, what makes the novelistic aesthetic experience such a vital place of discussion is the way it "accomplishes the project of universalizing the individual subject" and in so doing situates the novel as accomplishing important "ideological work" (898). Such experiences are thus not depicted uncritically. Often portrayed as distilled aesthetic moments of reflection, they, as David James puts it, "retrieve in poignant yet unsentimental terms moments of sublimity from the onrush of daily experience so as to explore how such moments become the occasion for both individual and shared discernment that arises out of quotidian wonder" ("Renaissance" 871). As largely narratives of everyday experience, these moments invite perceptual pleasure into otherwise banal encounters. The implications of crafting narratives of aesthetic experience ripple out in both style and substance: everyday parlance to a lyrical register and reflection and meditation become the usual mode of being and thinking. Although this constitutes at the very least the broad strokes of the argument, it contests the supposition that aesthetic experiences are to be described in aesthetic terms. However true for many of the aesthetic narratives discussed throughout this book, what also arises is a vocabulary that refuses to solely relinquish the realm of the aesthetic experience to lyrical expression. Recasting such experiences in less than aesthetic terms, therefore, while "striv[ing] to democratize, if not domesticate, the sublime," James argues, also "refuses to paint a picture of harmony between aesthetically attuned ways of seeing and good ways of living" (860).

It is precisely this set of ethical considerations behind writers' refusals to parse sentimental moments of the aesthetic that affirms literature as the repository for these experiences. Indeed, we entrust in literature our aesthetic experiences, even if in doing so they set about to disturb what we take the aesthetic to mean. As Jonas Grethlein suggests, "a possible answer to the question as to why experience currently attracts so much attention in aesthetic theory" is not only that it is "a powerful defence against the linguistic turn," but that "the notion of experience also lends itself to securing the ground that seems to be endangered by virtual realities" (310–11). In particular, it is "the anxiety of being disconnected from the 'real' world" that "draws our attention to the experiential dimension of our responses to art as well as to that of being in the world in general" (311). But these anxieties or other negative affects are not smoothed away. Depicting aesthetic experiences thus works to comfort and console, even when working in the shadow of the fresh wounds of global violence, environmental disaster, and personal suffering that provoke disturbances, both subtle and overt, to the novels' aesthetic worlds. Terrorism, hurricanes, and sexual violence work in relief to the aesthetic in these novels, yet these neither undermine nor trivialize the aesthetic. What they do occasion, though, is a conceptualization of aesthetic experience that is not detached from the politico-ethical concerns often levied against art.

AESTHETIC EXPERIENCE'S CRITICAL ATTACHMENTS

Despite the aestheticization of contemporary life, and the disintegration of the distinction between aesthetic and everyday experiences and affects, art novels still seek out aesthetic experiences in conventional places. The conditions of the contemporary art world, if not contemporary artworks themselves, are fruitful sources of the aesthetic in the construction of their everyday experience. Equally captivating, moreover, are pre-twentieth century artworks: paintings of Rembrandt figure prominently in Smith's *On Beauty*, which also features works of Hector Hippolyte and Edward Hopper; Hustvedt's *What I Loved* muses on a multitude of artists, including Goya; Lerner's Adam Gordon frequents the Museo del Prado in Madrid, gazing upon Hieronymus Bosch's *Garden of Earthly Delights* (1503–15), as well as Rogier van der Weyden's *Descent from the Cross* (c. 1435); Julius attends a concert of Mahler's Ninth Symphony (1908–09) in *Open City*, while the Belseys attend one of Mozart's *Requiem* (1791) in *On Beauty*. They do so, not to revert to a traditional style of aesthetic experience, but to show that these are not fruitful sources of aesthetic experience anymore. Hardly sentimental, contemporary aesthetic experiences instead frequently negate the profound, verge on the automatic, and are troubled by uncomfortable and anxious feelings.

These novelists are critics of various arts—from Justin Bieber to Christian Marclay—and also of twenty-first century life—from the Obamas to Trump to gender politics and war photography. From the one-off essay in *Frieze*, to regular columns in *Harper's*, *Artforum*, and the *New York Times*, to book-length collections of criticism, contemporary novelists are increasingly turning to the essay—in the words of Zadie Smith, both as "a form of relief" and "an attempt at a kind of clarity" ("Chaotic Mind"). This breed of novelist-critic also doesn't approach the two genres of the novel and criticism separately. Critical fiction names the political, ethical, and social modality of even the most conventionally styled novels in this book.

The contemporary art novel's theoretical investments are also deep. Teju Cole and Ben Lerner, for example, are founding members of what Nicholas Dames calls the "theory generation" or what Mitchum Huehls has termed "post-theory theory novelists." While Chris Kraus and Siri Hustvedt, both writers of an older generation, exhibit similar traits to original theory novelists of the late twentieth century—who not only "incorporate theory" but "reflect on it, complicate it, and sometimes go beyond it" as Judith Ryan argues in *The Novel After Theory*—a younger generation of novelists have "taken the theory novel's flattened caricature of theory and repurposed it, even revitalized it, for newly aesthetic ends" (Huehls 306). Joan Hawkins recasts Kraus's "lonely girl phenomenology" as "theoretical fiction," preferring not to emphasize its critical modality but to refer to the presence of theory within the very plot of the novel, "where theory and criticism themselves are occasionally 'fictionalized'" and "performed" by the novel's main characters (247). However, while theory may crop up in a writer's linguistic inflections—as Huehls argues, "freely incorporating different realisms into its more innovative forms and techniques" without giving itself over to the "struggle between realist and experimental modes" or "the language of theory" (308)—what might be illuminated if we extricated aesthetic experience in the contemporary novel from theory's stubborn grip? As the novelists throughout this book show, the language of aesthetic theory does very little to help our aesthetic experiences.

How do we write about living writers who illuminate the act of writing, frame and reframe their artistic processes, and examine their own aesthetic, formal, critical, theoretical, and sociopolitical investments? What are the stakes for our critical methods? When reading for affect and aesthetic experience, how do I negotiate my own experience of reading? Moreover, if novelists are urging for aesthetic experiences to evolve beyond critique, then what does that mean for our critical methods, and the attitudes and moods that pervade them? The old suspicious belief that authors and texts don't know what they are doing is now not simply passé but unproductive, particularly since, in the words of Elias, "so many artists today are theoretically savvy and have so much to contribute to criticism" (quoted in Hoberek et al. 46).[4] Is it "hubris and desire to mark off intellectual territory that causes us to believe that writers" (45) such as those in this book "have/had nothing to say about the fundamental formal, ethical, aesthetic, and political basis of art"? (46) Shifting the subject—especially when the self-reflexive networks that constitute artistic sensibility signify innovative methods of reading and looking—allows us to see when writers, too, assert their own "critical positionality," to borrow Timothy Bewes's formulation ("Reading with the Grain" 4). Their interconnected critical and novelistic praxes suggest the need for a similarly reflexive reading practice, one that reads the novelist-critic relationship to unravel how their novels negotiate the experience and destabilization of literary form's evocation of aesthetic experiences.

With the explosion of new reading methods—from surface, to moderate, to generous—comes a multiplicity of approaches that could help answer the evolving question of what we do with the theoretically informed, critically nuanced self-reflexivity of living art produced by living writers. To illuminate praxis-based reflections and interpretations of artistic sensibility, this book argues for a generous mode of reading that reads *with* writers rather than against them. In this territory, between the inside and outside of the aesthetic experience, my aim is to occasion productive new spaces for criticism and, more widely, to question how we conceive of the exigencies that contemporary social pressures on the artistic process place on aesthetic experiences. Reading reflexively is to read *between*: between the novel and what the novelists say about it, as well as their criticism.

As a relational way of reading, then, such a methodology is ideal for engaging with the networked parts of artistic and critical sensibility in how novelistic works are made. In her recent book *Forms*, Caroline Levine argued that "as defined patterns of interconnection and exchange that organize social and aesthetic experience . . . networks have structural properties that can be analyzed in formal terms" (113). Thinking about networks not as "self-enclosed totalities" but attending "to the patterns governing networks" (113) allows for spacious *formal* considerations "of what the affordances of each network can entail" (119) for the aesthetic modes of writing and reading novels now. Indeed, it was also for Deleuze and Guattari that "[t]here is no difference between what a book talks about and how it is made. Therefore a book has no object. As an assemblage, a book has only itself, in connection with other assemblages and in relation to other bodies without organs" (4). The method of reflexive reading developed in this book reflects this concentration on assemblages and networks, formally organizing complementary modes of seeing which "define patterns of interconnection and exchange that organize social and aesthetic experience" (113). Such a networked vision of the very contemporary novel that positions itself against the image "first and foremost affords connectedness," brokering alliances in sensibility and aesthetic understanding. It purposefully draws readerly lines of sight to the images within—both in novelistic description and in remediated photographs, film stills, and slides. Networked, intermedial forms build coherences in a nonlinear fashion; affects accumulate, overlap, reverberate.

In this sense, it pays attention to lateral, not vertical, relations—those that are networked, not hierarchical. But it is also interested in what happens in the space of relation, between two points of reflection, between A and B, as well as A and B themselves. Crucially, it is also a kind of reading embodied by contemporary writers who, themselves, read back their work in interviews—via autocritique—or in the novels themselves—as *speculative fiction* coming into being, rather than *meta*fiction commenting on the structure of its own status. Such fictional speculation is ubiquitous in disciplinary discussions, too. A dialogue between Mary Esteve, Elias,

Matthew Hart, David James, and Samuel Cohen, facilitated by Andrew Hoberek and published in *Postwar/Postmodern—and After*, sought to capture a snapshot of the multifaceted speculation that characterizes attempts to understand what terms like *postwar*, *post-45*, and *contemporary* conceptualize when they themselves are conceptually amorphous. It seems to me that, rather than settling on one definition or another, this nebulous fluidity can be mobilized productively as occasioning new spaces for reading arts that are, too, in the process of being shaped.

My ethos of reflexivity follows Rachel Haidu's model of transmission as necessarily tracing out lines of superimposition and influence. This practice is something that crops up every now and again as a worry for how scholars of the very contemporary negotiate the present when it's a field that is perpetually in the process of becoming history. Indeed, Andrzej Gasiorek and David James question whether "fiction [has] witnessed a new phase of development that should no longer be read primarily in relation to earlier twentieth-century phases of innovation, such as, most monumentally, modernism and postmodernism," or whether "novelists' formal commitments over the last ten years" should continue to be "very much in dialogue with preceding traditions?" (611). Should not criticism, in other words, consider very contemporary authors with an eye to future formal and experiential developments?[5] But because "[t]he time of artistic influence is *past*" and all but one of the novels this book examines were all published after 2000, what is transmitted and received happens "in *our* time—that of viewing, producing, reading, and writing" (Haidu 323; original emphasis).[6] Whereas "influence is what happens on the page, when I want to describe how two authors relate," for example, the work of the following chapters, as they construct synesthetic, transcriptional, recombinatory, discontinuous, or negative aesthetic modes, is the "broadcast, the larger, overlapping networks of audience members" of transmission; in other words, "their relat*ing*" (324; original emphasis). Where reading the contemporary novel is often an analeptic process, flashing back to fixed points in time, reflexive reading is proleptic, anticipatory, hoping to catch a glimpse of the future.

Such a method compels a suspicion of suspicion. Suspicion, as Felski reminds us in *The Limits of Critique*, signals a certain "constellation of attitudes and beliefs that expresses itself in a particular manner of approaching one's object, of leaning toward or turning away from a text, of engaging in close—yet also critical and therefore distanced—reading" (21). As a mood that characterizes the practice of critique, it generates attitudes of "guardedness rather than openness, aggression rather than submission, irony rather than reverence, exposure rather than tact" (21). She is right when she notes that moods like suspicion "are often ambient, diffuse, and hazy, part of the background rather than the foreground of thought"; they can be difficult to pinpoint and categorize, and "pervasive, lingering, slow to change" (20). It is easy to be suspicious of autocritique, not because it is a new phenomenon particular only to twenty-first century literature, but because we have been suspicious for a long time. It is difficult to cast aside the wariness of intentionalism that is still so prevalent in literary studies even if "there is more going on in literary studies than theoretical debates, political disputes, and close readings" (21). But when we're thinking and writing about the literature that is being published right now, is being wary of the perils of intentionalism still the best approach? While we might not want to be *too* intentionalist, perhaps a moderate amount might be exactly what we need.

Reading *postcritically*, as Felski terms it, is about "creating something new in which the reader's role is as decisive as that of the text" (174)—a notion more compelling in a climate where contemporary authors are increasingly conceptualized not only as writers, but readers of their own work. For one, it does not presume in the interpretation of the literary work that *author* is coterminous with *authority,* nor does it claim that the author's views and intentions are paramount to the critic's, particularly as writers like Cole freely acknowledge that "an intelligent and sympathetic critic can do as well as [he] can with the text" (Interview with Bady). Reflective reading is not, therefore, an author-centric reading, but rather one that occupies a space between the text and the author's critical and artistic sensibilities. In other words, it views the literary work flexibly, as having, to borrow Cole's terms, "some openness, some volatility," and certainly ample "space for interpretations" beyond the author's. Casting aside the ambivalence, at least, or antipathy, at most, toward artistic intention of scholarship past when reading contemporary novelists is therefore increasingly necessary. To be sure, what the contemporary writers discussed here say about their novels, and what the novels say about themselves, may be inexact; but although inexact, they are nevertheless indelibly precise, or what Ngai calls "a proliferation of precise inexactitudes" (*Ugly Feelings* 255).[7]

Even if what arises in these writerly observations is a tangible map to the work of art, this map is by no means more authoritative than any other. Self-reflexive interpretative frameworks operate as any other critical encounter—they remain suggestive, gestural, directive, fictional. As Lerner contends, "the instability and participatory nature of [literary] form is supposed to shift attention from the finished and polished artifact to the process of thinking and feeling in time—to let the struggle to express be expressive" (Interview with Rogers 236). Yet the reanimated critical enchantment with the critique structured by work and writer is not without its own distinct sense of unease. Lerner's disquiet is overt. Though compelling us to consider his own "fictions about [his] fiction or poetry" as "necessary" to the creative process, what "worr[ies]" him is "getting in the way" of "disciplin[ary] readings of the books themselves" (238). Above all, he observes, "there is something off-putting about an author who keeps saying that he wants the reader to participate in the construction of meaning and then keeps offering readings of his own work," something objectionable about writing that "already contains its own critical supplement, already comments on its procedures or investments" (238). If suggestions of "redundancy" create anxieties for authors and critics alike, it is no wonder that engagement with aesthetic frameworks as comprehensive and distinctive as Lerner's has seemed problematic to some. But what tends to be perceived as an intentional reading of the writer's own making might actually be an integral part of a critico-literary dialogue on the dissonance in aesthetic innovation and discordance of contemporary artistic sensibility.

For Felski, what this kind of reading "values in works of art is not just their power to estrange and disorient but also their ability to recontextualize what we know and to reorient and refresh perception. It seeks, in short, to strengthen rather than diminish its object—less in a spirit of reverence than in one of generosity and unabashed curiosity" (*Limits of Critique* 182). To read, say, autocritique alongside and with the fictional work then is to read open-mindedly, warding off, as David James argues, "the polarization between critical analysis and authorial sensibility," in favor of compelling "a means of combining interpretive methods with that sensitivity to artistic

INTRODUCTION 27

motivations" (*Modernist Futures* 31). This is to say that if I treated sensibility generously I would not seek to perpetuate a particular reading of the text that comes from the author. Nor does it mean that I am interested only in mediating the work in the author's terms. It would not mean that I am sympathetic to how authors read their own work, but that I am aware that even a highly revered author-critic (of an older generation) like Toni Morrison "explains less than she obscures" (Wu 780), her "interpretations of her novels often befuddl[ing] rather than clarify[ing]" (Serpell 119). Reading in such a way to be comfortable in authorial paradox and resistance involves inhabiting a double consciousness, that "neither subsumes" the authority of the writer "nor defers to it" (120)—especially when met with contradictions: "I have nothing to say," Tom McCarthy claims; "[i]ndeed, I'd go as far as to claim that no serious writer does" (*Transmission* 10). Smith has worried openly about the equivalence of intimate specialism and disciplinary qualification: in the foreword to *Feel Free* she discusses an "anxiety" that "comes from knowing I have no real qualifications to write as I do. Not a philosopher or sociologist, not a real professor of literature or film, not a political scientist, professional music critic or trained journalist. I'm employed in an MFA programme, but have no MFA myself, and no PhD" (*Feel Free* xi). However, there is something really important in the caveat that follows: "my evidence—such as it is—is always intimate" (xi). Not only for Smith herself, but for the novelist-critic more widely, it is vital to make the intimacy of writing about personal aesthetic and embodied experiences of looking, viewing, reading, listening, a part of the everyday, ordinary, quotidian. Rather than altogether sublime, such experiences are made accessible, democratic, and urgently necessary.

Serious or not, then, many contemporary writers have a lot to say about their artistic praxis and aesthetic, political, and ethical attachments. Reflecting on the field of the contemporary in 2013, Elias asked, "Instead of worrying the creative-critical divide, why not build a new kind of salon for critics and artists whose verbal and written interchange would have the potential to introduce us to new practitioners and to open up discussion of uberous and exciting new art forms, analytical methods, and conceptual frames?" (quoted in Hoberek et al. 47). When we are faced with writers who are reaching beyond literary practice, imbuing the form of the novel with intermedial relationships and critical observations, it falls upon critics to urgently experiment with new modes of reading, spurred on by artistic collaboration and scholarly dissatisfaction with the hegemony of critique. I agree with Elias that because "we live in an age of increasingly intermedial and multimodal art . . . the borders between the arts as well as the borders between art and criticism have blurred" (46). Novels such as those this book focuses on are not only intermedial, but "combine . . . craft and theory; likewise, installation art and conceptual art today very much merges visual and verbal media in artworks often deeply engaged with 'high theory'" (46).

The ambition underlying this book, then, is to distinguish a peculiarly novelistic mode of talking about art that makes clear these novelists' entanglements with theory, while also theorizing an experiential, everyday contemporary mode of experiencing the aesthetic. This mode at once privileges the experience over the object, derailing the hegemony of institutional responses to art—one that oscillates between modes of judgment, critique, examination, and analysis, and feeling, impression, perception—and makes those experiences weakened by negative feelings, quite unlike the sublime encounters that high theory attributes to art.

A kind of reflexive reading accounts for both the criticality of the contemporary novel and the growing body of art criticism produced by novelists. Intersecting also with recent developments in affect and contemporary American literature, this method balances the formal with the affective, commensurate with these writers' own complex investments in artistic form and emotional dissonance. Indeed, reflexive reading takes inspiration from how the book's novelists disturb the modalities through which we see, talk, encounter, and write about art to ask what wider implications these interartistic literary experiments have for our critical habits. Engaging with sensory aesthetic experience, they seek not only to refract and problematize such experiences but to interrogate expectation in compelling and fresh ways. By reading between their literary and critical works, this book maps the networks of the contemporary art novel since the turn of the millennium, illuminating how writers conceptualize and craft artistic form, how they negotiate their works once in print, and how they negate the mainstream novel form and conventional models of aesthetic experience.

Enstrangement, slant rhymes, synesthesia, transcription, and suspension are modes of against that grapple with form and affect, emerging

INTRODUCTION 29

as affective form and formal affect. How does the chiasmus signify both the formal rhymes between the image and text and an ethics of vision? Why is it so difficult to say anything after the act of looking? What forms might be able to capture a female phenomenology of chance, vacillation, and readerly affinity? How does synesthesia operate as a blended sensory experience and a plea for an embodied critical apparatus? What rhythms are traceable in methods of slow reading and suspension of feeling?

They are also modes that attempt to cohere aesthetic judgment and experience. Enstrangement encompasses the problem of habit in aesthetic encounters and the inability to say anything after artistic encounters. *Slant rhymes* refers to a chiasmic way of bringing together image and text to break from the mutual exclusion, described in the preface, of the antagonistic relationship that writers perceived between art and literature, but it also represents an ethics of vision. Synesthesia mixes touch and feeling as a mode of repairing the affective link in our critical methods. Transcription enables novelists to get as close to the real as possible, while also capturing a female phenomenology of chance, vacillation, and readerly affinity. Suspension delineates a method of slow reading that also negotiates suspended feeling. The moment of transformative aesthetic power each of these novels seeks is often short-lived or undermined to the point of never existing. Through extended close readings—of the novels, of interviews, of art and literary criticism written by novelists—this book not only refocuses the way we read contemporary literature, but how we reflect on our own aesthetic experiences.

ONE

ENSTRANGEMENT

Let's start at the end. In the final pages of Zadie Smith's *On Beauty* (2005), Howard Belsey wordlessly clicks through the images in his PowerPoint, lingering on each: "A picture came up. He waited a minute and then pressed it once more. Another picture. He kept pressing. People appeared: angels and staalmeesters and merchants and surgeons and students and writers and peasants and kings and the artist himself. And the artist himself. And the artist himself" (442). In the accumulation of images, the noiseless display of images appears as deliberate and evident curation: "The man from Pomona began to nod appreciatively. Howard pressed the red button. He could hear Jack French saying to his eldest son . . . *You see, Ralph, the order is meaningful*" (442). Then, finally, he zooms in on one painting until a "woman's fleshiness filled the wall" (443). And, in the face of the overwhelming surface detail, as Smith observes in her author's note, "Howard has nothing at all to say" (445).

Even though we know this performance is intended to stall for time—Howard has forgotten his lecture notes in the car—this ineffability points to what Peter de Bolla calls "*the* distinctive aspect of aesthetic experience"

(4). Ineffability as a sign of wonder might even deem this experience as sublime: as Philip Shaw notes, it is sublimity that specifically "refers to the moment when the ability to apprehend, to know, and to express a thought or sensation is defeated" (3). Indeed, in *A Portrait of the Artist as a Young Man*, James Joyce described this effect as "[t]he instant wherein that supreme quality of beauty, the clear radiance of the esthetic image, is apprehended luminously by the mind which has been arrested by its wholeness and fascinated by its harmony is the luminous silent stasis of esthetic pleasure" (179). In this "spiritual state," Howard's intellectual mind has quieted due to "the enchantment of [his] heart" (Joyce 179). Attending to the peculiarity of this not-so-peculiar response to art, de Bolla undermines the conventional explanation of inarticulacy as cognitive failure after the perceptual experience—that "since affective experiences do not lie within the realm of the cognitive, there is nothing, as it were, to communicate"—to suggest that it comes down instead to linguistic failure: "a fault in our language" (4). Here, Howard suffers a failure of both cognition and language: though his well-worn spiel does not come readily to mind, and he seems to have forgotten the very systems of art historical response his training has afforded him, for the first time in the entire novel Howard is overcome by intense aesthetic feeling.

This ineffability is an odd paradox of the very technique of ekphrasis, from the Greek *ek* (out from) and *phrasis* (to speak).[1] But *having nothing to say is a familiar trope in* On Beauty. Its characters' relationships tend to falter or come undone after failed or missed attempts at communication. So why start with an affective state that seems to fulfill the intensity of feeling that aesthetic experiences purport to engender? This moment in *On Beauty* is unusual in how it imbues art with the quality of intensifying perceptual and emotional effects, rather than perpetuating the exhausted aesthetic state in which the rest of the novel operates. "The new artistic immortality," as Michael Clune argues, doesn't desire "the survival of an object across chronological time" but "pits the survival of subjective intensities against the operation of habit, which turns time into space, lived experience into objects" ("Make It Vanish" 248). Because the recognition that the novel celebrates in its final pages erodes the vivacity of the experience or object, flatlining the possibility for new observations, "[t]oday's literature severs" the "bond" of recognition (248). Because reading backward from this point illuminates quite how much *On Beauty* negates the optimistic view of aesthetic experience. When this structure of trying and failing to speak occurs inside the aesthetic experience, it suggests less a mute wonder after seeing the image than a state of affective alienation.

This moment of aesthetic speechlessness is faithful to the common thinking that art releases the eye from the slow erosion of perceptual and sensory slackening caused by habit. Feeling like the humdrum of daily life is getting you down? Go and spend some time in a gallery or read a book; take time out and slow down. Reacquaint yourself with the act of looking. When you finish, you might just see things afresh. For Viktor Shklovsky in "Art as Device," the category of art is peculiarly immune to the fading vibrancy of other activities or mental processes, "exist[ing] in order to restore the sensation of life, in order to make us feel things" (3). Usually these experiences of lower aesthetic power amount to everyday activities and interactions, like doing the washing; usually the surfaces of paintings provide us with new ways of looking and feeling; usually, art becomes a technique for "intensifying the impression of the senses" (3).

But what happens when the art object occupies this lower register? When it is the art object that becomes desensitized? When the work of art is what is familiar, banal, and even boring? Smith doesn't like to be bored, and this is what worries Smith's novelistic and critical work. In "Fail Better," an essay published in 2007, Smith upended several failures of the prevailing literary culture, lambasting the cliché as "the simplest denomination of literary betrayal." Because "you have pandered to a shared understanding, you have taken a short-cut, you have re-presented what was pleasing and familiar rather than risked what was true and strange." Saying it fresh does not just yield to arguments about newness, but relying on a cliché "is an aesthetic and an ethical failure: to put it very simply, you have not told the truth." For Smith, "writers have only one duty," and that is "the duty to express accurately their way of being in the world," without "all the dead language, the second-hand dogma, the truths that are not your own but other people's, the mottos, the slogans, the out-and-out lies of your nation, the myths of your historical moment." With these removed, "what you are left with is something approximating the truth of your own conception," or at least "one person's truth as far as it can be rendered through language." Failing to do so risks not only repeating the small clichés like "somebody 'rummages in their purse'" in every novel (as Smith herself does), but because of what it suggests of stylistic ambition: "[t]o rummage through a purse is to sleepwalk through a sentence—small enough betrayal of self, but a betrayal all the same." Relying on "old, persistent friend[s]" through "laz[iness] and thoughtless[ness]" and other unideal states attenuates the literary self toward the worst kind of literary failure: inauthenticity.

"Old," "persistent," and "friend"—seeking their opposites ironically risks recycling the familiar modernist dictum of making it new again. This emphasis on the intensification of aesthetic experience calls into question the assumption that the category of art is immune to the fading vibrancy of other activities or mental processes—over time "becom[ing] habitual" and "automatic" ("Art as Device" 4, 5), "[s]o eventually all of our skills and experiences function unconsciously" (5). Though William James, too, emphasizes that "[t]he moment one tries to define what habit is, one is led to the fundamental properties of matter," its grounded materiality is beneficial for higher aesthetic states of mentation or feeling: "[t]he more of the details of our daily life we can hand over to the effortless custody of automatism, the more our higher powers of mind will be set free for their own proper work" ("Habit" 102). This chapter seeks to address these questions with regard to a novel that doesn't rebel against the inevitability of this process of habit, but succumbs to it.

While Jesse Prinz has shown that familiarity from repeated exposure of artworks "induces positive affect, and positive affect increases preference" (73), such habits of looking are vulnerable to the fade of flattening aesthetic effects. So, while aesthetic experiences are often drawn on as sources of profound comfort and consolation, my sense of aesthetic affect encompasses a wide range of negative affects. Negative or equivocal affects, such as disappointment, disgust, envy, irritation, or anxiety, as Sianne Ngai demonstrated in *Ugly Feelings* (2005), can hold equal sway over experiences of art. Although aesthetics might proclaim to prepare us for the ideal, she notes, "most of our aesthetic experiences are based on combinations of ordinary feelings" (Interview with Jasper). As I show throughout this chapter, Smith's *On Beauty*'s aesthetic experiences often feature disquieting moods and undercut their sublime ambitions, instead searching for ordinary feelings that might on occasion preference "ambivalent" or "non-cathartic feelings that index situations of suspended agency" over aesthetic intensity (Ngai, Interview with Jasper). Such aesthetic experiences that are "grounded in equivocal affects . . . on feelings that explicitly clash" can nevertheless wield surprisingly equal critical and aesthetic power (Interview with Jasper).

Here, habit gets a thorough airing—as repetition, as critical or literary training, as routine—as Smith negotiates the affective contingency of contemporary aesthetic experience. Remembering that art forms part of a daily experience is a significant motivating factor for Smith as she depicts situations where art has undergone the process of automatization, where it may be intellectually stimulating but lacks any emotive power. Never a quality of the object itself, however, this dilemma of seeing is attributed to the viewer's own affective deficiencies. *On Beauty* builds through repetition a drop-off effect, whereby experience over time leads to an increasing sense of emotive dissociation. Though Smith courts enstrangement formally, stylistically, and experientially, suggesting novelistic strategies for overcoming desensitization once it has occurred, never is this structure of disassociation preempted or foreclosed. Over the following pages, I take my cue from this simple realignment of values: what really matters about contemporary writing is the way it avoids the economy of institutional habit to instead express a desire for art to create something more intrinsic to aesthetic experience in ordinary life.

TURNING AWAY

After the psychological dynamics of the novel's modes of aesthetic ambivalence, perception is foregrounded as a remedy by the end of the novel. During the procession of images, "the lights begin to go down, very slowly, on a dimmer, as if Howard were trying to romance his audience"— indeed, looking out into the audience, he finds his soon-to-be ex-wife, Kiki, "in her face, his life" (442). The atmosphere is heavily expectant; lines of vision intersect palpably in the room as he pauses on the painting he later zooms in on, Rembrandt's *Hendrickje Bathing* (c. 1654, also known as *Woman Bathing*). First, between the audience, the painting, Howard, and Hendrickje, the woman in the painting:

> On the wall, a pretty, blousy Dutch woman in a simple white smock paddled in water up to her calves. Howard's audience looked at her and then at Howard and then at the woman once more, awaiting elucidation. The woman, for her part, looked away, coyly, into the water. She seemed to be considering whether to wade deeper. The surface of the water was dark, reflective—a cautious bather could not be certain of what lurked beneath. (442)

Even Hendrickje is expectant, "coy," and "cautious" and the water "reflective." But the suspense in the room is driven by the audience's desire for Howard to start speaking, to provide intellectual "elucidation." Even more anticipatory is the second intersecting triangle of vision, between Howard, Kiki, and the painting: Howard "looked out into the audience once more and saw Kiki only. He smiled at her. She smiled. She looked away, but she smiled. Howard looked back at the woman on the wall, Rembrandt's love, Hendrickje" (443).

This turn of the head, glance away, turn away is the action of the afterimage, where images of Hendrickje, Kiki, Howard, and the audience imbricate on top of one another. This action follows the general line of Henri Bergson's reflexive perception as an accumulation of "images photographed upon the object itself" (125). While some perceptions "are dissipated as soon as received," what Bergson calls "*attentive* perception" instead "involves a *reflexion*, in the etymological sense of the word, that is to say the projection, outside ourselves, of an actively created image, identical with, or similar to, the object on which it comes to mold itself" (102). It is in this moment of reflexion, turning "our eyes abruptly away" *after* "having gazed at any object," that "we obtain an 'afterimage' of it" (102). By overlapping image upon image, the afterimage describes both the immediate effects of looking and its attenuating affects over time, but as this process of perception continues, burgeoning "memory-images" start to complicate matters as they are "but the echo" of what has preceded (126, 125). If the afterimages produced in the immediate aftermath "are identical with the object" or scene, "there are others, stored in memory, which merely resemble it." Behind even them, are those "which are only more or less distantly akin to" the original. Nevertheless, in the moment of perception, "[a]ll these go out to meet" it "and, feeding on its substance, acquire sufficient vigour and life to abide with it in space" (103). In this convergence,

> Memory thus creates anew the present perception; or rather it doubles this perception by reflecting upon it either its own image or some other memory-image of the same kind. If the retained or remembered image will not cover all the details of the image that is being perceived, an appeal is made to the deeper and more distant regions of memory, until other details that are already known come to project themselves upon those details that remain unperceived. And the operation may go on indefinitely; memory strengthening and enriching perception, which, in its turn becoming wider, draws into itself a growing number of complementary recollections. (123)

But if Bergson's double take is intensified, Howard's memory-images lack the "sufficient vigour" needed to refresh "present perception"—the overlapping of image upon image upon image (from memory, resemblance, echo) instead deadens and falls away.

In the first class of the academic year, Howard turns to *The Anatomy Lesson of Dr. Nicolaes Tulp* (1632), one of the most recognizable paintings of the Dutch Enlightenment. Although "Howard had a long shtick about this painting that never failed to captivate his army of shopping-day students, their new eyes boring holes into the old photocopy," his own experience of *The Anatomy Lesson* is marred by the humdrum repetition of habit (144). If we are to follow Shklovsky's argument that "[t]he purpose of art is to lead us to a knowledge of a thing through the organ of sight instead of recognition" (*Theory of Prose* 9), then Howard's experience is failing horribly. That the original perceptual experience fades over time, afflicted by the imperfections and rituals of memory, raises significant questions about art's transformative potency. According to Michael Clune, too, "[t]ime poisons perception. No existing technique has proven effective at inoculating images against time. The problem itself is familiar. The more we see something, the duller and feebler our experience of it becomes" (*Writing Against Time* 3). If art is subject to the same erosion of our sensorial faculties, "[c]an art reliably return us to the intense duration of the first impression"? (11).

In *On Beauty* the answer is a hard no: the artwork is the object that the eye recognizes, and experiences of art can become devoid of all affective power. Rembrandt's cultural status is so well known and his paintings so ubiquitous that his aesthetic power has been thoroughly depleted. Here, the reproduction of the painting is itself "old"; Howard's "long shtick" is worn material, repeated year upon year, we presume, because of its success in charming prospective students who, by contrast, listen to his speech each year for the first time. In fact, "Howard had seen it so many times he could no longer see it at all. He spoke with his back to it, pointing to what he needed to with the pencil in his left hand" (144). As Bergson argued, "habit is formed by the repetition of an effort; but what would be the use of repeating it, if the result were always to reproduce the same thing?" (111). If "the true effect of repetition is to decompose, and then to recompose" (Bergson 111), Howard is stuck at the first hurdle: decomposition of perception. Even earlier remnants of radical thinking—Howard considers myths of "Art" to be "[n]onsense and sentimental tradition" and is writing a book, *Against Rembrandt*, whose arguments are expressed "along these almost automatic lines" (*On Beauty* 118)—have stalled. Habit has exhausted his affective perception to the point of apathy.

Howard presents Rembrandt as indicative of the false reassurance of aesthetic power over perception:

> He had offered them a Rembrandt who was neither a rule breaker nor an original but rather a conformist; he had asked them to ask themselves what they meant by 'genius' and, in the perplexed silence, replaced the familiar rebel master of historical fame with Howard's own vision of a merely competent artisan who painted whatever his wealthy patrons requested. Howard asked his students to imagine prettiness as the mask that power wears. To recast Aesthetics as a rarefied language of exclusion. He promised them a class that would challenge their own beliefs about the redemptive humanity of what is commonly called 'Art'. (154–55)

Howard's art historical sensibility is firmly rooted against the consoling and fictionalizing features of familiarity, even if herein also lies the joke: "'Art is the Western myth,' announced Howard, for the sixth year in a row, 'with which we both *console* ourselves and *make* ourselves'" (155). Does the yearly repetition of such aphorisms not form Howard's own comforting myth upon which he constructs himself? Smith makes Howard the butt of the joke: he attempts to make students cast aside what they know about *The Anatomy Lesson* in order to really see it.

38 CHAPTER ONE

The novel offers a specific painting in which these lines intersect. Consider the traditional view of a Rembrandt painting, such as his 1662 painting *The Sampling Officials of the Drapers' Guild*, or *The Staalmeesters*. One conventional reading might suggest that Rembrandt has caught each of the six officials in a "moment of cogitation," encapsulating on each of their faces exactly "what *judgement* looks like: considered, rational, benign"— a moment spurred on, some think, by a question from an unseen audience member (383). When looking at the digital image of this painting on his computer screen, however, Howard scoffs at such a sentimental project of critical benevolence:

> Iconoclastic Howard rejects all these fatuous assumptions. How can we know what goes on beyond the frame of the painting itself? What audience? Which questioner? What moment of judgement? . . .
> To imagine that this painting depicts any one temporal moment is, Howard argues, an anachronistic, photographic fallacy. It is all so much pseudo-historical storytelling, disturbingly religious in tone. (383–34)

But if Howard's *Anatomy Lesson* material is so worn as to have lost meaning, so too is this argument. The narrator, too, seems jaded: "So goes Howard's spiel," we are told; "He's repeated it and written about it so many times over the years that he has now forgotten from which research he drew his original evidence. He will have to unearth some of this for the lecture" with which the novel closes (384). Perhaps understandably, the thought of going over this same material again does not reinvigorate him but instead "makes him very tired." Here, life diverges from art: while Rembrandt depicts the thinking of the *staalmeesters* as slight bewilderment, as if registering something for the first time (if we follow the popular story Howard is fundamentally against), Howard is depicted as embodying the fading cognition that is produced by repeated viewing, even asking in a rare moment of self-awareness: "How many times has [he] looked at these men?" (384).

Experiencing art within this mode no longer retains any qualities of the aesthetic; bereft of affective reaction of any kind, Howard's automatization has inured him to the wonder of his initial impressions of the painting at age fourteen. Experiencing the painting for the first time "forty-three years ago" (385), "[h]e had been alarmed and amazed by the way the Staalmeesters seemed to look directly at him, their eyes (as his schoolmaster put it) 'following you around the room,' and yet, when Howard tried to stare back at the men, he was unable to meet any of their eyes directly" (384–85). Then, the staalmeesters had assessed "an uncultured, fiercely bright, dirty-kneed, enraged, beautiful, inspired, bloody-minded schoolboy," but now that Howard is the same age as the men in the painting, their judgment is unequivocally ambiguous. First, Smith traces this perceptual interaction—"Howard looked at the men. The men looked at Howard. Howard looked at the men. The men looked at Howard"—as reciprocal, but Howard quickly averts his gaze to "zoom, zoom, zoom until he was involved only with the burgundy pixels of the Turkey rug" (385). Intoxicatingly luminescent as Rembrandt's fabrics are, however, the swift and distracted way in which Howard looks elsewhere in the painting suggests precisely the extent to which his captivation with the painting has dulled, the fresh curiosity of his childhood eroded by his knowing, critical eye. His interaction with the painting following his interpretative account only recounts superficial biographical details of the men, rather than the compositional or material qualities observed by the narrator. What Howard is thus occupied by is the surface of the painting only, which is mediated through the computer screen in such a way that pigment becomes pixels.

Deconstructing the surface of the painting to its smallest components (pigment/pixels) suggests a new system of vision—for one, it suggests Howard is trying to see *again*, rather than remember what he already knows. Though his vision is still distracted and affectless, replenishing the painting's surface with pigment seeks to recover the materiality of the painting that was initially lost. Returning to the surface wipes it clean.

OVERCOMING

That it is through literature that the modes of responding to art need to be made new again (to adapt Ezra Pound's famous dictum) raises problematic questions of the ethics of ekphrasis's descriptive habits. Though "literature itself . . . has often aimed to unsettle entrenched perceptions so that we can see the world more clearly," as Caroline Levine has noted, "[n]ovelistic description, if it is going to disrupt rather than conserve, must unsettle those habits of dulled acquiescence" ("Strange Familiar" 588, 590). But as we know from Smith's critique of lyrical realism outlined in her now seminal essay "Two Directions for the Novel," the semblance of the perfect surface is both aesthetically dissatisfying and ethically compromising. In tune with what I'm tracing as *On Beauty*'s friction with the automatic structures of everyday life, Smith critiques a certain kind of overwrought aesthetic sensibility in contemporary writing: that which occurs "[o]ut of a familiar love" ("Two Directions" 81). For some novels, this is a love for "the rituals and garments of transcendence," even if their authors are well enough aware that such promises "are empty"—or, in other words, a love, in essence, for comforting delusions (81).

Such works, epitomized by a novel such as Joseph O'Neill's *Netherland* (2011), "indulge" in "the fears and weaknesses of its readers" to evoke temporal coherency and rely on heavy "verbal fancy" (Smith, "Two Directions" 82). Smith's disappointment is palpable: "our receptive pathways are so solidly established that to read this novel is to feel a powerful, somewhat dispiriting sense of recognition" (73). Our readerly "recognition" is not consoling, even if that's the desired aim—the novel "wants always to comfort us, to assure us of our beautiful plenitude" (80–81). Recognizing *Netherland*'s lyrical image is instead "dispiriting"; it is too perfect, too "precise" to be soothing. But what are the implications of the perceptual familiarity Smith describes? What might it tell us about the ethically strained lyricism in contemporary writing? In leveling familiarity against *Netherland* as critique rather than praise, Smith paints a picture of the road to this literary register as paved not by innovation but aesthetic habit—"so precisely the image of what we have been taught to value in fiction . . . throws that image into a kind of existential crisis, as the photograph gifts a nervous breakdown to the painted portrait" (73). As Mark McGurl has discussed, "[t]o the extent that 'lyrical' simply means a beautiful voicing of individual perception, adding that kind of value to the raw matter of the world will probably always seem a good bet for writing something worth reading" ("Forking Path").

Worse still, Smith claims, such emotionally barren habit is a product of a shared desire for artistic complacency—"it's the post-911 novel we hoped for . . . . It's as if, by an act of collective prayer, we have willed it into existence" (72)—even if the design of the resulting work only produces a "cheap longing" (74) of the sort we find in "bedtime stor[ies]" (73). Regardless of whether novelistic surface is itself a problem—*Netherland*'s corollary, Tom McCarthy's *Remainder*, too, "is more than sufficient" as surface, indeed "surface *alone*" (96)—surely artifice is: in contrast with McCarthy's novel, *Netherland* is "only superficially about 9/11 or immigrants or cricket as a symbol of good citizenship" (82). For Smith, it is in such semblance of depth that we find the false consolations of the "relentlessly aestheticized" novel (78); as Kiki Belsey notes uneasily in *On Beauty*, "our memories are getting more beautiful and less real every day" (*On Beauty* 174).

In this disconnection between the beautiful and the real lies the novel's core suspicion of the contemporary novel's aestheticizing tendencies. Although such a model encourages a "reenchantment" of the commonplace, as Martin Jay argued, "as if any object or event, however mean, were a legitimate occasion for aesthetic experience" (16), Smith is far from indiscriminate in her efforts to illuminate the moral consequences of aesthetic excess. Neither new at the time nor resolved since, Smith's central critique of lyrical realism has nevertheless become representative (unwillingly so if you ask its author) of the ethical concerns of the consoling ambitions and expectations of literary expression. David James, writing in defense of lyrical realism, has critiqued Smith's equivalence between lyrical realism and readerly comfort. Casting doubt on Smith's assertion that lyrical realism causes ethical discomfort, James argues that "lyrical realism has no truck with mere bedtime stories" because "it triggers assessments of fiction's capacity for tackling tough material without transmuting it into something more bearable" ("In Defense" 87).

Smith's uneasiness about the ethics of literary aestheticization privileges a common, though reductively schematic, narrative about the aesthetics of contemporary life. Lyrical realism signals both an intensification and exhaustion of the aesthetic. Though novels that conform to the stylistic patterning of lyrical realism tend to represent the aestheticization of contemporary life in prose, they also portray "a state of exhaustion in our frames of aesthetic experience" (Gumbrecht 315). Indeed, in her essay "Fail Better," the aesthetic and ethical are diametrically opposed: "[w]riters feel . . . that what appear to be bad aesthetic choices very often have an ethical dimension." Located in what is for her, as Dorothy Hale notes, "the defining feature of literary art" ("*On Beauty* as Beautiful?" 827), "bad aesthetic choices" result when the writer does not prioritize style over subject; accurate representation of the "ethical dimension" of the scene must take precedence over the way it is represented. But outside of this context, might we not also consider the inverse to be a mark of a "bad" style? As we know from "Two Directions," a form's stylization has its own "ethical dimensions." Smith takes style seriously: it is neither "merely a matter of fanciful syntax, or as the flamboyant icing atop a plain literary cake, nor as the uncontrollable result of some mysterious velocity coiled within language itself," but "the only possible expression of a particular human consciousness" ("Fail Better"). Stylization, however, offers in effect a false "refinement" of consciousness, overriding the function of style as "a writer's way of telling the truth." Considering Smith's critical work, Hale argues that what we notice is "a serious attempt to articulate a theory of the positive value of literature as an ethical discourse, which is to say an aesthetic discourse that raises the question of its own status as a social discourse" (826–27). Putting it a different way, I suggest that in reaffirming the value of the novel, Smith does so by refracting it through its negations and refusals of the aesthetic—advocating not for the smooth surface of lyrical realism, but for the meaning that is found in aesthetic and ethical disturbance.

So, these disturbances are not large-scale disruptions to plot or narrative but are proliferated in stylistic nuance. Critiquing this preference for lyricism, Chimamanda Ngozi Adichie's *Americanah* (2013) echoes Smith's worries about the dangers descriptive overload poses for contemporary literary praxis: "if you're going to write about race, you have to make sure it's so lyrical and subtle that the reader who doesn't read between the lines won't even know it's about race. You know, a Proustian meditation, all watery and fuzzy, that at the end just leaves you feeling watery and fuzzy" (335–36). We know precisely what Adichie is referring to by "watery and fuzzy"; after all, as Smith tells us, lyrical realism prioritizes "baroque descriptions of clouds, light and water" ("Two Directions" 72). Indeed, "isn't it hard to see the dark when it's so lyrically presented?" (79). But a painterly sensibility and an "adjectival mania is still our dominant mode" (79), however often it results in "a nicely constructed sentence, rich in sound and syntax, signifying (almost) nothing" (81). Whether we choose to view Adichie's use of the word "lyrical" as telling or not, what she (along with Smith) is uneasy about is the desire for the niceties of the familiar and the aesthetic conventions that such desires direct the novel into as a consequence. To be sure, this novelistic familiarization creates comfort, but an ethically compromising kind of comfort where there ought not to be any at all—"if a character is not familiar," as Shan points out, "then that character becomes unbelievable" (*Americanah* 336). "Nothing escapes" ("Two Directions" 78), not even matters of race, terrorism, and trauma: in *Netherland*, for example, "[t]here was the chance to let the towers be what they were: towers. But they were covered in literary language when they fell, and they continue to be here" (82). Habit's stultifying effects have frozen lyrical realism's coordinates not simply because it falsely comforts us through the replication of recognizable images, but because any generative meaning—aesthetic, ethical, epistemological, or otherwise—has been emptied out of the subject.

If we are to take Smith at her word, novels working in this mode are in danger of creating assurances where there ought to be violent ruptures; like lyric realism's alternative path, it needs to "retain . . . the wound" ("Two Directions" 79). In what follows, though, I want to pursue this path by considering how the critical care Smith urges literary practitioners to employ through description bears on a genre of description that exhibits a pervasive debt to lyricism. Ekphrasis is not immune to description's "aesthetic offence[s]," nor does it avoid "highly stylized uses of language" (79). Published two years earlier than "Two Directions," *On Beauty* internalizes the very critical sensibility this essay projects. While many have thought of *On Beauty* as working within this lyrical realist mode (a fractured image of the aesthetic or not, it is on beauty after all, and what else does lyrical realism strive to emulate than what's aesthetically pleasing?), Smith's novel takes as its subject, not style, but two core problems of aesthetic experience today: first, the slow erosion of affective exhaustion caused by repeated encounters with art, and, second, the uncertainty with the affective language of aesthetic judgment.

DIZZY, UNCERTAIN PATHS

Given *On Beauty*'s critique of the familiar, what is it about Rembrandt that proves so attractive as a subject? In performing art history, the novelistic congregation around this one painter (occasionally even the same painting as W. G. Sebald's *Rings of Saturn* exhibits) demonstrates the currency of Western culture's fascination with the myth of Rembrandt's "genius" (as Howard claims) at least, and a sense of underlying resonances between social and artistic values in Rembrandt's paintings and those of the present, at most. But far from wanting to make broad claims as to precisely why Smith chose Rembrandt's paintings to engage with fictionally, what interests me more here is how the novel models different engagements with the work of art. From the satirical banal to the joyous, the novel's vision is segmented through eyes plagued by uncertainty: eyes that are flawed, prone to distraction, and that often cannot tell one painting's surface from another.

Seeing through unfamiliar eyes is often privileged as a hallmark of Smith's ethical approach to literary perspectivalism, as the familiarization of the social other by focalizing their experiences—part of the problem of lyrical realism, as we have seen, is that it only shows us what we know we *want* to see, or, what we have already seen. To the extent that this constitutes an ethics of perspectivalism, when ekphrasis enters the frame, it sustains an equally significant aesthetics of perception. Ekphrasis, too, allows us to see anew, even if what it is describing is familiar to us. As Jaś Elsner argues, such a descriptive strategy is mired in the gap between the visual and the verbal—the ambition of making "the reader or the listener 'see' more than they saw before, when they encounter the object next" while also acknowledging the object's "uncanny ability to be verbalized in a myriad of ways" (26). As Smith deploys it, ekphrasis thus invites us to break out of habit and see the art object anew.

But if one part of this struggle is located in the ekphrastic "gap" between the visual and the verbal, another is found in the gap between modes of responding to art. Hale reminds us that *On Beauty*'s title, a direct citation of Elaine Scarry's *On Beauty and Being Just* (1999), does not replicate a philosophical point of view but "signals the difference between the philosopher's notion of beauty and the novelist's by calling attention to the social discursivity through which the meaning of beauty is produced" ("*On Beauty* as Beautiful?" 815–16). In so doing, Hale argues, "Smith affirms the perspectivalism upon which the aesthetics of alterity rests" (820). So if against Rembrandt's paintings themselves, Howard's singular ekphrastic passages thus allow us to see the paintings as if for the first time— refracting his specific sensibility to bring us closer to the art object—Smith's ekphrasis through perspectivalism augments this process. Amy J. Elias has noted how today's "proliferation" of keywords like "relationality; activated spectatorship; intersubjective relationship; remix; participation; collaboration; connectivity," among others, "imply that intersubjective communication is an aesthetic as well as an ethical imperative that has deepened through, and after the turn of, the twentieth century" ("Dialogical Avant-Garde," 739). Twenty-first century arts are stretching beyond the postmodern efforts of "see[ing] and hear[ing] the Other" using "tropes of difference and in the mode of irony," instead querying "how to speak with the Other and how to set discourses in dialogue" (739). Smith's ethical perspectivalism tracks this aesthetic dialogue in form.

Partway through *On Beauty*'s second section, "the anatomy lesson," the novel moves swiftly from Howard's objective critical register to a "subjective affective response" that Smith has explored in her critical work as something she used to find "sentimental" and ultimately "irrelevant" to critical study ("Love, Actually"). For Katie, a sixteen-year-old student, Rembrandt "is the second most amazing human being" she "has ever come across" (second to Picasso), having long "dream[t] about one day attending a college class about Rembrandt with other intelligent people who loved Rembrandt and weren't ashamed to express this love" (250). In attending Howard's classes, however, the vocabulary of critique "escapes" her to "stream through her toes as the sea and sand when she stands at the edge of the ocean and dozily, stupidly, allows the tide to draw out and the world to pull away from her so rapidly as to make her dizzy . . ." (253).

While the novel moves frequently between characters, Katie's brief appearance is unusual; we see through her eyes only once, with the clear aim of disrupting the extremely flat tone of Howard's critique. We are told she "has spent a week staring at" the "photocopies" of two images, indeed "thinking deeply about them" (250). The painting, *Jacob Wrestling with the Angel*, "Katie finds impressive, beautiful, awe-inspiring" (251), noting its "vigorous impasto that works counter-intuitively to create that somnolent, dreamy atmosphere" (250). She admires the tonal palette of "earthly colours," locates the Bible passage to which the painting refers, and ruminates on the wings, which seems to be painted as "almost an afterthought." Nevertheless, she does not find the painting "truly moving" (251). Identifying with the "faith battle" Rembrandt is aiming to depict in the painting, Katie finds a lack of "struggle"—enough to question whether the painter has depicted a battle at all: when she looks at the figures of Jacob and the angel, "Jacob looks like he wants sympathy, and the angel looks like he wants to *give* sympathy" (251). But if her thoughts on *Jacob* represent the distant curiosity of intellection, it is her experience of *Seated Nude* that resembles Smith's subjective affective response. Looking at it "makes Katie cry" (251). The subject of the "misshapen woman, naked, with tubby little breasts and a huge distended belly" is for most commentators "technically good but visually disgusting"; men in particular "are repulsed" by her embodiment of the "grotesque." But for Katie, who is shocked by the etching "at first" glance, on deeper inspection, it is "all the exterior, human information, not explicitly *in* the frame but implied by what we see here" that is so moving: "the crenulated marks of absent stockings on her legs, the muscles in her arms suggestive of manual labour. That loose belly that has known many babies, that still fresh face that has lured men in the past and may yet lure more." Identifying again with the figuration in this work—this time it is personal—Katie "can even see her own body contained in this body" for "[t]his is what a woman *is*: unadorned, after children and work and age, and experience—*these are the marks of living*" (251–22). *Seated Nude* makes Katie *feel*.

Though critics have found Katie's entry into Smith's perspectivalism "almost gratuitous" (Hale, "*On Beauty* as Beautiful?" 835)—her appearance proving to be all too brief and her aesthetic perception ultimately crushed under the weight of "the white, male academic's perspective" (836)—our brief encounter with her, however, does serve to underline the novel's skepticism of academic knowledge ("Poor Zora—she lived through footnotes" [70]). The friction *On Beauty* exposes between the sensibilities of art historical critique and subjective pleasure played out here echoes Smith's own worry about sentimental moralism in the university in her essay "Love, Actually" (2003). Recounting how youthful impressions of literary fiction located in the realm of personal subjectivity disappear when we become "intellectually responsive to the text," Smith claims that "[t]here is something about love that does not sit well with the literary academy." When we enter the academy, she argues, "a peculiar thing happens":

We find that our initial affective responses are no longer of interest to the literary community in which we find ourselves. We are as Heraclitus described us: "Estranged from that which is most familiar." Suddenly this incommensurable "Love," and this other, more vague surmise—that the novel we loved was not simply "good" but even represented a Good in our lives—these ideas grow shameful and, after some time, are forgotten entirely, along with the novel that first inspired them. For no sensation empirical as love can have any importance as a "response" to novels qua novels. Can it?

Within the university, "[a]n admission of love . . . would only be seen as weakness"—perceived in this way, we "grow shameful" of our notions of a novel's "Good" and our "incommensurable 'Love'" for them. It is this attitude that disheartens Katie after her "third class," enough to make her "curse . . . her stupidity and her youth" and go "back to her dorm" to cry (252). But even away from the pure environs of art historical critique, the expectation to evaluate art through analysis rather than appreciation does not dissipate. Discussing the symbolism of Hector Hyppolite's painting *Maîtresse Erzulie* (c. 1945–48) with her friend Carlene Kipps one afternoon in her library, ex-nurse Kiki feels pressured "to remember a thesis of Howard's . . . to reproduce as her own" (175). The longer they spend admiring the painting, the greater Kiki's impulse to replicate a pattern of intellectual response she has heard many times before from her husband: "Because . . . we're so binary, of course, in the way we think. We tend to think in opposites, in the Christian world. We're structured like that—Howard always says that's the trouble." Despite the cautious everyday speech, the implication of the attempt is plain and, as a result, Carlene's response feels quietly, but equivalently, pointed—"That's a clever way to put it. I like her parrots" (175). For Carlene, there is no need for token theological musing; simply acknowledging aesthetic preference is enough.

But why does Kiki feel compelled to tread the "uncertain path" of technical language? Indeed, other characters are "doubtful" too (175). Later in the novel, Claire Malcolm "uncertainly" repeats "Idealize?" in response to Zora's question, "But how do you avoid falling into pastoral fallacy—I mean, isn't it a depoliticized reification, all this beauty stuff about landscape? Virgil, Pope, the Romantics. Why idealize?" (218). Claire's language of craft was "tiresome" to Zora, committed as she is to poststructuralist theory: "Claire didn't know anything about theorists, or ideas, or the latest thinking. Sometimes Zora suspected her of being barely intellectual" (219). Meanwhile, Warren, Claire's husband, felt a "scientist's reticence when using the language of artists" (54). Though Kiki initially declares the painting's resplendent figure as *"fabulous"* (174; original emphasis) and conversationally exclaims, "Phew. That's a lot of symbolizing" (175), she is nevertheless drawn to speak about art in an idiom both unfamiliar and uncomfortable. We can wonder, of course, about how femininity exerts its own pressures on this scene, and about Kiki's earlier recollections of how "[s]he let Howard reinvent, retouch" (174) throughout their marriage. More broadly, however, it is not difficult to read into this exchange some of Smith's advocacy for sentimentality. After all, Carlene uses primarily an appreciative register when speaking about the painting: she asks Kiki whether she is "admiring" Maîtresse Erzulie (174) and "looks stricken" when Kiki reveals that the Belseys "don't have any paintings in [their] house" as Carlene's many paintings are "her company . . . the greater part of [her] *joy*" (175; original emphasis). But a heftier ambition is the novel's ability to make significant the democratic potential of depicting different encounters with art and modes of understanding them. Through the eyes of Katie, Kiki, and Carlene, the novel retrieves art, if only briefly, from the "rarefied language of exclusion" of "Aesthetics" that Howard claims his classes aim to reevaluate (while, it's important to note, nonetheless continuing unashamedly in the same manner).

By placing critique with love to cultivate a kind of reading, as well as looking, Smith recovers critique from the blunt language of suspicion. Even through the novel's satire one can sense a genuine ambition in its aesthetic commitments. As she describes in "Fail Better," "[s]tyle is a writer's way of telling the truth. Literary success or failure, by this measure, depends not only on the refinement of words on a page, but in the refinement of a consciousness, what Aristotle called the education of the emotions." Recalling the productive critical movement that began to pick up steam with Eve Kosofsky Sedgwick's reparative reading, the kind of criticism that we end up with by the end of the novel gestures toward repair—both the repair of human relationships and the restoration of a dynamic aesthetic vision. As Heather Love argues, the kind of weak theory that reparative reading represents "prefers acts of noticing, being affected, taking joy, and making whole" rather than "organiz[ing] vast amounts of territory and tell big truths" ("Truth" 238, 237). What Katie knows intuitively, what Kiki figures out as she is in the process of divorcing Howard, and what Howard eventually discovers in the final scene reminds us that it matters that although aesthetic experience involves weaker acts than aesthetic judgment, feeling is not itself weaker than intellection. If as Marjorie Garber notes, "[t]he job of the critic is to account for love" (51), *On Beauty* shows precisely how much Smith is a firm believer.

EXPRESSIVE FAILURES

As does Smith's criticism. As we move toward the end, I want to take a detour through "Crazy They Call Me," an essay Smith wrote on Billie Holiday. Writing against Jerry Dantzic's photographs of Holiday for the introduction of *Jerry Dantzic: Billie Holiday at Sugar Hill* (2017), Smith's reflection riffs off the photographs, blending fictional voice with historical episodes.[2] The photographs were taken in April 1957, two years before Holiday's death, when she was performing at the jazz club Sugar Hill in New Jersey. Holiday had been banned from singing in New York jazz clubs ten years earlier, having been charged with a drug crime. Noting in an interview with Cressida Leyshon that she had "never seen them before," Smith points out that "the piece is my direct response—I never would have written it otherwise." Dantzic's photographs captured a variety of "unexpected attitudes," so to Smith the image of Holiday was enstranged, as if she were "[s]eeing an old friend from a new angle."

Like listening to jazz, some might say, "Crazy They Call Me" is tonally inventive, rhythmically hypnotic, and, at its heart, improvisational. Though she confesses in an essay on Joni Mitchell to not being particularly musical—"my parents loved music, as I love music, but you couldn't call any of us whatever the plural of 'muso' is" (*Feel Free* 100)—there is an aesthetic ambition about this essay that recalls the off-kilter tonality of Holiday herself. "Well, you certainly don't go out anyplace less than dressed, not these days," the essay begins, "[c]an't let anybody mistake you for that broken, misused little girl: Eleanora Fagan. No. Let there be no confusion" ("Crazy" 7). Just as Holiday famously wanted to turn her voice into an instrument,

Smith continues her "Billie impressions" from her younger days singing in bars and "old people's homes": "[y]ou can replicate the phrasing but you can't come anywhere near that tension between delight and pain that she had" (Interview with Leyshon). However, it isn't just Dantzic's photographs that enstrange the familiar image of Holiday; Smith's inventive ventriloquism skews internal cognition as external perception: "Once, you almost said—to a sneaky fellow from the *Daily News*, who was inquiring—you almost turned to him and said *Motherfucker I AM* music. But a lady does not speak like that, however, and so you did not" ("Crazy" 12). No tired observations about composition, form, or history here: "Hair takes a while, face takes longer. It's all work, it's all a kind of armour. You got skinny a while back and some guys don't like it, one even told you that you got a face like an Egyptian death mask now. Well, good! You wear it, it's yours" (11). No more Keatsian Grecian urns: it's ekphrasis, stream-of-consciousness style, reimagined for the twenty-first century.

Though she "intended to write a straight biographical introduction to the photographs," "Billie's voice is so distinct" she "couldn't find a way to write about it from any distance at all": "[i]n the end I just looked at the pictures and felt my way in" (Interview with Leyshon). Though Smith has reflected that essay writing is both "a form of relief" and "an attempt at a kind of clarity" ("Chaotic Mind"), it is significant that she turned away from the essay to speak directly to Holiday: "every angle seemed too formal or cold" (*Feel Free* 164). Writing about these photographs could only take the form of ventriloquism. In fact, no essayist compels us to feel as much as does Smith. Reviewing her first collection of essays, *Changing My Mind* (2009), Peter Conrad noted how for Smith, "criticism is a bodily pleasure, not an abstracted mental operation." Her second essay collection is no different, where *Feel Free* is as much an invocation to feeling as it is to freedom. We wouldn't be wrong to register the implicit jab at inauthenticity here. We know that Smith, as a novelist "who came of age under postmodernity, is naturally skeptical of the concept of authenticity"—"after all, how can any of us be more or less authentic than we are?"—because they "were taught that authenticity was meaningless." Despite this, however, the kind of contemporary literary failure writers like Smith ruminate on attends to "a betrayal of one's deepest, authentic self" ("Fail Better"). We've already seen that by enstranging the concept of authenticity from the cynicism of postmodernism, Smith argues for literary style that reflects the authenticity of the self: avoid clichés, get rid of the baggage, and make it strange. Most importantly, though, as *On Beauty* and her criticism tell us, make it *feel*.

Like David Foster Wallace and Dave Eggers, Smith is what Lee Konstantinou would call a "believer" (163). Just as "Wallace sought to defeat bad institutions that give rise to toxic incredulity," so does Smith (Konstantinou 215). By creating a writing and reading practice that cultivates real feeling in place of a belief in the institution—of postmodernism, of the university, of critique—Smith wants us to believe in not only literary but critical empathy: "I always think critical writing should meet its subject in sympathy. If you write about Borges, get a little Borgesian. If you write about Bergman, write Bergmanly. And so on. The stronger the voice of the artist under consideration the more I feel this" (Interview with Leyshon). Being Smithsonian means becoming a writer-critic in the "fantasy literary republic" she envisioned in her essay "Read Better," where "[e]very critic is an artist." Rather than cynical, "a great critic is, in the end, imagining the novelist." Instead of "corrective criticism" (no doubt a veiled jibe at James Wood's "hysterical realism" ["Human"]), "[h]e is piecing together, retroactively, the beliefs and obsessions and commitments that powered the novel into existence in the first place"—itself a process of "speak[ing] the truth about an individual experience with a novel" ("Read Better"). It is fitting that Smith's mode of experience involves surrendering to enstrangement, for enstrangement doesn't involve stepping back, taking distance, only to re-enter and see afresh. It doesn't involve peering from the side or glancing askance. Enstrangement invites a closeness unmediated so we can experience unfiltered as pure feeling.

Democratizing aesthetic experiences, however, is largely depicted without caution. Attending a free, outdoor concert of Mozart's *Requiem* with Howard and her children, Kiki encounters a strange, disassociating experience:

> The experience of listening to an hour's music you barely know in a dead language you do not understand is a strange falling and rising experience. For minutes at a time you are walking deep into it, you seem to understand. Then, without knowing how or when exactly, you discover you have wandered away, bored or tired from the effort, and now you are nowhere near the music. You refer to the

programme notes. The notes reveal that the past fifteen minutes of wrangling over your soul have been merely the repetition of a single inconsequential line. (70)

Indeed, the closest the novel really gets to a sublime experience of art comes immediately after this. As "Kiki tip[s] back her head on her deckchair and trie[s] to let go of her curious anxiety," she notices her eldest son, Jerome, crying:

She opened her mouth with genuine surprise and then, fearful of breaking some spell, closed it again. The tears were silent and plentiful. Kiki felt moved, and then another feeling interceded: pride. *I* don't understand, she thought, but *he* does. A young black man of intelligence and sensibility, and *I* have raised him.

Unsurprisingly, Howard is dismissive—asking "Everyone been touched by the Christian sublime? Can we go now?" (71)— and we don't ever find out where these tears are coming from (Jerome has, after all, been humiliated by a rejected marriage proposal), but Kiki's wonder signals that it is at least possible that there could be something aesthetically enriching about the experience of listening to Mozart.

Tracing out this experience through Kiki's distracted eyes draws our attention to three distinct aspects of the contemporary aesthetic experience. First, the inaccessibility of the intense feelings of aesthetic experience can come down to a lack of aesthetic knowledge ("*I don't understand*"). This is particularly the case with classical music, as Gumbrecht has argued; despite the ubiquity of, say, Mozart and the efforts of democratizing through free outdoor events, "the enormous amount of knowledge and sophistication required to grasp the form and to enjoy the beauty of modern classical music has the effect... of transforming conditions of inclusion into mechanisms of social exclusion" (315). Second, artworks that elicit an aesthetic frame, such as classical music, are difficult to experience aesthetically—there are program notes to contend with, information you feel you're not able to access, and more often than not, it is difficult to maintain the arrested attention of the aesthetic experience for longer than a few minutes before boredom, tiredness, or distraction interrupts. Lastly, daily, minor feelings, such as the pride you feel for your children, might just have the greater capacity for aesthetic experiences today than art's sublimity. When perception is rerouted through the lens of aesthetic sentimentalism, the stultifying effects of aesthetic habits dissipate, even if only momentarily.

As both a phenomenological position and a narrative disposition, then, uncertainty captures the general tenor of the novel's aesthetic experiences. Indeed, at its simplest, contemporary literature treats aesthetic experiences with affective uncertainty. This is similar to what C. Namwali Serpell describes as "refer[ring] to either the object or the cognitive state of the observer. It is the quality or 'state of not being definitely known' or 'the state or character of being uncertain in mind'" (8). Unlike "*ambiguity, difficulty, indeterminacy*," which Serpell argues "tend to get attributed solely to the literary object," uncertainty "captures the interactive, temporal, and experiential qualities to reading" (8; original emphasis) and to encounters with art more generally. Characters go into aesthetic experiences uncertain not because they don't know what to expect but because they do—because they know that aesthetic experiences ought to transform the subject's emotions for the better, because this is what aesthetic experiences are meant to do. And so they generally emerge feeling the same way, because these experiences generally don't resemble these assumptions in any way, shape, or form. Here, characters are unsettled because their relationships with art become antagonistic.

Consistency isn't key, nor is intensity. Rather than being predetermined or fixed, such dissonant affective states fluctuate atmospherically in the way William James described:

> In the case of our affectional experiences we have no permanent and stead-fast purpose that obliges us to be consistent, so we find it easy to let them float ambiguously, sometimes classing them with our feelings, sometimes with more physical realities . . . [I]n practical life no urgent need has yet arisen for deciding whether to treat them as rigorously mental or as rigorously physical facts. So they remain equivocal; and, as the world goes, their equivocality is one of their great conveniences. (*Essays* 74)

As Michael Clune points out, "[m]oments of ekphrasis are always useful occasions for reflecting on art's desire—on what art wants to be and do" ("Make It Vanish" 246). But here, even the novel's seemingly optimistic foray into sublime aesthetic mutism succumbs to ambiguity. After observing the vivid textures of *Hendrickje*—"[t]hough her hands were imprecise blurs, paint heaped on paint and roiled with the brush, the rest of her skin had been expertly rendered in all its variety—chalky whites and lively pinks, the underlying blue of her veins and the ever present human hint of yellow"—the novel ends by abstracting concrete detail into an ambiguous "intimation of what is to come" (443). This kind of *bathos* is characteristic of the negative affective register of *On Beauty*; the final words undercut what "intimation" sets up as an elevated profound conclusion; we can never know "what is to come."

Nevertheless, *On Beauty*'s turn to aesthetic experience exhibits what Clune calls "radical subjectivity," the "dominant form" of which "is the narrative of private experience," not least because the novels transcribe in minute detail intersubjective experiences and feelings that occasionally "seem to enter and colonize" readers' own perceptions ("Make It Vanish" 242). These structures of perception take on metacritical significance in the "new art" of the twenty-first century, in which "experience nibbles away at institutions, objects, individuals, old politics, modernism, postmodernism," and even the modes in which we write about aesthetic experiences. "Today's most vital art, today's most *revolutionary* art, attacks objects" through "the transmission of private vision: absorption, authenticity, intensity" (244). The novel's dissatisfaction with habitual relations between art, reader, and world reflects what Clune refers to as "[t]he new artistic immortality" (244–45). The "utopia" of such novels is "a community not founded on recognition," but "a world where subjectivity encounters no border, no seam" (244). Smith's reinvestment in such perceptual experiences indeed revisits what Viktor Shklovsky claimed one hundred years ago in "Art as Device," whereby "[t]he perceptual process in art has a purpose all its own and ought to be extended to the fullest. Art is a means of experiencing the process of creativity. The artefact itself is quite unimportant" (6). Such a phenomenological position asserts that even though the art object may be "without emotion," aesthetic experience is not.

This brings me to the final pivot of the novel's aesthetic enstrangement. By refusing a single reading or speech altogether, the art object itself has an antagonistic function. As Elsner argues, ekphrasis is a site of contest between an object's "glorious resistance to being fully verbalized" and "its uncanny ability to be verbalized in a myriad of ways, equally valid and sometimes mutually exclusive" (26). Some posit that this muting function allows us to see anew, even if what it is describing is familiar to us—it "brings us back up against the object" (26). When coupled with the shifting subjectivities of perspectivalism, ekphrasis finds a vital and vibrant function: "to make the reader or the listener 'see' more than they saw before, when they encounter the object next. That search for words to make us 'see' is at the heart of the creative struggle against the ways in which what we have learnt can go stale, and it is an attempt to open to the new" (26). But not as Smith deploys it. Instead, *On Beauty* insists "speech is beautifully useless" (153).

And so, we'll end in the middle with an inadvertent contest of expressive failure. When Jack (the dean of humanities) and Claire meet by chance in the photocopy room, the latter gives the former an old poem of hers to read.[3] As a broken pantoum, "On Beauty" consists of lines that repeat, double back, and negate each other. "The beautiful don't lack the wound" pivots to "speech is beautifully useless" and, pivoting again, "the beautiful know this." Jack and the reader of the novel read the poem together, but unlike the novel's reader, "Jack was now faced with a task he dreaded: saying something after reading a poem" (154). True to Smith's sharp eye for irony, he lands on "Beautiful," the only word he could think of, even though "it was in the shady groves of dictionaries that Jack fell in love" with "the bizarre etymology of the intransitive verb 'ramble'" (154). "Beautiful" ends up being "beautifully useless." Claire, at her turn, simply replies offhandedly, "it's just old crap" (154). They're poor afterimages of the poem; the vivacity of the art object is already fading.

TWO

SLANT RHYME

Photography's metaphorical weight has tended to be buried beneath a raft of claims of its indexicality and referentiality, but Kaja Silverman has recently characterized a photograph as an *analogy*—a structure that bridges the chiasmus of sameness and difference between our perceptions of world and self.[1] So let's begin with a metaphor. In an interview with Teju Cole in the *New Yorker* in 2014, the photographers Rebecca Norris Webb and Alex Webb described how they imagine the conversation between their photographic works as slant rhymes: "subtle echoes" "such as a shared palette or an affinity for surreal or surprising moments." In the introduction to their most recent book, which has taken this metaphor of relation as its title, Alex Webb expanded on this earlier description, observing how their "paired photographs strike a similar note . . . although often in two different keys": "[i]f my photographs tend toward a bluesy A minor, like Albert King's *Born Under a Bad Sign*, then Rebecca's work favors an elegiac D minor, like the Bach partita she so loves" (*Slant Rhymes* 7).

Once a poetic technique, the slant rhyme has come to refer to a peculiarly twenty-first century interartistic mode. Despite the preponderance of free verse in the twentieth century, Susan Stewart has argued that "[f]ar from a constraint, rhyme endows us with certain freedoms—among them: the vernacular, including the locality of the poem itself, released from the standard; the monolingual in dialogue with the multilingual; sound opened up by vision, and sound released from meaning entirely; expectation released into surprise; and pattern drawn from the oblivion of time" (48). As the slant rhymes of Webb and Norris Webb's photography show, rhymes are not only semantic and aural but visual too. The mode of slant rhyming, as visual and textual, echoes the feel of poetry: "perfect, imperfect, total, and partial at once" (Stewart 48).

The musical, visual, and textual resonances in this use of the slant rhyme are held in formal and affective tension in Cole's work, too. The slant rhyme indicates the modulation of two different keys, whether intermedial (textual and visual or textual and musical) or tonal variation in a single form (between images). Cole's artistic practice thrives in this intervallic territory: a writer and photographer, he has recently taken on the roles of performance artist, Instagram innovator, and Spotify virtuoso, documenting aural moodscapes in playlists such as "A History of Jetlag" and "27 Roads," inspired by Robert Adams's photographic ode to the road.[2] Though I mostly focus on the slant rhyme that occurs between the photographic and the textual in order to tease out how Cole's works *see*—he has himself professed these two modes to be "expressions of the same instinct," noting that "both are my way of aspiring to lyric poetry" (Interview with Vikaas)—the aural residue of the rhyme hovers in the background of his slanted vision. Indeed, recent works have involved collaborating with jazz musician Vijay Iyer, first the "Open City Suite" in 2013, inspired by his debut novel, and, most recently, "Blind Spot," which was performed during Iyer's residency at the Met Breuer in New York in March 2016. Such multimedia collaborations—the latter piece combined Iyer on piano, Patricia Franceschy on vibraphone, and Linda Oh on double bass, accompanied by a curated selection of Cole's photographs and spoken text—accumulate form and media upon one another to take on, as one reviewer remarked, "a more personal, even quotidian feel, obliging listeners to reflect on individual failures of sight" (Walls). Resisting reductive labels and categorization simply as a writer or photographer, as Nigerian or American, Cole has argued that such collaborative performances "respond . . . to something other than the needs of the exigencies of the marketplace"—a space of artistic innovation and improvisation where "some other thing can happen" (Interview with Marschke).

Since the publication of his debut novel *Open City* (2011), Cole's artistic practice has been built on bifurcated lines. As a writer, he has complemented his debut novel and his novella-cum-travelogue, *Every Day Is for the Thief* (2014), with an expansive body of critical essays covering political, literary, and aesthetic subjects. But as a trained art historian and celebrated photographer, Cole is as prominent in the world of visual art as he is in the world of letters. The published companion to his major 2016 exhibition, *Blind Spot* (first published in Italian as *Punto d'Ombra*, then in English in 2017), has been celebrated as the "fulfillment of an intellectual project" in a review for *Slate* that emphasized the "stunning subterranean unity" (Muhammad) that links his writing, criticism, and photography—"the fourth in a quartet of books about the limits of vision" (*Blind Spot* 325), as Cole himself puts it. The continuity of the photographic and the literary within his work is not always as overt as this implies: while the two converse openly in *Every Day Is for the Thief*, in which Cole's own photographs of Lagos echo and disturb the written text, poetic fragments converse more elliptically with photographs in a work like *Blind Spot*. On other occasions, most notably in *Open City*, the photographic is an artistic metaphor that draws aesthetic elements from the practice and technology of photography into novelistic style.

From the "voiceovers" inspired by Instagram to the novelistic slant rhyme, Cole has frequently theorized the way in which text and image work together, noting in a recent interview how he has "always been interested in the complications that ensue when images and texts meet" (Interview with Hatfield). In this case, the slant rhyme denotes a specific formal relation, but also an aesthetic mode. That photographs embedded in fiction can be used "in a way that has imprecise connections to the text" (Interview with Hemon) only intensifies what such imprecision occasions for aesthetic experience. This aesthetic imbrication recalls W. J. T. Mitchell's formulation of "Image X Text," which captures the slant rhyme in notational form. Twenty years previously, in *Picture Theory*, Mitchell created three categories in which to capture the range of relationships between image and text in three forms: "image/text," "imagetext," and "image-text" (194). Signifying the "[r]upture, synthesis, relation" of all three original variations, however, "Image X Text" denotes "the traumatic gap of the unrepresentable space between words and images" (*Image Science* 39). Out of the six modes of "[r]upture, synthesis, relation" that the X symbolizes, three are relevant to slant rhyming. The first is "X as the sign of chiasmus in rhetoric, the trope of changing places and dialectical reversal, as in 'the language of images' providing 'images of language'" (40), a linguistic mirroring that makes micro-adjustments to image and text. The second positions "X as an image of crossing, intersection, and encounter," marking the space of the formal or conceptual join. The third, and most resonant for this chapter, imagines "X as a combination of the two kinds of slashes (/ and \)," or the two typographical slants. This overlap "suggest[s] opposition directionalities in the portals to the unknown, different ways into the gap or rupture between signs and sense, indicating the difference between an approach to words and images from the side of the unspeakable or the unimaginable, the invisible or the inaudible" (40). Crafting an intermedial ethics, the visual echo of text and image hint at what is unseeable and unsayable. Indeed, as noted in the introduction to a recent collection on "the coexistence" of the two art forms, the remix of *image times text* "has always generated a kind of uncertain energy, the kind of energy we find in the realm of the experiment, the crossed border, and the bastard outcomes of surprising encounters" (Beckman and Weissberg xii).

The notational slant captures the formal gap between media, but also gaps in sight, memory, and truth—spaces of negation, absence, and failure. Alix Beeston has construed the "crossed border" between writing and photography in American modernism as "construct[ing] its own intervallic bridgework: a composite diction that bears its gaps and reiterations, its associative and additive logic, on the page" (28). This chapter picks up on an intervallic structure that is both aesthetic—the formal slant—and ethical, which, in turn, calls to mind Emily Dickinson's double terminology of *slantness*. "There's a certain Slant of light," she opens one poem, recalling the etymology of *photo* (light) and *graph* (write): a slant of light that enables us to see, but only see partially; we can only write what we can see. "Tell all the truth but tell it slant," she opens another, gesturing more toward the purposeful and potentially deceptive angle of subjective experience (506).

As a novelist deeply "concerned with structures of consciousness," Cole mulls extensively on faults in perception, emotional discordance, and ethical dilemmas (Interview with Nair). Louise Hornby has described the photographic image as inherently "a form of negation," an artistic position that figures "a way of obscuring sight" (23). What interests me is that the photographic, as evident in Cole's oeuvre as both an artistic medium and a literary aesthetic, emphasizes a negative relation—what is beneath, hidden, what is *realizable* rather than *realized*. Harnessing the tension of negative relation, Cole's artistic practice carefully places image and text, memory and event, against one another in such a way as to displace rather than solidify continuity to conjure a mode of ethical and affective resonance.

Before examining the stylistic modes of aesthetic experience in *Open City*, and Cole's broader aesthetic practice, I turn to *Open City*'s photographic aesthetics. As I explore in the following pages, although there are no photographs within the body of *Open City*, the novel's stylistic and tonal variation is nonetheless commensurate with a decisively photographic aesthetic. Photography manifests not as an artistic medium within Cole's debut, but rather as three distinct aesthetic effects—slowness, shock, and shadowing—within which we can find Cole adopting a path toward a theory of the negative: at times attentive to harmony, while at others alert to political dissonance and the ethically incongruous. In the vein of its aesthetic predecessors, Sebald, Ralph Ellison, and James Baldwin, *Open City* is meditative and existential. These reticent formal considerations are reflected in Cole's own description of his style as structured around "quiet foreshadowings" ("Pitch Forward") and "the failure of mourning" (Interview with Liu). Playing into "the uncertain relation to truth created by the multifaceted act of writing with photography" that Beckman and Weissberg claim "offers a crucial resource to writers attempting to capture and respond to not only personal but also collective history," Cole joins a group of twentieth and twenty-first century writers like Sebald for whom "to write with photography is to acknowledge the difficulty of accessing the real, of reading or writing history responsibly and truthfully, as well as the necessity of attempting to do so in spite of the seeming impossibility of the task" (xiv–xv). For Beckman and Weissberg, the slanted relationship between writing and photography "seems particularly to attract authors grappling with phenomena that are unknown and at times unknowable" (xv). Describing echo as "very important," emphasizing its role as "a good way to intensify that region of localized weather that we call a novel," Cole similarly figures mourning as the act of "writing allusively" (Interview with Liu). Both stylistic functions necessitate a certain reticence: "the repetition of motifs" and "the slight alteration of what's been said before" requires a subtlety commensurate with that required when "consider[ing] the suffering of others" (Interview with Liu). Yet, not all is doom and gloom; there is an energetic sense of artistic and formal play that underpins such ethical investments. "Into the space created by that reticence," he declared in the same interview, the artist can "bring in those things that best help us confront ambiguity: music, painting, film and so on."

THE STILL IMAGE

If the photograph's uneasy stillness after the birth of cinema is one of the form's crucial aesthetic functions, how does the photograph work against the flow of narrative time? Set against the narrative momentum of novel form—even when novelists aspire to slow or stop time—the photograph's "stillness is a category of resistance—it impedes motion, gets in the way of forward trajectories, opposes, obstructs, arrests, freezes, halts, waits, interrupts, stagnates, pauses, suspends, delays, remains" (Hornby 1). As we'll see again in chapter 5, photographic images that appear in novels generate a particular rhythm that works to suspend formal time: a pause or breath. Even novels like Rachel Kushner's *The Flamethrowers* (2014), which registers photographic effects through an aesthetics of *speed*, use photographic documentation to contain the debris of experience in stillness. Although the photograph pictures the object world, a world apart from human experience, for writers who imagine their forays into intermediality in terms of imparting stillness or suspension into the flow of narrative, time necessarily reasserts a "subject-centered point[s] of view"—a position traditionally "unseat[ed]" by "the medium's claims" to objectivity or indexicality (3).

By openly describing himself as "very deeply interested in bringing slowness into basically everything that I do" ("Pitch Forward"), Cole registers an aesthetic interest both experiential and formal, novelistic and photographic. This concern is an unsurprising side effect of his training in sixteenth century Dutch art history, where "if you spend enough time with a still image, it can be drawn out, it has things to say to you" ("Pitch Forward"). Cole's pursuit of the literary "still image" performs in many ways as the key photographic mode in *Open City*—the slow pace at which the novel moves elicits the effect of a series of photographic stills or a series of still-life scenes. The close attention to objects as points of access into historical inquiry or personal memory indeed recalls Northern Renaissance still-life painting where composition, combined with the painting's subject, requires one when looking to search for details. In regard to literary practice, Cole identifies the impulse to create such an effect by questioning "how can you do something that's a little bit arresting and not merely beautiful but that creates a capacity for a doubt and for rereading," an impulse that seeks "to capture that surreal lyric moment" ("Pitch Forward").

Attending to this "surreal lyric moment," we might rightly recall Zadie Smith's critique of lyrical realism. We might also feel uncomfortable with novelists' lyrical ambitions in light of Jonathan Culler's warning about the perils of "novelizing account of the lyric" in his compelling work *Theory of the Lyric* (2015): that doing so "fails to respond to what is most extravagant and distinctive about" lyric form (3). But when contemporary novelists such as Cole, Smith, and even Ben Lerner claim a lyrical ambition for the contemporary novel, it nevertheless suggests "we need a more capacious notion of lyric to counter modern notions of lyric intelligibility linked to the voice of the subject" (Culler 82). Angela Leighton, while describing "the lyric" as "a capacious form" that is, more often than not, poetic, also accounts for the *lyrical* as "a quality that might be found in almost any literary genre. It refers to those moments when sound takes over from sense, and we hear, as it were, the lure at work in the words" ("Lyric" 171). Leighton's description of the lyrical "makes us think 'with the ears,' and that, perhaps, requires another account of what it means to think at all" (171). The lyrical directs Cole's prose simultaneously toward resonance, where "it is enough if one note is played beautifully," and silence, where it is "trying to find a way to turn the volume down"; in other words, "[e]very form finds its own spaces and silences" (Interview with Blignaut). It also pushes the novel toward the experience of the lyrical subject: the "I" in search of aesthetic experience.

When narrative propels time forward, how can a work such as *Open City*, drawn together by an organizing photographic aesthetic, achieve stillness?

The authorial wish "to slow down the timeline of the person reading" the novel is an aspiration only for reading in actual time, not phenomenological time (Cole, Interview with Brockes). For readers as well as for the narrator of the novel, slow time occurs in order to "give an account of what's happening when a person is looking at something—not necessarily an art object, but some sort of object that is somehow removed in time" (Interview with Brockes). In these moments, "there's something that happens—not just aesthetically, but psychologically, too" (Interview with Tepper). Writing, for Cole, is "about the space that you create in which other things might happen to the reader" (Interview with Tepper). The psychological minutiae of aesthetic experience "speak[s] out from a buried visual subconscious" ("Disappearing Shanghai") to capture not only the event of consciousness but the "structures of consciousness" (Interview with Nair): the levels of perception involved in the continuous act of experiencing. While we might notice a similar preoccupation with the "neurobiological defeat of time" within Michael Clune's Romantic tradition, in which we see "writers' acknowledgement of temporal limits of actual artistic form and their expression of a desire to transcend these limits" (*Writing Against Time* 112–13), or observe an aspiration toward the archaeological gaze that the photographic eye is often accorded, neither truly finds a suitable analogue here. Rather than being concerned with achieving experiential timelessness or with recuperating time, *Open City* experiments with the parallel experience of the present and imagined past in order to achieve an expansion of time—in other words, time that is *full* of time. Such a condition necessarily compresses as much as it expands, or as Cole argues:

> All photography is a record of a lost past. Photography does not share music's ability to be fully remade each time it is presented, nor does it have film's durational quality, in which the illusion of a present continuous tense is conjured. A photograph shows what was, and is no more. . . . There are no instantaneous photographs: each must be exposed for a length of time, no matter how brief: in this sense, every photograph is a time-lapse image, and photography is necessarily an archival art. ("Disappearing Shanghai")

The syntax of this final sentence performs its own time-lapse: three clauses sitting in parallel overlay the "instantaneous" with "length" and with "lapse." Such stylistic decisions give us insight into how a conserved image of a fleeting impression can be fully reconciled with narrative movement, or how the onward rush of durational time might pause in stillness for even a moment.

Slow aesthetic time is at its most discernible when the novel's narrator, the psychiatrist Julius, visits two art galleries. The novel constantly offers images of this lyric subject in galleries—senses are attuned to subtle shifts in environment. Early in *Open City*, Julius visits New York's American Folk Art Museum: rather than a ritual experience, he retreats inside the museum by chance in order to escape inclement weather. Described as exhibiting "the art of a country that had an aristocracy but did not have the patronage of courts: a simple, open-faced, and awkward art," the museum's curatorial program "featured" artists who "were, in almost every case, working outside the elite tradition," and who "lacked formal training, but [whose] work had soul" (*Open City* 36). Recalling one exhibition in particular, which featured the work of the deaf artist John Brewster, Julius hones in on silence as a kind of formal consolation. "[B]rought to life by an incisive gaze," he notes, "[t]he effect was unsettling. The key, as I found out, was that John Brewster was profoundly deaf, and the same was true of many of the children he portrayed" (37). Indeed, the paintings are rendered as if behind glass: "[e]ach of the portraits was a sealed-away world, visible from without, but impossible to enter," a peculiar quality of silence and stillness that for Julius is reserved for narratives of profound quietness of the deaf (37). He muses: "Standing before Brewster's portraits, my mind quiet, I saw the paintings as records of a silent transaction between artist and subject. A laden brush, in depositing paint on the panel or canvas hardly registers a sound, and how great is the peace palpable in those great artists of stillness: Vermeer, Chardin, Hammershøi" (38). For Julius, "Brewster hadn't resorted to indirect gazes or chiaroscuro to communicate the silence of his world," while Vermeer, Chardin, and Hammershøi had; rather, the subjects' "faces were well lit and frontal, and yet they were quiet" (38), while "his images were imbued with what that long silence had taught him: concentration, the suspension of time, an unobtrusive wit" (39).

Here, the aesthetic subject begins to mirror the paintings' affects: the stillness of the viewed work overflows into Julius's experience of it. But what are galleries but spaces of silence? Julius's experience of the space is figured in terms of the colonial context of Brewster's work, where the gallery's "row of slender white columns running through its middle" and "floors [of] polished cherrywood" are "elements" that "echoed the colonial architecture of the New England and Middle Colonies" (36). The silent and self-contained aesthetic observed in the portraits, moreover, corresponds to the solitude that Julius experiences in the space: "[t]he silence was even more profound, I thought, as I stood alone in that gallery, when the private world of the artist was total in its quietness" (38). Indeed, Julius's solitary and introspective experience of the space, as "the only person there," resonates with the artwork, "heighten[ing] the feeling of quietness" that he "got from almost all the portraits," to the point where, although the "stillness of the people depicted was certainly part of it, as was the sober color palette of each panel," Julius nonetheless begins to attribute aspects of the space to the artwork, explaining that "there was something more, something harder to define: an air of hermeticism" (37). The space that the art creates draws him out of the present moment, where "[t]he sense of having wandered into the past was complete" (36), and he had "lost all track of time before those images, fell deep into their world as if all the time between them and [him] had somehow vanished . . . eventually walk[ing] down the stairs and out of the museum . . . with the feeling of someone who had returned to the earth from a great distance" (39–40).

To represent aesthetic transformation is precisely to delineate a state of outsiderness. When Julius visits the International Center for Photography later in the novel for an exhibition of the Hungarian photographer Martin Munkácsi, Cole amplifies the feeling of displacement. The gallery is white, employing a contemporary aesthetic model: a bareness that, depending on who you ask, elicits either contemplative response or boredom.

Feeling like a voyeur, Julius in his nervousness spurs an art historical aside—a common trope when the novel enters uncomfortable terrain—referring to essays by Henri Cartier-Bresson, Roland Barthes, and Walter Benjamin on the photographic instant. "Photography seemed to me," he pondered, "as I stood there in the white gallery with its rows of pictures . . . an uncanny art like no other," where "[o]ne moment, in all of history, was captured, but the moments before and after it disappeared into the onrush of time" (152). In his 1928 essay "A Small History of Photography," Benjamin suggested that the photographic aesthetic is "to focus [on] the moment rather than hurrying on past it; during the considerable period of the exposure, the subject as it were grew into the picture, in the sharpest contrast with appearance in a snap-shot" (*One Way Street* 245). Indeed, as Benjamin argues, photography could "find the inconspicuous spot where in the immediacy of that long-forgotten moment the future subsists so eloquently but we, looking back, may rediscover it" (253).

It is specifically with regard to Benjamin's term of the "snap-shot" that Julius frames Munkácsi's photography. Describing them as "snaps," Julius observes a resonant tension in the photographs, suggesting that "Munkácsi's journalism was dynamic" and held a certain "alertness" (152). That the photographs "were so carefully composed but always seemed to have been taken on the go" prompts Julius to consider the works explicitly in regard to its aesthetic origins, noting that "[i]t was from him . . . that Henri Cartier-Bresson had developed the ideal of the decisive moment" (152). Introduced in his influential 1952 essay "The Decisive Moment," Cartier-Bresson had structured his early work around the concept of the *instant decisif* (a concept perhaps inspired by his interest in Zen aesthetics), explaining that "[o]f all the means of expression, photography is the only one that fixes forever the precise and transitory instant" and "deal[s] in things which are continually vanishing" (44). Carlos Fuentes identifies this core temporal principle in Cartier-Bresson's Mexican photography in particular, as "[a]rt that is simultaneously instant and eternal" (11). If Cartier-Bresson developed his snapshot technique specifically as a means of capturing the transitory and the ephemeral, the novel's evocation of this tradition alerts us to its own aesthetic ambitions.

And yet, the ethical disturbances caused by this aesthetic stilling of time are palpable. While it has the capability to capture a moment in time, when the event that is preserved holds incalculable social weight, it also catches its viewer easily in silent horror:

> The mood of Munkácsi's photographs darkened as the 1920s became the 1930s, and the soccer players and fashion models gave way to the cool tensions of a military state. This story, told countless times, retains its power to quicken the heart; always, one holds out the secret hope that things will turn out differently, and that the record of those years will show wrongs on a scale closer to the rest of human history.

> The enormity of what actually happened, no matter how familiar it is, no matter how often it is reiterated, always comes as a shock. (154)

And so it happens that "there was the image, at once expected and unexpected, in the middle ground of a row of soldiers, of the new German chancellor. Walking close behind him, with his contorted nightmare of a face, was Goebbels" (154). Julius's experience quickly becomes unendurable on noticing a young Jewish couple looking at the same photograph. The reason for this is partly shame at intruding into an experience that Julius perceives as private: "I needed to move away, immediately, needed to rest my eye elsewhere and be absent from this silent encounter into which I had inadvertently barged... I couldn't bear to look at them, or at what they were looking at, any longer" (154). But present here is also a sense that the extreme emotion elicited by this photograph is what is private, and thus impenetrable for Julius: "I had no reasonable access to what being there, in that gallery, might mean for them; the undiluted hatred I felt for the subjects of the photo was, in the couple, transmuted into what? What was stronger than hate?" (154). "Reasonable" seems to be the operative word here: precisely because the couple's experience is incomprehensible in distant and logical terms, Julius subsequently feels he has no reason for accessing Munkácsi's photographs at all: "[t]he show turned on that axis. It became something else, and couldn't be saved" (154). The novel positions this sudden ethical dilemma as the catalyst for exposing a certain kind of weakness in aesthetic vision that occurs during affective overload. The squint, the grimace, the sidelong view cuts off the rest of the scene, so that what we see and how we see are limited: a shot snapped shut.

LIKE A PINPRICK

Not to recoil at the horror of these images would involve for Susan Sontag in *Regarding the Pain of Others* (2003) a failure of "imagination, of empathy" and a failure to "hold this reality in mind" (7). In an interview for the *Aerogram*, Cole too insists that "a good photograph" should shock us, should be "like a pinprick." Disregarding its aesthetic accomplishments or aesthetic economy, "it draws blood, it quickens, it's uncomfortable, and it reminds you in a small sharp way that you're alive right now." In order to be beautiful, he suggests, a photograph must elicit a "momentary shock to the consciousness or a sudden rush of blood to the head" (Interview with Vikaas). To readers of Roland Barthes, the photographic resonances are clear. One can draw a neat line from Cole's "shock to the consciousness" (or, an intellectual disruption) that also "draws blood" (in other words, a somatic attack) to the *punctum*: an "element" that is not sought out by the viewer, but which "rises from the scene, shoots out of it like an arrow, and pierces me" (Barthes 26). Acting as a "disturb[ance]" to "the *studium*," the *punctum* has a multitude of meanings: to "sting, speck, cut, little hole—and also a cast of the dice. A photograph's *punctum* is that accident which pricks me (but also bruises me, is poignant to me)" (Barthes 23). In other words, he remarks, "because the photographs I am speaking of are in effect punctuated, sometimes even speckled with these sensitive points; precisely, these marks, these wounds are so many *points*" (23). In part, what allows literature or photography the capacity to wound is the human propensity for forgetting, covering, occluding, and ignoring.

In the essay "Object Lesson," Cole makes a case for the anti-spectacular in conflict photography, venerating instead the quieter documents of conflict, which encourage us to "look at them for the way they cooperate with the imagination, the way they contain what cannot otherwise be accommodated, and the way they grant us, to however modest a degree, some kind of solace" (*Known and Strange Things* 139). They might not "ever effect the political change we hope for from highly dramatic images" (138), he argues, but "we look at them anyway, for the change that they bring about elsewhere: in the core of the sympathetic self" (139). Responding to Sontag's anesthetization of vision that occurs when we look at conflict images, Cole finds emotional impact in the quietly forceful object photography of Sam Abell, Sergei Ilnitsky, Glenna Gordon, and Gilles Peress. Solitary objects left behind, "worn through use" or "frayed" by "the hours of some person's life" (138), linger for longer on the memory than "yet another horrific photograph of a corpse" (137). The question he poses is an ethical one: "what . . . are we to do with a thrilling photograph that is at the same time an image of pain?" (135). Rather than "bring[ing] us into a state of productive shock," which he claims is what they are supposed to do, the "cinematic images" of conflict photography supply "aesthetic satisfaction, as well as a jolt of outrage" (135) without alluding equally adequately to the actual reality of the content of what is being depicted. Not that a political image need cede its aesthetic qualities or artistic condition: to borrow Walter Benn Michaels's assertion, "if we think that political art should provide identification rather than 'beauty,' we're making" a mistake (*Beauty of a Social Problem* 38).

Airs of indexicality haunt the medium specificity of photography—its ability to "index" events, action, and people in the tangible world imparts on novels an equal burden of veracity that is both ethically and aesthetically contested. This argument also preoccupied Sontag, who claimed in *On Photography* that "reality has always been interpreted through the reports given by images" (153). Such photographs are viewed to be mimetic to the actualities of the world. But it is no wonder that the medium's claims to truth are so evocative, equally distilling reality as it defamiliarizes our view of reality: while "[p]hotographs are a way of imprisoning reality, understood as recalcitrant, inaccessible; of making it stand still," they are nevertheless also able to "enlarge a reality that is felt to be shrunk, hollowed out, perishable, remote. One can't possess reality, one can possess (and be possessed by) images" (163). We perceive the camera to be a neutral instrument, as Cole has recently argued regarding American photojournalism, despite our simultaneous contradictory belief that "the camera is an instrument of transformation" (*Known and Strange Things* 212). In other words, while "images, unlike words, are often presumed to be unbiased," our sheer belief in "[t]he facticity of a photograph can conceal the craftiness of its content and selection" (212). A photograph "can make what it sees more beautiful, more gruesome, milder, darker, all the while insisting on the plain reality of its depiction" (212). But while it is a separate artistic medium, as theorists, critics, and photographers alike have argued, "the photograph's distinctive relation to the real doesn't guarantee it any distinctive relation to the true" (to borrow Walter Benn Michaels's specific wording [*Beauty of a Social Problem* 13]), and with written accompaniment the dilemma is amplified. Within the context of war, as Cole has argued, the epistemological crisis is all the more pressing; selected coverage of "war, prejudice, hatred and violence pursues a blinkered neutrality at the expense of real fairness" (*Known and Strange Things* 217).[3] And when "the photograph and the words arrive simultaneously," the photograph and words "guarantee each other" in a closed self-perpetuating system: "[y]ou believe the words more because the photograph verifies them, and trust the photograph because you trust the words" (212).

While at times Cole's own propensity for occlusion performs artistically—when in his photography, say, the fluid form of a sheet covers a building structure, or a curtain is drawn through an open window—at others, particularly in his writing, recovering the disregarded confronts unsettling crises. Not only does 9/11 quietly (almost silently) reverberate in the novel, so does an accusation of rape late in the novel. The absence of photographs is never more starkly felt than when the novel's denouement begins. Attending a party with Moji, a woman he knew from his childhood in Nigeria, Julius is confronted by her unexpectedly. Rising "around six," Julius "tiptoed over the slumbering bodies on the floor of the living room . . . made some tea" and "sat on the glassed-in terrace, overlooking the Hudson," at which point "Moji came to join" him, "look[ing] out over the river, narrowing her eyes" (244). At this moment *Open City* quivers quietly on the edge of that early-morning silence:

> And then, with the same flat affect, she said that, in late 1989, when she was fifteen and I was a year younger, at a party her brother had hosted at their house in Ikoyi, I had forced myself on her. Afterward, she said, her eyes unwavering from the bright river below, in the weeks that followed, in the month and years that followed, I had acted like I knew nothing about it, had even forgotten her, to the point of not recognizing her when we met again, and had never tried to acknowledge what I had done. This tortuous deception had continued until the present. But it hadn't been like that for her. Indeed, I had been ever present in her life, like a stain or a scar, and she had thought of me, either fleetingly or in extended agonies, for almost every day of her adult life. (244)

Just as Moji's tone is "emotional in its total lack of inflection," so is Julius's reaction to her words. While Moji's accusations are to Julius the unfolding of "her precise memory of what had happened," he does not express denial, regret, shame, or guilt. Having gone "on in this vein for what was probably six or seven minutes" (244), Moji claims that "things don't go away just because you choose to forget them" (245). Despite the novel's earlier extended meditations on the ethics and aesthetics of historical and contemporary experience, Julius's reaction is underperformed. Is it disinterest? Fear? Shame? The silence of dredging up repressed memories? The syntax of "I had forced" and "I had acted" distances and dismisses Moji's reported speech. The way in which the prose recalls it is in the abstract, as if spontaneously inserted into the narrative, and his acknowledgment of the rape is equally suspended.

If, for Moji, voicing her experience of the rape is an act of resistance against forgetting, what is it for Julius? Speaking with Aaron Bady, Cole explained:

> I wanted to ask: what is taken for granted in the matter of being a man? And since I feel that one answer is "far too much," I tried to convey that answer novelistically . . . But let's think about rape and justice. Beyond the very obvious—a woman's body belongs to her, there's nothing to discuss here—there's also the maelstrom of that comes with every incident of sexual molestation. It is one of the most narratively complex things that can happen in a community. People take sides, and it's often quite saddening what sides people take. But rape is also one of those situations where, as a man, your wiser self says: shut up, dude. Believe her, and shut up. Men opine entirely too much about rape, while managing not to ever say enough.

This poses a complex ethical question about memory and the experience of remembering through writing—one for fiction to consider where its social viability lies. Formally, Cole has described this in an interview with Christopher Bollen as "invit[ing] the ambiguity"—a technique that plays on the opacities of memory—into prose that otherwise seems certain of its own certainty. In the case of Moji's accusation, not only does this incident occur at the end of the novel, but it is not even described during the passage about the party. Instead, Julius's experience is discursively elided, only mediated after he returns home. His description of the event begins: "Each person must, on some level, take himself as the calibration point for normalcy, must assume that the room of his own mind is not, cannot be, entirely opaque to him" (243). He continues by emphasizing the subjectivity of narrative:

> And so, what does it mean when, in someone else's version, I am the villain? I am only too familiar with bad stories—badly imagined,

or badly told—because I hear them frequently from patients . . . But what Moji had said to me that morning, before I left John's place, and gone up on the George Washington Bridge, and walked the few miles back home, had nothing in common with such stories. She had said it as if, with all of her being, she were certain of its accuracy. (243–44)

But if Moji is certain, Julius is not. Whether through shock or denial, the incident is not referred to for the remainder of the narrative, as if it never happened. The novel shows how shock can occlude as much as it can reveal, as an interruption or suspension of sensory perception as well as a means of jolting us out of the everyday. This bears comparison to what Clune calls the aesthetic of "leaving out"; "a certain abstraction," he argues, "is basic to the mimesis of things as they show up in a world" (*Writing Against Time* 117). Indeed, this economical "version of novelistic description" ought to be differentiated "from the idea of the novel as a project of complete description." While this kind of description—"to describe a thing as it shows up for someone familiar with it"—requires "leaving this kind of perceptual detail out" (117), though, leaving out the psychological details of such an experience takes the "*abstraction* of novelistic description" (119; original emphasis) one step further: this is not an experience familiar to most. Considering Cole's photographic aesthetic, however, the technique of leaving out these perceptual details expresses *more* rather than less.

Here, saying a lot without becoming effusive requires a certain reticence of narratorial voice, and as such, Julius's reportage of Moji's speech is a clear act of unexpected devocalization. He provides himself with no voice; his experience of the accusation is entirely inexplicit. While mimetic of Moji's experience, it is a deliberately vague portrayal of Julius's. As such, this scene is a remarkably strange disruption of the narrative flow of the novel as a whole. Indeed, in many ways, given that this development occurs late in the novel, it *implores* rereading. You feel as though you've missed something; you've ignored signs of a disturbed pathology. What the novel becomes on a second reading, with this knowledge, is ostensibly altered: Julius's solitude becomes suspicious, even potentially sinister; his professional role as a psychiatrist, morally ironic; that one of his patients commits suicide, worrying; the dissolve of his relationship with his ex-girlfriend Nadege at the very beginning of the novel is colored by a new ethical incongruence.

Whether or not the rape accusation works within the plot—the way in which Julius does not address it has been pointed out by critics as unsatisfactory or odd—his ethical failures revitalize the reader's experience of the prose; failure is aestheticized and the reader's view of the novel is rendered anew. The spectral hold this scene has on the novel's subject implies an imaginary and unarticulated narrative that overlays the one that exists in the literal pages of *Open City* and which implies an alternative aesthetic mode to invisibility. The virtual register accounts for the abstraction of the self that Julius experiences—or, rather, the rupture that the reader experiences—following Moji's accusation. Indeed, Cole remarks about Moji's accusation that "it's absolutely true. I can't imagine Julius's story without it. I knew right from the beginning the book would end like that. Three vicious thwacks of the hammer, and then a soft exit to strings. I'm attracted, in art, to things that trouble the complacency of the viewer or reader" (Interview with Liu).

Cole believes events like "crashing a plane into a building full of people, or people on account of their sexuality or race being marched off to camps and killed in large numbers" ultimately "defeat language"; while "[i]ndividual tragedies come close to defeating language . . . [m]ass tragedy does" (Interview with Somerset). Crafting a form of negative aesthetics that unsettles the senses, the novel delineates an affective mode that Lauren Berlant has called "underperformed emotion," an emerging "cultural style that appears as a reticent action, a spatialized suspension of relational clarity that signifies a subtracted response to the urgencies of the moment" ("Structures" 191). In the crucial moment of accusation, the "subtraction" of reaction signifies all three qualities of Cole's negative aesthetics: time is slowed, shock is produced, and Julius's flawed memory distorts the "historical moment" of the event, while the narrative threatens us with the imminent closure of the story without resolution. Julius's preciously tightly woven consciousness now unraveling represents "a crisis of experience" (193)—a façade readers now feel silly, at best, or morally compromised, at worst, for having believed.

Berlant describes this "recessive style" as "just as likely to point to tragic or traumatic situations" rather than a "casualization of emotion" (194).

More than just an ethical form, then, Cole is searching for an *empathetic* form, one that adheres to banal, ordinary emotion, rather than conforming to the pressure of "melodramatic reengagement" (Berlant, "Structures" 198). Despite claims to objectivity, photography too has a capacity for being an empathetic or relational medium. As Margaret Olin notes, photography's "meaning [is] determined not only by what it looks like but also by the relationship we are invited to have with it" (3). In other words, when *what* is said is mirrored by *how* it is said—despite the possibility of its eventual failure—the slant rhyme form of writing and photography comes close to being consolatory by treating traumatic experiences simply and economically.

Across Cole's quartet, we can see this attention to care evolving beyond a curatorial interest to something more like affective responsibility that opens up when we do not just look closely, but look again. The negative views of *Open City* and his photography place pressure on the reader to become a "rereader"; looking again "affords an affective, aesthetic, and ethical mode distinct from that ever elusive 'first reading,'" in the words of Serpell (81). Rereading opens up our aesthetic vision to "a softer layering of subjunctive possibilities," which, as Serpell argues, might just ameliorate our ethical faults on the first reading. Although we may resist it, "an ethics of complicity might be the best we can offer" (81). All the same, by forcing readers to address their complicity in Julius's silence in *Open City*, Cole casts a sharp, and often unforgiving, light on the assumption that moments of silence, darkness, and no description are empty: they are "information at rest" (*Blind Spot* 322).

Certainly, the aesthetic experiences within *Open City* critically interrogate how fictionalizing can, but also fails to, transform ordinary experiences into subjects for art. Both novels aim to create a new experiential language not just for the spectator of artworks, but for the reader of fiction. Indeed, Cole's aim in writing the novel—as "something that could conceivably be passing through the mind of an admittedly acute and over-educated protagonist"—emphasizes the novel's experiential narrative. He describes his intention in these terms, noting that he aimed to "tell the story in a way that reflected the way a certain *we* live today—the experience of buying books, reading books, going to museums" (Interview with Tepper), giving the novel its peculiarly immersive quality. But this immersive quality is built up through affective and perceptual accumulation, not the decisive moments of the photographic image that so occupies Julius in the International Center for Photography. Cole has described that it is "generally true of art" that it is "made to reveal more the more you look at them." It is through this process of perceptual revelation that he "wanted to broach Julius's encounters with people and places"; in other words, "[i]f you keep looking at a place, it begins to give you more. Or: If you have an encounter with another human being, in a sensitive way, you begin to get more" (Interview with Tepper). Whatever this "more" constitutes, although vague here, it occurs both on the level of style (in observing detail, whether formal, technical, or otherwise) and emotion (what is discovered draws from the viewer a particular affective response).

AESTHETICS OF COLLECTIVITY

The ethical resonance of empathy for Cole demonstrates the extent to which his oeuvre as a whole is invested in the tension between individual perception and collective community. *Open City* in particular is interested in the negation that occurs when individual experience attempts but fails to achieve collectivity.

The conventionally aesthetic experience, as we have seen, insists upon the individual's subjective and solitary perceptions, particularly if it wants to achieve complete absorption. Julius achieves this ideal state in front of Brewster's paintings:

> I lost all track of time before these images, fell deep into their world, as if all the time between them and me had somehow vanished, so that when the guard came up to me to say the museum was closing, I forgot how to speak and simply looked at him. When I eventually walked down the stairs and out of the museum, it was with the feeling of someone who had returned to the earth from a great distance. (39–40)

Juxtaposed against this aesthetic detachment from everyday life, Julius leaves the museum into the pouring rain. He gets into a cab without so much as a hello to the driver, his mind and voice elsewhere. As an attempt at an apology for his silence, he gives his address "to the cabdriver" with "So, how are you doing, my brother?" (40). The driver immediately "stiffen[s]." Why this simple gesture of hardening, of closing off to others?

But where Julius is deep in what Peter de Bolla calls a "poetics of wonderment," occupying the aesthetic "feeling for that which lies beyond thought and language" (3), the driver misreads his silence as a bitter and deliberate negation of perceived shared experience: "Not good, not good at all, you know, the way you came into my car without saying hello, that was bad. Hey, I'm African just like you, why you do this?" (40). Although Julius feigns a quick apology—"my mind was elsewhere, don't be offended, ehn, my brother"—the driver refuses to engage with him, saying "nothing" and stays silent for the rest of the cab journey (40). A moment of potential recognition and connection—Julius's "brother" and the driver's "I'm African just like you" both reference claims to a shared narrative of origins and of marginality—has been inverted into a series of refusals. Julius internally revokes his apology ("I wasn't sorry at all"); with rising anger, he rejects the driver's expectations ("I was in no mood for people who tried to lay claims on me"); the driver then takes Julius "to the wrong address, several blocks from [his] apartment" and refuses "to correct the error," stating: "No, that's it" (40).

Reflecting on Ellis Island much later in the novel, Julius acknowledges how "Blacks, 'we blacks,' had known rougher ports of entry" into New York: "this, I could admit to myself now that my mood was less impatient, was what the cabdriver had meant. This was the acknowledgment he wanted, in his brusque fashion, from every 'brother' he met" (55). Attempted and failed connection here references what Stephen Best calls "[m]elancholy historicism" (10) in his brilliant *None Like Us: Blackness, Belonging, and Aesthetic Life* (2018). Best points to what "registers with and in me, concerning art and life, as the minority subject's sense of *unbelonging* (e.g., forms of negative sociability such as alienation, withdrawal, loneliness, broken intimacy, impossible connection, and failed affinity, situations of being unfit that it has been the great insight of queer theorists to recognize as a condition for living)" (10), a history of self-negation he locates in both black and queer accounts of self. Here and in the novel, we can see "a kind of crime scene investigation in which the forensic imagination is directed *toward the recovery of a 'we' at the point of 'our' violent origin*" (21; original emphasis). However, as Best extrapolates, "[w]hatever blackness or black culture is, it cannot be indexed to a 'we'—or, if it is, that 'we' can only be structured by and given in its own negation and refusal" (22). For blackness in *Open City*, *we* becomes a social and grammatical site of false and vexed connection. In Julius's denial of their shared blackness, the cab driver senses the long history of white identity achieved at the expense, the *negation*, of black identity; rather than their becoming allies in a shared isolation, Julius's accidental blindness positions them on either side of a contest over visibility.

To this site of failed connection the novel offers one exception. Experiences of music are not beset by the same political and personal crises, anxieties, or aesthetic expectations, even if these are the states that music is mobilized to remedy. Because no art form resists the desire to seize impressions more than music does, as Michael Titlestad argues, "writing or speaking about music is regularly cast as an apocalyptic lifting of veils through which one approaches, but never reaches, the thing itself. Situated as the elusive other of language, as an aesthetic process and object untainted by speech, music becomes something like a discursive space of wishing" (2). Music's abstraction defies concrete explanation in such a way as to bring together conflicting or unresolvable feelings. In this way, music has long been thought to be reparative; from Kant to music therapy, music is an art form that "takes the language of the affects" (Titlestad 2), transposing emotion into art in a way that language cannot. For Julius, music bypasses the intellect to more easily engender somatic and affective responses more conducive to collectivity.

If Cole's photographic aesthetics prick us, do *Open City*'s experiences of music offer us consolation from moments of shock? Throughout the novel, music acts as a counterimage of what we have seen as photographic negation. While time is still slowed, stillness gives way to movement, darkness to illumination, and ethical distress to solace. Embodying this ontological agitation, Cole is self-consciously aware of the difficulties of the novel's capacity to embody affective form, questioning how "a novelist [can] sit down and write something . . . that can equal Brahms four," or something that can "take you to all sorts of places emotionally and just feel complete, without you having to worry about a plot, because the spaces they take you are psychological" ("Consummate Mahlerian"). Nevertheless, the very structure of *Open City* was conceived of in musical metaphor: ending, as we've seen, with "three vicious thwacks of the hammer, and then a soft exit to strings." While we've seen the "three vicious thwacks of the hammer" in the novel's unexpected turn to Moji's rape accusation, let's turn now to what constitutes the "soft exit to strings."

Although today's aesthetic experiences tend to anything but sublime, music seems to offer an exception. The novel culminates with such an intense aesthetic feeling following a performance of Gustav Mahler's Ninth Symphony at Carnegie Hall in New York. Let's set the affective scene with Cole's description of his experience of Mahler's Ninth from an interview for Radio Open Source. The piece opens as a "vast force," with "soft and hesitant sound ... sighing," becoming the motif of a "falling figure" that "the entire first movement, and in fact the whole symphony, is built on." At first "gentle," then bringing in "different instrument groups [that] carry different versions of this figure," the movement develops an "incredible complexity" of sound and sentiment: for Cole, "the core of it is essentially simple, almost as if it's saying life, death, life, death ... every complication comes out of this binary." Sorrow, after all, was what Mahler considered to be his "only consolation" (quoted in Lebrecht 17). The second and third movements are comparatively lighter, "interrupting the [previous] music with more folkloric elements, with more parodic, more satirical elements" ("Consummate Mahlerian"). It is the final movement, however, that offers Cole his own kind of consolation. As in Lewis Thomas's "lovely brooding meditation," *Late Night Thoughts on Listening to Mahler's Ninth*, listening to this music is "a solitary, private" act, in which the listener can find a kind of "metaphor for reassurance." Cole emphasizes that this is "because we know exactly what that feels like to have music going through you in the still small hours of the night." Listening in a large concert hall, however, does not have to be a sociable experience: at the end, "the music has died out ... reluctantly, like one's last breath. And you just want everyone to hold that moment with you ... to be with that crowd in absolute silence, so that you can all experience this together." Operating on a level of "complexity and completeness" that allows for a collective experience, it develops from "something that is complex but then absolutely resolves into becoming part of your own inner logic," connecting things so that "the weave of existence is tight" ("Consummate Mahlerian").

Norman Lebrecht has also expressed the way in which Mahler can cultivate privacy in this way:

> He expressed intimate, furtive, even shameful feelings in pages that were written for a hundred players and an audience of thousands. This contrast of message and medium is innate: it may also lead us towards the secret of Mahler's intensive appeal. Mass society overwhelms the individual in us with the encroachments of ephemeral fashion. Mahler turns that formula on its head, using orchestral mass to liberate the individual unconscious. Among these thousand people in a concert hall you are always alone when Mahler is played. (6)

Music thus allows for a collective experience of solitude. It is this sublime function of music that Cole aims to encapsulate in his central Mahlerian image. "When something is shadowed," he argues, "it is not just black in an undifferentiated way, but . . . there are places where light then shoots through" ("Consummate Mahlerian"). Mahler's music, for Cole, achieves something close to ideal aesthetic form: shadowed light, or, conversely, illuminated shadow, produces a "natural instinct for montage [that] makes sense to the environments that we function in; life cannot be just one thing or another. The sublime and the ridiculous are always interspersed with each other in life."

Turning back to the novel, then, Julius's encounter with Mahler's Ninth Symphony at the culmination of the novel has structural significance, containing one of the few markers of specific time in the novel: "Last night," Julius recalls, "I attended the performance of the Ninth Symphony" (249). Julius's experience of music allows the novel to "catch up" with the present, with "real" time. Music thus takes possession of Cole's form.

An end for the end then—Julius remarks how Mahler "made himself a master of the ends of symphonies, the end of a body of work, and the end of his own life" (250), or, in other words, of creating a perpetual aesthetic end. His last years were like clouds that "sometimes race across the sunlit canyons formed by the steep sides of skyscrapers, so that the stark divisions of dark and light are shot through with passing light and dark," while his final works "are vast . . . lively works," that "overwhelming[ly] impress" upon Julius "the light of a passionate hunger for life, the light of a sorrowful mind contemplating death's implacable approach" (250). It is here that Julius's encounter with Mahler's Ninth finds an analogue in

Vinteuil's *Septet*: experiencing art allows the viewer, reader, or listener the perceptual ability to "see . . . through another's eyes." While for Marcel, it is "in order to counter the habit that dulls our perception with time," to achieve "permanent novelty" (30), for Julius, experiencing his music like this creates an imagined existence for Mahler that colors his own experience; his encounter with this symphony is coincident with Mahler's experience of composing it. Julius imagines that "[a]ll the darknesses that surrounded him, the various reminders of frailty and mortality, were lit brightly from some unknown source, but even that light was shadowed" (250). Imagining this perception of mortality so lucidly transforms his musical experience from object to subject; the sublimity afforded by this experience is rendered intensely vital.

The concert scene begins with the description of other people. Helpfully, because Julius had "bought [his] ticket for yesterday's concert too late . . . [he] was up in the fourth tier above ground level" of Carnegie Hall, "a beautiful conch shell of a space, with a ceiling studded with fixtures and recessed lighting," an ideal position to observe the entire scene (250–51). Remarking on the "overapplied perfume" of the "person next to [him], a beautiful woman, dressed in an expensive coat," and "[h]er companion, a tall, tanned man in a blue suit and a checked white shirt, a European-looking type with merry grey eyes," he turns his attention to the orchestra as it tunes: "first with the oboist sending out a clear A, and then the sounds of the string instruments drawing themselves out of beautiful cacophony into unison"; then "the woodwinds tuned, and they were joined by a flurry of strings" before "a hush fell on the hall" (251). Noting the racial composition of the audience—"[a]lmost everyone, as almost always at such concerts, was white" (251)—he suggests that "Mahler's music is not white, or black, not old or young, and whether it is even specifically human, rather than in accord with more universal vibrations, is open to question" (252). Cole's music, even before it has begun, is a form that has the ability to transform individual consciousness and experience.

Julius's experience of Mahler is perhaps the novel's most concerted use of aesthetic experiences. While he describes the "first movement of the Ninth Symphony" as "a great ship slipping out of port: weighty but nevertheless entirely graceful in its motion"—"it began with sighs, a series of hesitations, a repeated falling figure that stretched out at the same time that it became more frenzied" (252)—the third movement, "the rondo, was loud, rude, and as burlesque as it could conceivably be" (253). His experience of listening is enacted "both with my mind and my body, entering into the familiar details of the music, discovering new details in the score, points of emphasis and articulation that I had not noticed before, or that had been brought to the fore, for the first time, by the conductor" (252). For Julius, experiencing familiar art is not as Smith, Viktor Shklovsky, William James, and the rest, worry—Edmund Burke, too, worried that "when we accustom our eyes to it, a great deal of the apprehension vanishes" (99)—but continues to enrapture because even the most familiar works can offer perceptual renewal; his "sensory engagement," in Clune's phrasing, does not dull because he knows the contours of the work, but brightens because the art work "prolongs intense perceptual experience" (*Writing Against Time* 11). Experiencing this particular music, moreover, has the capacity to defeat the diminishing intensity of familiarization, because Julius perceives it as a new work: he experiences it as it is being re-created. Music is an art form that presents as, in essence, aesthetically fresh each time it is performed:

> Then, out of a calmness that seemed to have all in the auditorium holding their breaths, the sweet, hymnlike opening of the final movements, carried by the string instruments, filled the hall. I was stunned: I had never before noticed how similar the melody in this movement was to "Abide with Me." And that revelation steeped me in the deep sorrow of Mahler's long but radiant elegy, and I felt I could also detect the intense concentration, the hundreds of private thoughts, of the people in the auditorium with me. (253)

Mahler's music can still astonish. Indeed, Julius's captivation has a hallucinatory effect on his perceptions:

> In the glow of the final movement, but well before the music ended, an elderly woman in the front row stood, and began to walk up the aisle. She walked slowly, and all eyes were on her, though all ears remained on the music. It was as though she had been summoned, and was leaving into death, drawn by a force invisible to us . . . As she drifted to the entrance and out of sight, in her gracefulness she re-

sembled nothing so much as a boat departing on a country lake early in the morning, which to those still standing on the shore, appears not to sail but to dissolve into the substance of the fog. (253–54)

The music itself then dissolves into "[p]erfect silence," and Julius considers those "flooded with that silence" to possess "illuminated faces." The cessation of this music is linked with aesthetic enlightenment; musical experience allows Julius, as it does earlier in the novel, to be emotionally transformed.

This change in perception continues its effects even after Julius leaves the hall. Lost both in thought and in the reverberations of the music, he accidentally locks himself out of the hall on a "flimsy" fourth-tier fire escape, from which "[t]here was to be no respite from the rain and the wind" (255). Precariously suspended "[i]n the darkness above a sheer drop" to the street, Julius "face[s] solitude of a rare purity." Upon finding another door, he looks up and sees that "there were stars. Stars!" (256). In what was previously a "situation of unimprovable comedy" (255), this realization marks the singular experience of transcendence in the novel. Like Mahler's music, which joins the "sublime and the ridiculous," seeing stars when he "hadn't thought [he] would be able to see them"—because of "the light pollution perpetually wreathing the city, and not on a night on which it had been raining"—constitutes the effect that the performance had on him. Indeed, the chiaroscuro of Mahler's music becomes a metaphor for Julius's experience of the stars:

> The miasma of Manhattan's electric lights did not go very far up into the sky, and in the moonless night, the sky was like a roof shot through with light, and heaven itself simmered. Wonderful stars, a distant cloud of fireflies: but I felt in my body what my eyes could not grasp, which was that their true nature was the persisting visual echo of something already in the past. In the unfathomable ages it took for light to cross such distances, the light source itself had in some cases been long extinguished, its dark remains stretched away from us at ever greater speeds. But in the dark space between the dead, shining stars were stars I could not see, stars that still existed, and were giving out light that hadn't reached me yet, stars now living and giving out light but present to me only as blank interstices. (256)

Julius finds comfort in his view of the sky. "I wished I could meet the unseen starlight halfway," he muses, and despite his being unable to do so, the "starlight . . . was coming as fast as it could, covering almost seven million miles every hour" (257). Not even the thought of the end of the world frightens him; starlight would persist nevertheless, and "cast its illumination on other humans, or perhaps on other configurations of our world, after unimaginable catastrophes had altered it beyond recognition." Cole's inability to linguistically transpose Mahler's music directly is not in and of itself a failure; it, at the very least, expresses the formal limitations of literary and imagined aesthetic experience: as lyrical as it may seem at times, literary prose can never harness the sonority of music. And yet, this passage creates an aesthetic experience coincident with how we would imagine musical experience to unfold all the same; the description of the intensity of the perceptual experience of a lyrical subject—"it was as though I had come so close to something that it had fallen out of focus, or fallen so far away from it that it had faded away"—affords the novel the power to mediate music.

Such is the affective power of music. Here, Cole's musical image is a technique that appropriates Mahler's aptitude for perpetual completion. Not only a feature of the Ninth Symphony, Mahler's elegiac movement represents the "falling figure" of perceiving starlight, and precipitates, in the terms of sublime aesthetics, the collapse of humanity. The devastating sublimity of Julius's perception of Mahler heightens his sensibility of other "real" objects, transforming what could have been, without music, an object of experience—he views the stars; the stars are beautiful objects to him—to a subject of experience: he *feels* the stars "in [his] body" as an abstraction of aesthetic experience itself; it becomes coincident with the end of the world. Cole's literary mode is not, therefore, only representational, nor does it rely upon literary description to denote the experience of music; across the novel, both mass tragedy and aesthetic experiences are equally inexpressible. Instead, this mode performs as an experiential idiom that can transform perception and, whether experienced alone or in company, ultimately aims to achieve something resembling collective experience.

READER AESTHETICS IN THE INTERNET AGE

If the experience of novel reading is largely seen as a solitary affair in the twenty-first century, and the experience of social media is almost the complete opposite, is there something to be gained in occupying the slant between the two? Many contemporary writers use Twitter experimentally; many contemporary photographers employ Instagram as a gallery of the creative process. Part of both camps, Cole used Twitter for a period of time in 2012 to reinvent the modernist practice of the *fait divers*, before moving to Instagram, a visual platform on which his photography exhibitions *Blind Spot* and *Black Paper* took shape. In the essay "Serious Play," Cole positions Instagram as a site where relational media creative practice is visibly ongoing as relational art. The Instagram feeds of photographers act as their "studio," where "we see how an obsession develops and not simply what it looks like once it is on the walls of a museum or between the pages of a book":

> Once we've fallen in love with an artist's work, isn't one of the things we most long for to get inside that artist's head, to somehow get closer to the creative process? This is why we read interviews, it is why we look at sketchbooks, it is why we pore over contact sheets. Instagram, at its best, can replicate aspects of this directness; it can be a conversation that unfolds gradually, over weeks and months.

This relational attitude inverts Nicolas Bourriaud's conceptualization of relational aesthetics as peculiar to the realm of visual art. According to Bourriaud, this is "because it *tightens the space of relations*, unlike TV and literature which refer each individual person to his or her space of private consumption" (15–16; original emphasis). Art spaces like exhibitions create spaces "and time spans whose rhythm contrasts with those structuring everyday life, and it encourages an inter-human commerce" (16). For Cole, Instagram ties together intimate and collective experience and reflection: "[o]ne part of the thrill is knowing that it is not happening anywhere else with such intimacy or immediacy. Another is the bittersweet fact of its evanescence" ("Serious Play"). It is a relational art form that does not occur in physical social space, but "[l]ike all conversation, it happens when it happens, and when it's gone, it's gone" ("Serious Play"). Indeed, writing about Gueorgui Pinkhassov's Instagram practice in 2012, Cole reinforces not only the intimate pleasure of viewing art privately, but how work viewed in this space "regains its aura" (*Known and Strange Things* 157). Stripping the work of the old sites of social space, the immediacy of Instagram is "a pleasure for the pure lover of the image: while lying in bed in the morning, you can see the latest work from a photographer you find interesting. The image comes to you" (157).

Harnessing this immediacy, all of Cole's artistic practices are born-digital. *Every Day Is for the Thief* (2014) began online as a blog, and although *Open City* appears to be a traditional novel without images, between September 2010 and March 2011 Cole posted several images and written quotes on a Tumblr site titled *op cit*.[4] Not only an abbreviation of the title of the novel, or a play on words that refers to the abbreviation for the Latin term *opere citato*, meaning "in the work cited," *op cit* evinces the self-reflexive, irreverent use of digital platforms of contemporary literary and artistic culture. As an early version of the kind of digital studio Cole describes, *op cit* quotes text from writers, philosophers, and dictionaries that corresponds to certain sections of what Julius is ruminating on in the novel, as well as featuring images that recall certain things and places that the novel describes and the artwork that Julius encounters (like Brewster and Munkácsi). Using a medium that is more interactive than the novel form not only allows Cole to make accessible "real" experiences of art—as well as visual artwork, he posted a link to a recording of Mahler's Ninth Symphony—but allows the novel to gesture outside of itself to actual conditions of aesthetic experience and, indeed, allows the reader a paratextual apparatus that stages the immediacy of the aesthetic experiences to occur in parallel with the novel.

The 150 photographs that form *Blind Spot* (2017), now a book, began as a solo exhibition of Cole's photography at the Fondazione Forma per la Fotografia in Milan in 2016 (it has since toured the United States), but even before then, *Blind Spot* developed on Instagram as #_blindspot (fig. 3).[5] Each photograph (using 35-mm film) is accompanied by a short, lyrical meditation on the image, functioning less as a caption and more as a voice-over. Indeed, "the length of the text" of the voice-overs "was partly shaped by writing on Instagram" (Interview with Hatfield). The project amplifies the recurring image of the blind spot that repeats throughout Cole's aesthetic practice. An essay that recounts his experience of papillo-

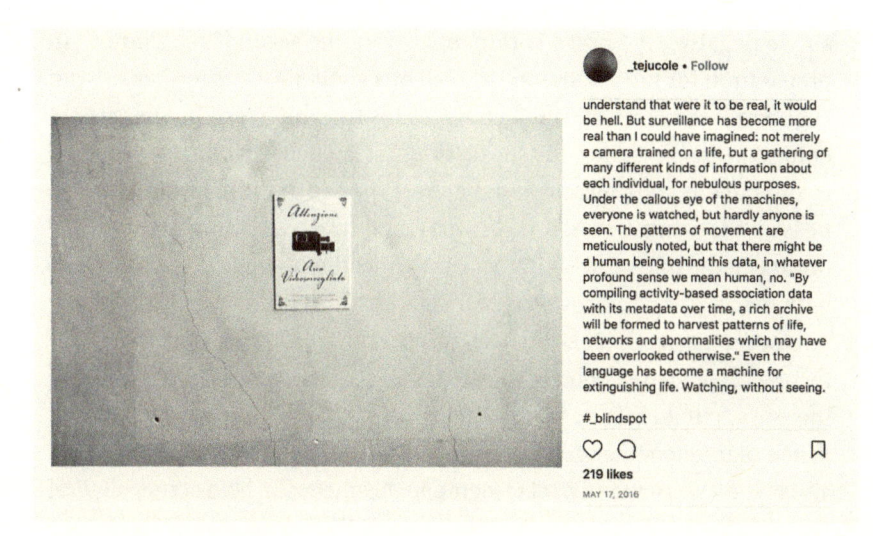

Teju Cole, *#_blindspot* (May 17, 2016). Instagram. Printed with permission from the artist. © 2016 Teju Cole.

phlebitis, otherwise known as "Big Blind Spot Syndrome," closes his essay collection *Known and Strange Things*. And yet despite Doctor L. convincing Cole during his first episode of papillophlebitis that, medically speaking, the "Big Blind Spot is benign" (384), as a human condition the blind spot persists as an ethical malignancy. Indeed, as much as it is remedied by a sensitive photographic eye that can alight on what is disregarded, photographic technology is not always a reliable antidote. We will see a similar emphasis on blind spots in Siri Hustvedt's work in the next chapter, where we find that, like Cole's, her essays are interested as much in the limits of perception as in the detail of our vision.

Two photographs from his *Blind Spot* exhibition—both taken in Brazzaville in February 2013—show a young boy knee-deep in the Congo River, gripping a red bar, vivid against the murky white water. He is wearing Crane sports gloves and a light blue-gray shirt, and he rests his head against his right thumb. The only difference between the two images is that in the first, there are no distinguishable facial features—"his eyes disappear" (*Blind Spot* 322). The second reveals his face. And yet, although there are two different photographs of this image, they are two scans taken from a

SLANT RHYME 87

single negative, the first a commercial scan, the second "re-scanned" in preparation for the exhibition. "But all of a sudden," Cole remarks, "with slightly altered settings, I could now see his face, his eyes. Darkness is not empty." Here, he claims, the "boy is double visioned": in other words, "[h]e is looking out, looking outward, but here, poised at the edge of the crisis, he is also looking inward, looking in" (322). Indeed, "being caught by the unexpected" (Interview with Vikaas) is an aesthetic equally sought after in both his artistic practices. Part of this fascination is the literary use of the photographic aesthetic, which suggests a progressive expansion of both forms. He perceives photography to be "in its moment of crisis," whereby there is a "curatorial uncertainty" in its artistic value ("Google's Macchia"). When placed together, the two photographs, while catching us off guard, also invite a small moment of recognition. Aesthetically, both occupy a lyrical register (the froth of the water, the sweep of the bar across the frame, the tenderness of the boy's expression), and yet when placed side by side, they ask the viewer to recognize a nascent partiality in an everyday technology. As Walter Benn Michaels claims, "photography has more political meaning as art than as documentary, more political significance when it seeks to be beautiful than when it seeks to be relevant" ("On Photography and Politics").

Politics of vision are located, too, in aesthetics of blackness. In "A True Picture of Black Skin," Cole draws attention to how "the dynamic range of film emulsions, for example, was generally calibrated for white skin and had limited sensitivity to brown, red, or yellow skin tones. Light meters had similar limitations, with a tendency to underexpose dark skin" (*Known and Strange Things* 146). Even with the invention of digital photography, "there are reminders that photographic technology is neither value-free nor ethnically neutral" (146)—a point that we can't help but align with contemporary US politics. Aspiring toward a lyrical mode of photography that also attempts to be ethically and ethnically observant then does not only expose subjective blind spots but encourages us to remember, to borrow Cole's words, that "darkness is not empty" (*Blind Spot* 321). In other words, darkness and absence are not coalescent. With his new project *Black Paper*—an Instagram project, #_blackpaper—created "in response to the US election," his own photographic practice is taking charge of these critical concerns, as "responsive work" documenting an "ongoing" crisis (Interview with Hatfield).

What the slant rhyme of digital and traditional forms of literary publication illuminates, then, is a new path for contemporary artistic practice. No longer reliant on the book form that historically wed the two forms together, it allows opportunities for more complex intermedial investments to take place. Take Cole's "soundscape" made for *Black Paper*, recorded and mixed by Cole between August and November 2017, or the Spotify playlist for *Known and Strange Things*, called "Known and Strange Songs."[6] Although "at the present moment, books have a near monopoly on the literary reward system (if not on actual literary production)," he likens the impact that technological advancements have had, and will have, on writing to the similar evolution of musical composition: just as the predominant classical soundscape developed into the variety of forms of the contemporary music scene, he "expect[s] that the rewards of literary production will inevitably include people whose work is embedded inside these newer technologies" (Interview with Hemon). Blogs, Tumblr, and Instagram leave "no space for brooding about the death of the author"—relational spaces such as these show how the "author, if not dead yet, will die" just as the "reader will die and be replaced by another reader" (Interview with Bady). Before he left Twitter in 2014, he transformed the ephemerality and impermanence for which Twitter is generally criticized to become his very subject. For Cole, there are "[s]ituations [that] can get to the point where what needs to be said must be said very simply," for which "Twitter is paradoxically" unhelpful—it is "not good at helping us express the most needful things" because "[t]here's so much foolishness around." He acknowledges that it can be, however, sometimes "very good about . . . saying plainly what needs saying," where "all of a sudden, a pristine line emerges and I forget to breathe." Twitter's capacity for linguistic precision, moreover, evinces his "poetic impulse" (Interview with Bady). While Twitter offers an open and unfiltered forum that poses a complex alternative to traditional methods of literary production—if used effectively—the way in which the platform has the capacity to mediate aesthetic form into the culture of prosaic experience not only facilitates the spontaneity and improvisation of Cole's artistic experiments but becomes itself an aesthetic mode.

A hint of déjà vu, the double take, the half chime: slant rhymes signify a way of understanding the intermedial relationships between text and image, but also a way of conceiving of the surprising encounters of networked contemporary artistic practices like Cole's. More than just new aesthetic forms, however, Cole's slant rhymes search for an empathetic form. Where Zadie Smith's empathy requires finding new ways to look afresh, slant rhymes offer Cole a mode of locating perceptual weaknesses; what we avoid, refuse to see, or ignore. Putting it simply, Cole reflects how he "see[s] the literary" "as a modest contribution to closing the empathy gap"—and while often it achieves "[l]ittle more than that," the aim is "important anyway" (Interview with Bady). This is what makes Cole's born-digital artistic practice, according to Jessica Pressman, "distinct from the majority of born-digital art—a commitment to literariness and a literary past" (2). Despite their intermedial investments, "[t]hey support immanent critiques of a society that privileges images, navigation, and interactivity over complex narrative and close reading"—they are "aesthetically difficult, and ambivalent in their relationship to mass media and popular culture"; rather than a celebration of "all that's new in new media, these works challenge contemporary culture and its reigning aesthetic values" (2). That Cole's artistic practice does so while being intermedial is important, as it is altogether more "convinc[ing]," in Sebald's words, in "captur[ing] and document[ing]" experience than solely photographing or writing (106); such a practice "contain[s] the secret" (Interview with Scholz 107). In a world of political precarity, for Cole "[t]here's a refuge in those things—in poems, in novels, in tweets—that contain no clear policy recommendations" (Interview with Bady), but also no conventional restrictions. The slant rhyme between the novel and digital platforms like blogs, Twitter, and Instagram doesn't only show us how aesthetic practices are evolving, but affords us new modes of reading. Looking slant, beyond the novel, or looking slant *at* the novel, allows us to air out the cupboards that usually remain firmly closed.

THREE

SYNESTHESIA

In the opening scene of Siri Hustvedt's *What I Loved* (2003), Leo Hertzberg is carried away by a compulsion to touch. Simply by caressing the painting he has just brought home leads to sexual anticipation:

> It was then that I noticed a bruise just below her knee. I had seen it before, but at that moment its purple cast, which was yellow-green at one edge, pulled my eyes towards it, as if this little wound were really the subject of the painting. I walked over, put my finger on the canvas, and traced the outline of the bruise. The gesture aroused me. (5)

Though at this time, early in their marriage, Leo and his wife Erica "lived in a state of almost constant sexual excitement," "[o]n that afternoon" in particular, they "made love *because* of the painting" (*What I Loved* 6; my emphasis). Or, more precisely, because of the bruise that proved too irresistible not to touch.

For Erica, this "erotic" encounter with the painting isn't shame inducing. How can Leo resist the instinctual urge to feel its edges, when he imagines that the painter "loved doing it, like he wanted to make a little wound that would last forever" (6)? The bruise encapsulates that "[w]e're easily cut and bruised," that "[s]kin is soft," and that such minor injuries are "black and blue" traces of "ordinary" connection. Under the spell of what Hustvedt calls "the aesthetic frame," the bruise enfolds three occasions of touch: the moment the bruise is formed, Bill's act of painting the bruise, and Leo's act of touching the painted bruise.

This desire of the wound occurs both in the making and experiencing of art: the painter "loved" making a bruise on the woman's leg, just as Leo felt compelled to touch it. Watching Bill painting her, Violet, too, wants to be touched; she recalls in a letter years later that "I wanted you to turn around and walk over to me and rub my skin the way you rubbed the painting. I wanted you to press hard on me with your thumb the way you pressed on the picture, and I thought that if you didn't, I would go crazy, but I didn't go crazy, and you never touched me then, not once. You didn't even shake my hand" (3–4). Playing on what Sara Ahmed has called "the *economies of touch*," Bill's "refusal of touch is . . . a means of forming and de-forming some bodies in relationship to other bodies" (*Strange Encounters* 49). By painting Violet's body—a not-quite mirror image—Bill forms an image of her body; his refusing to touch Violet threatens affective dematerialization.

The scene evinces both the sensual excitement of anticipating touch but also the fear of being undone by touch: Leo and Erica share a haptic state of empathy that Bill's refusal negates. In Adam Smith's formulation in *The Theory of Moral Sentiments*, this is the "pleasure of mutual sympathy" (14). While for Leo, "nothing pleases us more than to observe in other[s] . . . a fellow-feeling with all the emotions of our own breast," for Violet, we see the shock of "the appearance of the contrary," its absence (14). And as Smith explores, sympathy occurs not only in the mind, but in the body: "[w]hen we see a stroke aimed and just ready to fall upon the leg or arm of another person, we naturally shrink and draw back our own leg or our own arm; and when it does fall, we feel it in some measure, and are hurt by it as well as the sufferer" (3). In the essay "Becoming Others" (in *Woman Looking*), Hustvedt explores how she herself has experienced this blurring of sensory borders, whereby the subject mirrors the sensations of both pleasure and pain another is feeling (self and *other*), or where colors and sounds evoke particular sensorial responses in the body (self and *object*). A sensation often "described as empathy for touch" (Goldman 31), mirror-touch synesthesia, as a neurological phenomenon and an aesthetic of *against*, effects perceptual and sensorial aesthetic experiences:

> One can argue that there is a synaesthesic quality to all art experiences, that art revives a multimodal-sensory self. While looking at a painting, for example, don't we *feel* the brush? Studies have shown that mirror systems are active when people look at visual art and are also activated by written accounts of actions or emotional situations. If we do not feel our way into works of art, we will not understand them. I do not sense the touch of persons depicted in paintings, but I do have strong felt responses to the marks left by the painter's brush.... (*Woman Looking* 375)

Rereading the opening scene of *What I Loved*, we find that Violet, the artist's model, has this feeling as she is being painted: she wants the painter "to press hard on [her] with [his] thumb the way [he] pressed on the picture" because she senses what that touch would feel like. Leo, too, feels the bruise before he touches it, because of the desire already emanating from the picture due to the way it was painted.

To feel and to feel: the ambition of the synesthetic approach. As both "a noun and a verb," feel/touch is constantly in a grammatical, affective, and perceptual overlap: as David Maclagan notes, "[w]e do not in fact always know which comes first, the perception or the sensation, or the emotional response" (12). There is a touch of Merleau-Ponty's synesthesia hinted at here: "[t]here is a circle of toucher and touched, the touched grasps the toucher; there is a circle of the visible and the seer, the seer is not outside visible existence; there is even an inscription of touching in the visible, of seeing in the tangible, and vice versa" (in Maclagan 12). If Teju Cole's blind spots require reshuffling our ethics of visibility, Hustvedt's require the use of all the senses to feel with the body. Indeed, "looking at a painting, reading a poem or a novel, listening to music requires a *natural* loosening of sense boundaries, a blur that invigorates artistic experience" ("Becoming Others," in *Woman Looking* 376). By attenuating the perceptual significance of sight, Hustvedt ignites these "intersensual qualit[ies]" of the *synesthetic* as a mode of aesthetic feeling that brings both affective, physical, and narrative forms to touch. I take what neuroscientists call a monistic view of synesthesia—a more capacious model than synesthetic dualism or pluralism. As Lawrence E. Marks explains, monism "abolishes any distinct boundary separating synaesthesia from quasi-synaesthetic perception or synaesthetic tendencies, positing . . . what is essentially a continuous dimension (or multi-dimensional space) of synaesthesia-ness." This approach accounts for metaphor and other cross-modal "perceptual similarities" (31). By queering the visual toward the haptic, synesthesia seems to offer itself as a cure to repair the link between self and art. But as we'll find, synesthesia, even in the crossover, insists upon the impossibility of union.

MIXING

In the novel, the synesthetic ambition of overlapping and enfolding touch and feeling is expressed through Violet's theory of mixing. This phenomenon, which categorizes the embodied self as porous, is "the way of the world"—denoting a fluid mode of experience in which "[t]he world passes through us—food, books, pictures, other people" (89). According to Violet's analysis, sometimes this is "normal and good, and sometimes it's dangerous"; while "always mixing with other people" (89) intensifies feelings of connection in love, the porousness that makes this possible also renders the self vulnerable. Nevertheless, Violet's mixing demands a reorientation of the sympathetic relation of bodies in space: "defin[ing] ourselves as isolated, closed bodies who bump up against each other but stay shut" is no way to live (91). In Brian Massumi's account of the virtual, "[e]very given experience is already many-mixed" (158). Indeed, *mixing* is the core quality of sensation, as the consequence, the "fallout from perception": "a state in which action, perception, and thought are so intensely, performatively mixed that their in-mixing falls out of itself" (97–98).

The danger that Violet referred to earlier is that this porousness, to use her own words, "testif[ies] to an idea of the body as extremely vulnerable—one with failing thresholds, one that is under constant threat" (162). Harriet (Harry) Burden, the artist at the center of Hustvedt's 2014 novel *The Blazing World*, aspires to occupy both the inside and outside of perception. Framed as a biography of sorts, the novel spins around the mind of the artist as she comes back to making art after months of "agitated mourn[ing]" following the deaths of her husband, mother, and father (16). Though we'll see how it explores the obsessive and ultimately destructive compulsion to rebuild the bodies of the dead, the novel also demonstrates how art making performs the important function of aesthetic memorialization through metaphorical cannibalization.

With influences that are drawn from artists Hustvedt admires, even the novel notes how "her art runs in a tradition—Louise Bourgeois, Kiki Smith, Annette Messager: round feminine shapes, mutant bodies, that kind of thing" (277).[1] Hustvedt has written essays on all three of these artists, in which she consistently returns to the body. Harry's compositions highlight what Hustvedt calls the "emotional power" of Bourgeois's work—"how it stirred up old pains and fears, summoned complex and often contradictory associations, or echoed my own obsessions with rooms, dolls, missing limbs, mirrors, violence, nameless threats, the comfort of order, and the distress of ambiguity" ("Louise Bourgeois," in *Living* 247)—terrifying her grown children with "totems, fetishes, signs, creatures like him and not so like him, odd bodies of all kinds" (*Blazing World* 13). Even her giant figures, "soft stuffed bod[ies]" that resembled Felix at first, and later her father and mother bring to mind Bourgeois's *Personages*, those "first shown in 1949," if not in texture and material, then in impressions made by atmospheric sensation, as "abstract tower/beings or 'presences' [that] inhabit a room in relation to one another and to the visitors who come to see them" ("Louise Bourgeois," in *Living* 248). Though embodied, they "resemble three-dimensional signs or characters from an unknown language inscribed in space."

But if, for Hustvedt, Bourgeois's *Personages* "are stand-ins for what isn't there, tactile ghosts" rather than human forms (248–49), Kiki Smith's anatomies are "in part derived from looting traditions of representation and then altering them for her own purposes," so much so that "[b]ody parts are sometimes depicted as discrete units" (*Living* 270). Dissected anatomies, too, haunt Harry Burden; her figures, which she names her "elusive ones," sometimes come out as "mergings of desire, maddening beloveds mixed up," large and small, husband and father, "husband dolls" and a "penis with wings" (*Blazing World* 27). Reflecting on Kiki Smith, Hustvedt prefaces Harry's own artistic philosophy by turning to an art practice underpinned by dreaming. Where the author believes "that making art, whether it's visual art, music, or fiction, is a form of conscious dreaming, that art draws from the boundlessness, brokenness, merging identities, disjunction of space and time, and intense emotions of our unconscious lives" (*Living* 273), Harry asserts that "[n]onexistent, impossible, imaginary objects are in our thoughts all the time, but in art they move from the inside to the outside, words and images cross the border" (*Blazing World* 27).

What is imaginary and what is actual haunt the novel: in the claims Harry makes about the authorship of the art in her controversial project *Maskings*, and in the intensity of her belittlement in the art world, but most of all in her extensive musings on creative practice. As Harry reflects, her works of "resurrect[ion]" made way after a year for "the creatures that lived in my memory, not only actual persons, but those borrowed from my vast collection of books" (31). Memorializing the "critters" from her imagination, her "metamorphs" hint at another painter floating in the background of Hustvedt's descriptions of artistic practice. With its ardent images of monsters, Francisco Goya's famous painting *The Sleep of Reason Produces Monsters* (1799) echoes the epitome of Harry's theory of artistic creation—as she tells her daughter, Maisie, "there are more dreams, I'm afraid, and they must out" (26).[2] The novel is tinted with Edmund Husserl's theory of empathy, Søren Kierkegaard's play with pseudonyms and thinking on delusion, Fernando Pessoa's heteronyms, and Bourgeois's experience as a female artist. Returning to Bourgeois ten years after her first essay on her work, Hustvedt is well aware of her influence on creating her "invented artist" (*Woman Looking* 30): "[t]hey work at their art like maniacs even when they are not recognised for it, but they both desperately want recognition. And they are keenly aware of the fact that women remain marginal in the art world" (31). Obsessed with the political reading of the female body in art and as artist, Hustvedt captures this process of influence as another form of compulsion: "we consume other artists, and they become part of us—flesh and bone—only to be spewed out again in our own works" (30).[3] The body of work of other artists, too, is embodied as corporeal.

If Harry's figures cannibalize her husband, father, and mother, chewing them up and spitting them out anew, then *Maskings* cannibalizes Harry. Reflecting on the novel three years after its publication, Hustvedt sums up her artist's intentions as her "grand game about perception and expectation, a play with and on the ironies of being a woman artist" (*Woman Looking* 31). Early in the novel, Harry confesses that her "diverse fantasies were driven . . . by a growing sense that I had always been misunderstood and was madly begging to be seen, truly seen, but nothing I did made any difference" (*Blazing World* 37). However much she wants to seek restitution against the art world, refusing to come to terms with its injustices, Harry doesn't "want to live as a man" nor is she "interested in experimenting with my own body, strapping down my boobs and packing my pants" (35). Instead, as she argues in a diary entry, "[w]hat interested me were perceptions and their mutability, the fact that we mostly see what we expect to see" (35). Rather than embodied anew in another form, she theorizes how to disembody herself: "I wanted to leave my body out of it and take artistic excursions behind other names, and I wanted more than a 'George Eliot' as cover. I wanted my own indirect communications à la Kierkegaard, whose masks clashed and fought, works in which the ironies were thick and thin and nearly invisible" (35).

That the desire to be seen is brought about through the use of masks sounds like the height of performative paradox. Though Harry intended the project to "not only expose the antifemale bias of the art world, but to uncover the complex workings of human perception and how unconscious ideas about gender, race, and celebrity influence a viewer's understanding of a given work of art," as Oswald Case (the journalist that covers the scandal of demasking the authorship of her three installations) remarks, "for all practical purposes, she had been invisible" (1). Here, we recall that the controversy caused by the fraught claim to authorship of her third and final mask is exacerbated by the gendered somatic cliché that female art is soft while male art is angular. When Rune denies that Harry had anything to do with their installation *Beneath*—a twisting maze of corridors with windows inset into the walls and floor, with documentary film footage and peepholes that reveal dancing figures wearing black masks—one art dealer affirms it "empirically" because it was "hard, geometrical, a real engineering feat," completely unlike the style of Harry's previous artworks, made of "round feminine shapes" (277). Indexing how "[e]xpectation is crucial to perception" (*Living* 224), the novel's betrayal traffics in the cruelty of failed or corrupted modes of anticipation. As Hustvedt wrote in 2009, "[w]e see what we expect to see, which is shaped in part by our memories of having seen things before and in part by our brains' innate neural wiring for vision. But we also see what we pay attention to, and we cannot pay attention to everything in an image at once" (*Living* 235–36). Indeed, expectation is governed by the image of preempted perception. These observations hold true in the world of the novel, where because Harry has not produced a work like *Beneath* before, her critics don't expect her to. And because she is not expected to, perceptually speaking, many can't see how she has conceived of it, even though her use of masks was to fulfill her desire for people to "look at [her] work. Look and see" (*Blazing World* 221).

Of course, such circular logic isn't necessarily true to the twenty-first century structures of the art world, but what the novel "demand[s]" nevertheless, as Jennifer Levasseur put it, is "that we spend more time thinking deeply, making connections, seeing what is hidden in a distracting, surface world." We all "live in a circumscribed phenomenal world" (*Living* 224), according to Hustvedt, and as the novel argues, no more than in the insular New York art scene do we see such *"inattentional blindness"* (223; original emphasis). As writes one of Harry's pseudonyms, Richard Brickman, in a letter to the editor published in the *Open Eye*, a fictional journal of art and perception studies:

> Studies on change blindness (subjects missing blatant alterations in their visual field) and inattentional blindness (subjects who fail to notice an intrusive presence when attending to a task) suggest that, at the very least, there is much around us that we simply do not perceive. The role of learning in perception has also been crucial to understanding predictive visual schemas, which lend some support to constructionist theories of perception. Most of the time we see what we expect to see; it is the surprise of novelty that forces us to adjust those schemas. (*Blazing World* 267)

What makes the body as art a feminine subject, and structural art a masculine one, and what makes both these categories an expectation we have? Is there something about *Beneath*'s hardness that makes it implausible that a woman might have created it? Writing about Karl Ove Knausgård, Hustvedt notes that "[e]motion and its open expression have long been associated with femininity and the corporeal" (*Woman Looking* 86). Is there something open, intimate, and feeling about the corporeal softness in Harry's art that is lacking in *Beneath*? Art history would tell us otherwise, but the novel's art dealer falls susceptible to what Hustvedt remarks is the "conservative and biased" nature of perception, "a form of typecasting that helps us make sense of the world" (82). It's no wonder that Margaret Cavendish is Harry's inspiration for both *Maskings* and the final work she made before she died. Caught between seventeenth-century gender stereotypes, Cavendish often "staged herself as a mask or masque" (*Blazing World* 220), railing against expectations of her as a woman so much so that she was considered to be "an embarrassment, a flamboyant boil on the face of nature" (221). Dramatizing Hustvedt's critical observations about contemporary artistic life and practice, the novel both stages these debates in fictional terrain, while paying homage to one of the thinkers that has "become fundamental to [her] own thought over time" (221). Soft, feminine exteriors and hard, intellectual interiors breathe life through Harry as Cavendish's reincarnation, assuming her presumed desires as her own: "How to live? A life in the world or a world in the head? To be seen and recognized outside, or to hide and think inside? Actor or hermit? Which is it? She wanted both—to be inside and outside, to ponder and to leap" (221).

The liminal grammar of Harry's attempts to be both inside and outside resonates with her later assertion that "[e]very dying person is a cartoon version of the Cartesian dualist, a person made of two substances, *res cognitas* and *res extensa*. The thinking substance moves along on its own above the insurrectionist body formed of vile, gross matter, a traitor to the spirit, to that airy *cogito* that keeps on thinking and talking" (*Blazing World* 336). The desire to be both inside and outside suggests that on some level one's inside and outside are naturally disconnected. Cavendish's own musings in *Observations upon Experimental Philosophy* from 1666 limit "all knowledge" to "the mind" and "none" to "the senses" (153). Bodies and their interiors appear at an even greater remove when the exterior starts to fall apart, the novel tells us, as the mind observes an illness that is happening to the body and not to it. But once Harry learns she is dying, this split comes back to the fore. She already perceives her own body to be malaised; like Cavendish, her big and brutish image betrays her enough to find a way outside of it, to make it Other.[4] Reading between disarticulated systems of the multiplicity of being, synesthesia attempts to produce a new aesthetic category of experience reliant upon the affective and haptic overlap of mixing.

Synesthesia, then, is a mode of mixed perceptual experience. From their shared roots in the Greek *syn* (joining) and *aesthesis* (sensation), the many definitions in modern neuroscience all converge around "a merging/mixing/union/unity of the senses" (Cohen 64). From the rare conditions of hearing color and tasting words, to the more common scenario of seeing texture, synesthesia expresses "sensory transfers" between different modalities, transfers made possible by the fact that "sensory systems act in concert and not in isolation" (Marks 15). Massumi notes that when we remark that something *looks soft*, "vision has taken up a tactile function" (158), so "we can see texture" (157). To be sure, "this ability to see new tactile qualities depends on past touchings of other textures and movements providing continuous visual-tactile feedback. You have to know texture in general already before you can see a specifically new texture. But that doesn't change the fact that once you can generally see texture, you see a texture directly, with only your eyes, without reaching" (157).

But in the novel, an extra turn happens. As Leo is compelled to touch the bruise in the painting, his vision anticipates the texture of the bruise and, in turn, produces an affective feeling. The grammar of experience here is not only multimodal, but synesthetic, turning from sight, to touch, to affect.

CHIASMUS

Aspiration toward connection becomes the novel's cruel rub. In perfect tense, the title, *What I Loved*, jars against the opening scene's raw aesthetic and physical pleasures to suggest a palpable separation from the present time of writing the novel and a fixed past, while as a relative clause, it implies the imminent departure not of a person but of the sensations, objects, and experiences that constitute what he loved and has now lost. Love is in the past. In painting, however, nothing is lost. What she loves about painting, Hustvedt explains, is how its capacity for "immutable stillness" allows it "to exist outside time in a way no other art can": though "[h]ours may pass . . . a painting will not gain or lose any part of itself. It has no beginning, no middle, and no end" (*Mysteries* xv). The implication that "[p]ainting is there all at once" (*Mysteries* xv) is reminiscent of Cole's description of *acheiropoieta*, those images in Byzantine art that were "believed to have come miraculously into being without a painter's intervention" (*Known and Strange Things* 36). But while painting seems to give "an illusion of an eternal present" (*Mysteries* xv), the time and influence of making is not completely erased. Certainly, as Leo's wife pointed out, part of what so aroused him about the painting of the woman is how the bruise is painted for its permanence in a *now* that never ages, yet that it was made impacts the experiences of it: *his* desire to bruise the skin now speaks to Leo as he touches it. Indeed, he, too, has "always loved paintings for that reason": as he tells his eleven-year-old son who wants to become an artist, "[s]omebody makes a canvas in time, but after it's made, a painting stays in the present" (*What I Loved* 129). Though their materials, canvases, wooden panels, and paints will age and need restoring, paintings have the ability to capture the "*now*," even though "it's impossible to measure" (129).

Describing paintings in this way ends up being awfully poignant, as Leo comes to face the reality of this predicament when his son dies just over a week later. Testing out this theory, the novel gives Jean-Baptiste-Siméon Chardin's quiet *Glass of Water and a Coffee Pot* (1760) the capacity to break Leo from months of sensory "shallowness," experiencing the world "as though my vision had changed and everything I saw had been robbed of its thickness" (137). Freezing ("I didn't read or cry or rock or move" [138]) had become a bone of contention in his marriage; just as he came to "hate" his wife's tears (146), his wife came to resent how he too had "gone dead" (145). As he discusses the painting with his students one warm April afternoon, the affective resonance of the scene quivers:

> I began by pointing out how simple the painting was, two objects, three heads of garlic, and the sprig of an herb. I mentioned the light on the pot's rim and handle, the whiteness of the garlic, and the silver hues of the water. And then I found myself staring down at the glass of water in the picture. I moved very close to it. The strokes were visible. I could see them plainly. A precise quiver of the brush had made light. I swallowed, breathed heavily, and choked.
>
> I think it was Maria Livingston who said, "Are you alright, Professor Hertzberg?"
>
> I cleared my throat, removed my glasses, and wiped my eyes. "The water," I said in a low voice. "The glass of water is very moving to me." I looked up and saw the surprised faces of my students. "The

water is a sign of . . ." I paused. "The water seems to be a sign of absence."

I remained silent, but I could feel warm tears running down my cheeks. My students continued to look at me. "I believe that's all for today," I told them in a tremulous voice. "Go outside and enjoy the weather." (147)

The tenderness of the scene—the open windows in the room, "the sunshine, the breeze," the "atmosphere of languor and fatigue"—is gathered into Leo's reaction to the "light" made by the "precise quiver of the brush" (146). But more than Chardin's evocation of light itself, as he explains to his students, it is the glass of water that affects him so deeply. Though his students could be "surprised" for many reasons given the situation, we can trace how caught off guard they are by Leo's pathos here. Moreover, with the mere mention of his students' "surprised faces," soft and pitying as they appear to be, Hustvedt merges the compassionate description of Leo's fragile pain with a quiet nod to the incontrollable power experiences of paintings have over our emotions: indeed, holding on until his students had left, "I tried not to make any noise, but I know that I did. I gulped for air and I gagged and deep ugly sounds came from my throat as I sobbed for what seemed to be a very long time" (147).

Writing about this same painting in an essay that first appeared in *Modern Painters* magazine in 2000, Hustvedt asked, "[W]hy do I feel like weeping over a glass of water standing near a coffeepot?" (*Mysteries* 35). Almost identically to Leo's experience, she describes how "when I look at this painting, even in reproduction, even in a black-and-white reproduction, it inspires in me an almost inexpressible tenderness that is close to pain." But while the personal touch in Leo's experience in the novel imparts a lived quality to the prose—the warmth of the sun and the brush are intensified through the novel's loving prose register—what the novel showcases is the effects of his tragic circumstances on this reaction. While for Hustvedt, "[a] real pot and glass of water would never have this effect on me, unless perhaps these objects had belonged to a beloved person who had died" (35), Leo's experience is so keen precisely because, though he has lost his son, it is a painted glass of water, not a real glass of water, that provokes a memory of "the glass of water that stood underneath" the lamp on his son's bedside table (*What I Loved* 148). But again, it wasn't the memory of his son that caused him to go "to pieces": "the image of a glass of water rendered 230 years earlier had catapulted me suddenly and irrevocably into the painful awareness that I was still alive."

Unlike in Hustvedt's essay, however, the novel grants *Glass of Water and a Coffee Pot* the capacity to push Leo's psychological distress to manifest as physical movement precisely by recognizing its symbolism as life stilled. Even the way Leo describes his response to the painting is alert to the body, as "the glass of water is very moving to me." Indeed, as he gazes at the glass of water, he "moved very close to it," as if he were being drawn in or if the act of being nearer to the painting brought him comfort. These sensations continue beyond this April afternoon through the summer, as Leo, no longer deadened to the world, experiences "months of hypersensitivity" (149) in which "light, noise, color, smells, the slightest motion of the air rubbed me raw with their stimuli" (148).

In grieving, art thus pushes characters toward life by emphasizing the haptic. What we first witness in the novel with Leo's son returns when Bill, Leo's artist friend, dies suddenly of a heart attack. In the aftermath of this sudden loss, the novel dramatizes art's transformative capacity, but this time, rather than altering what we are sensitive to on the canvas, it transmutes the object itself into bodily form: "[w]henever an artist dies, the work slowly begins to replace his body, becoming a corporeal substitute for him in the world" (257). Because "[a]rt, useless as it is, resists incorporation into dailiness, and if it has any power at all, it seems to breathe with the life of the person who made it" (257). Bill is present within his work beyond remnants of his intentions or sensibility; gone is the subtle draw of his desire for Violet in the bruise on her leg, replaced instead by an almost magical realist quality underpinned by base human desire. So, even non–art historians in the novel know this much; when Bill's brother, Dan, hugs a painting "under his shirt" to be "next to his skin," it is a desperate attempt to have "no separation between himself and the little painting, because somewhere in the wood and canvas and metal he imagined that he was touching his older brother" (258). When Dan yearns for his brother, his desire is able to transform art into person. Though it deals with an altogether different form of desire, the novel confronts its opening premise of art made flesh by reminding us that both arousal and grief arrive from the same space of longing. Hustvedt's devoted characters are under no impression that art provides a magic salve to grief, but they nevertheless implicitly know that their encounters with it are instructive. Painful as the experiences may be, they are alert to what W. J. T. Mitchell meant when he noted in *What Do Pictures Want?* that "[i]mages both 'express' desires that we already have, and teach us how to desire in the first place" (68). For in love, as James Elkins elucidates, aesthetic experiences are "entangled in the passions," from adulation to sorrow (11).

But Derrida would disagree:

> How to touch upon the untouchable? Distributed among an indefinite number of forms and figures, this question is precisely the obsession haunting a thinking of touch—or thinking as the haunting of touch. We can only touch on a surface, which is to say the skin or thin peel of a limit . . . But by definition, limit, limit itself, seems deprived of a body. Limit is not to be touched and does not touch itself; it does not let itself be touched, and steals away at a touch, which either never attains it or trespasses on it forever. (*On Touching* 6)

Touch oscillates around liminal space, feeling its way between body and mind and between subjects and objects. Haunted by touch, Leo and Dan only experience the surface as inherently "deprived of a body": for the former, Violet's leg is off limits (the painted bruise can only be painted), and for the latter, Bill's body is in the ground (Bill's paintings can never actually be Bill). As Violet's earlier unrequited desire for Bill's touch denotes, touch isn't necessarily a connective force.

Or at least, it is not a connective force in the physical sense. As Derrida also posits when discussing touch's somatic qualities, there is a performative, almost imperceptible turn to metaphorical feeling. In a metacritical reflection, he observes that "[n]ever to this degree have I felt how enigmatic, how troubling idioms are in their necessity, in expressions such as 'touch to the heart,' 'touch the heart,' whether their value is properly literal or figurative, or sometimes both" (ix). To meditate on Jean-Luc Nancy's treatment of touch, as he does in *On Touching*, then, necessitates that the critic also reach out "to touch him, and thus touch someone, address oneself to him singularly, touch someone in him, a stranger perhaps?" (ix). Though a painted image of a person could actually *be* the person, the novel uses this desire to telescope between the desperation that it could come close and its ultimate impossibility. Touching the bruise, Leo touches Bill's hands painting the bruise; putting Bill's paintings on his skin, Dan touches Bill's hands.

The painting thus becomes a chiasmatic site of touch: a crossed point where painter and perceiver touch. Both "interpersonal" and "intersubjective," in Hustvedt's words, the "relation established" in experiences of art is not "between a person and just a thing," but "between a person and a part-person-part-thing" (*Woman Looking* 26). By this she means that "[a]s soon as a fork or chair or mirror is imported into a work of art, it is qualitatively different from the fork in your drawer or the chair in your living room or the mirror in your bathroom because it carries the traces of a living consciousness and unconsciousness." Even still lives like Chardin's become emotionally redolent because of "the aliveness we give to art," rather than its inherent figuration. Mapping Hustvedt's own experiences that she describes in essays onto novelistic plot, *What I Loved* lends an embodied structure to a kind of seeing that Elkins describes as "like hunting and like dreaming, and even like falling in love," where it "alters the thing that is seen and transforms the seer" (11). In Elkins's formulation, and arguably in Hustvedt's, "[s]eeing is metamorphosis, not mechanism" (12)—rather than ekphrastic prose that constrains seeing to literary artifice, the novel enlivens art's complex potential for offering a visceral kind of solace that refuses to neatly soothe grieving wounds, but nevertheless gives some grace to the void left by loss.

SYNESTHESIA AS REPAIR

In the turn to affect, critics often return to Susan Sontag's turn against. Pleading for an "erotics" rather than "hermeneutics" of art in "Against Interpretation" (1964), Sontag famously argued that "[i]nterpretation takes the sensory experience of the work of art for granted, and proceeds from there" (*Against Interpretation* 14, 13). When she notes that "[w]hat is important now is to recover our senses," her grammar implies a lack or gap in critics' sensory faculties. Indeed, though she might not be signaling a complete absence, there is enough of a loss to require that "[w]e must learn to see more, to *hear* more, to *feel* more" (14). Sontag's repudiation of critical detachment in favor of affective attachment has set the scene for the recent "method wars," to borrow Elizabeth S. Anker and Rita Felski's term (16), which has put pressure on the task of the critic, carving out a space where touch, emotion, and affect have taken hold as popular modes of approaching our critical experiences of art. As Anker and Felski have described, the rise of postcritique in the 2010s has drawn out the long dissatisfaction of affect theorists "who challenge the rationalism of critique and its frequent neglect of emotion, mood, and disposition," while also deeply embedding what feminist theorists have been practicing all along: "experiential and embodied dimensions of the viewing experience" (11). Against the image, criticism has attenuated to a hands-off approach.

If you read enough of Hustvedt's art criticism, you notice that she returns often and admiringly to Henry James's maxim that "[i]n the arts feeling is always meaning" (*Woman Looking* 185). Just a quick glance across her critical oeuvre shows how instrumental this formulation is to her own understanding of the aesthetic experience: feeling "is crucial to understanding a work of art" (185). When she acknowledges the complex relationships between subjects and objects in her novels, in Maclagan's terms, the "edges" between the emotional, perceptual, and physical become even more "blurred" (12). Though emotion is deeply embedded in her conceptualization of art, Hustvedt's *art feelings* refer not simply to the metaphysical states, but to the bodily sensation of touch, so much so that "an artwork becomes senseless without it" (*Living* 6). From lingering over how "[t]he artist affects us at a deep and wordless level of human experience that goes back to infancy—being held and touched" (*Living* 234) when writing about the Italian still-life painter Giorgio Morandi, to elsewhere proclaiming that "[a]ll works of art, including the novel, are animated in the body of the spectator, listener, or reader," for Hustvedt the comfort (or threat) of touch hovers in the vicinity of artistic production and aesthetic experience (*Woman Looking* 441). Experiencing art thus does not only require the faculties of sight, but the ability to feel the effects of art within the body. Setting bodily sensation in tension with perceptual experience, a form of affective criticism accounts for just how much states of aesthetic absorption are informed by the modalities of desire.

From the image of the body to embodied experiences of images, the physical touch imparted by the artist bleeds through the painting to imbue the experience of it with the sometimes real, sometimes metaphorical sense of touch. The experience of art is set against the making of it: by focusing on the hands and sensibility behind the object, as well as the affective and bodily responses of the perceiver, Hustvedt reinvigorates a form of experimental aesthetic discourse that sees perception as embodied. This is not to say that aesthetic experiences are not thought to be embodied, particularly when these are also emotive responses. As Jerrold Levinson has argued, "emotion is best thought of as a bodily response with a distinctive physiological, phenomenological, and expressive profile, one that serves to focus attention in a given direction" (41). Though, as we have seen, forms of aesthetic judgment necessarily rely on cognitive processes—"from mere registering of presence, to ways of seeing or regarding that which is registered, to propositional conceptions of the object responded to, to articulate beliefs about or attitudes toward the object of response" (41)—the kind of "emotional responses typical of engagement with art," too, "tend to be of the moderately, or highly, cognitively involved sort" (42). Put a different way, even though responding emotionally to art requires a level of cognition, this process is bound together within the body. Similarly, in her criticism, Hustvedt has acknowledged the dualism of emotion and perception: just as "[e]motion is always a part of perception" (*Woman Looking* 6), "[a]ll perception is accompanied by feeling" (*Living* 239).

A critical practice that is itself a form of touching points us in the direction of Sontag's erotics of art—a way of sensing (this time in its cognitive rather than somatic sense) the "luminescence" of the work of art without needing an interpretative interface. More recently, Eve Kosofsky Sedgwick's method of reparative reading represents a desire for readers to approach texts as though "commun[ing] through such haptic absorption" (22–23). Reading reparatively, and thus against paranoid structures of the hermeneutics of suspicion, involves reaching out to the object to touch it: "to touch is always already to reach out, to fondle, to heft, to tap, or to enfold, and always also to understand other people or natural forces as having effectually done so before oneself, if only in the making of the textured object" (14). Repairing the link between self and art, haptic reading "makes nonsense out of any dualistic understanding of agency and passivity" (14) and "records the intuition that a particular intimacy seems to subsist between textures and emotions" (17).

Echoing Sedgwick, Hustvedt toes the line between the "double meaning, tactile plus emotional" present in both *touching* and *feeling*, "the dubious epithet 'touchy-feely,' with its implication that even to talk about affect virtually amounts to cutaneous contact" (Sedgwick 17). Across several essays, she has written fervently against the stale, cold affectations of critical discourse. In an up-front indictment of the watered-down affect of disciplinary engagements with art in the introduction of her latest collection of essays, *A Woman Looking at Men Looking at Women*, she reflected that "[m]ost art historians are . . . queasy about emotion and instead write about form, color, influences, or historical context" (6). Even aesthetic terminological metaphor isn't safe from scrutiny of thinking through the absence of the body in aesthetic discourse: "Why do I not like the word *taste* when applied to art? Because it has lost its connection to the mouth and food and chewing" (228). Though she does not suggest we begin to eat art, "[i]f we thought about actual tastes, the word would still work": rather than seeing as feeling, "a crossing of our senses" would still occur so that "seeing" would become "tasting" (228). What this wordplay suggests about Hustvedt's aesthetics, and what is my concern here, is that embodiment seeps into every crevice of encounters with art: from the making of art (the object becomes "an embodied *intentionality*" [*Living* 342]) to where the body is when it experiences art, as well as the physical effects of art on our emotions and how our emotions in turn cause bodily reactions.

This lack of reliance is precisely the generative power of synesthesia; it reads the blur and repairs what Sarah Jackson has termed the "experiential borders of the body" (20). Like other modes of reading I have discussed in this book so far—slant rhyming and transcription—synesthesia reads not one against the other but the space between. And that space? To defer to Violet: "[w]hen does one thing cease and another begin? Your borders are inventions, jokes, absurdities" (298).

FOUR

TRANSCRIPTION

In an interview between the two writers in 2013, Sheila Heti described the effect of reading Chris Kraus for the first time:

> I know there was a time before I read Chris Kraus's *I Love Dick* (in fact, that time was only five years ago), but it's hard to imagine; some works of art do this to you. They tear down so many assumptions about what the form can handle (in this case, what the form of the novel can handle) that there is no way to re-create your mind before your encounter with them. (Kraus, Interview with Heti)

The experience of encountering a life-changing novel is construed here as a kind of afterimage: beyond this point "there is no way to re-create your mind before your encounter with them." But in the wake of such a pivotal encounter, what form is left? This is the question that occupies the two novels at the center of this dialogic art practice. Tracing the formal residues between the two, reading each through the other, demands a flexible comparative reading. Finding form by stretching the capacity of what the novel looks like, as these writers do, demands an equally elastic conceptualization of writing. Yet, if the novel signals an epiphany for the reader, Kraus is against the sublime "emotional transformation of the narrator above other kinds of experience. I hate that. The epiphany of the individual against the backdrop of other lives. It's so false! And it plays into such petty narcissism. And it's not what people feel all the time. People feel boredom. People feel a lot of things that don't find their way into those narratives." This love of boredom emerges stylistically, too: "I've always been a fan of plain writing. I hate metaphor-laden, heavily larded, lyrical writing" (Interview with Heti). Anti-sublimity, anti-lyrical, pro-boredom, and yet both Heti and Kraus's novels, as we'll see, are invested in the game of finding aesthetic categories that harness the experience of contemporary life. As I'll discuss in this chapter, transcription is the mode that emerges as best suited to capturing the banalities of everyday life today: a merging together of experience and novel form that brings the present into both writing and reading.

Initially secreted away in art circles, Kraus's debut *I Love Dick* has since achieved indisputable cult status, with a generation of readers treating it as if it had been written in the 2010s. Published originally in 1997 by Semiotext(e), a publishing house that Sylvère Lotringer (both a character within the novel and a real person, Kraus's former husband) set up in the late 1970s, it shot to enormous commercial and critical acclaim almost two decades later when reprinted, gaining its first UK release, in 2015. In a review for the *Guardian*, Joanna Walsh identifies "a hint of retrospective gratitude" in the effusive way the novel has been received: "[w]ithout her challenge to what she called 'the "serious" contemporary hetero-male novel . . . a thinly veiled Story of Me,' Sheila Heti might never have asked *How Should a Person Be?*, and Ben Lerner might never have written *Leaving the Atocha Station*. A whole generation of writers owes her." More than a "hint," then. Along the same lines, Jenny Turner for *London Review of Books* has claimed it as "an instant-classic feminist Künstlerroman" (37), and Emily Gould has showered it with unfathomable praise as "the most important book written about men and women written in the last century." Heti is not alone, then, in viewing *I Love Dick* as a feminist fiction sine qua non.

When reading the two novels side by side, we may find it humorous that Kraus attributes "Heti's use of real art-world names, real events, real conversations and correspondence . . . to the work of the late Kathy Acker"

("What Women Say"). Though there is a third line of influence from Acker to Kraus herself—an obsession that you can trace in Kraus's biography of the former—the disparity between Heti and Acker, for Kraus, is the affective tenor of the process through which the writer finds form, so that while "Acker's work was written mostly in scabrous rage, Heti's worldview is more conciliatory. Throwing fragments of chaos into the air and arriving at order, Heti's work mimics a Shakespearean form, while Acker's métier was closer to the bloody and bawdy revenge dramas of John Ford and Christopher Marlowe" ("What Women Say"). There isn't a mention in this review of Kraus's own work—not surprisingly, as tracing her own influence on a generation of writers isn't Kraus's style—but the core formal distinction between Heti and Acker here recalls the experiential shape that *I Love Dick* takes in organizing artistic failure and earnest-though-cerebral attempts to connect to lovers, friends, confidants.

Experiential form of the kind I want to elucidate by reading the two novels together is essentially performative. But it diverges from the kind of performance of the self we see in the mode of memoir or autofiction. Kraus says that though writing is "a performance" it is "not necessarily of one's life, or the facts of one's life, but of moods, feelings, thoughts and disposition" (Kraus and Gubbins). If Kraus thinks of herself "writing through a character mask" (Kraus and Gubbins), for Heti it "is like a form of acting" (Interview with La Force). The affective authenticity of both novels works in effect by transposing method acting as writing praxis:

> So as I'm writing, the character or self I'm writing about and my whole self—when I began the book—become entwined. It's soon hard to tell them apart. The voice I'm trying to explore directs my own perceptions and thoughts. But that voice or character comes out of a part of me that exists already. But writing about it emphasizes those parts, while certain other, balancing parts lie dormant—and the ones I'm exploring become bigger, like in caricature. That sounds really orderly but I never realize it's happening, because who is "the first person" becomes confused. Of course, this transformation happens very gradually over many years. Then, months after the book is done, all that falls away—the ways I was behaving and thinking while writing the book—and a different self from the origi-

nal one is left, with the qualities I was emphasizing much less prominent than originally. (Interview with La Force)

Kraus, putting it slightly differently, agrees: because "memoir implies the neoliberal illusion of the autonomous individual," it lacks the capacity to evoke the transformative potential of art, "as if one person's crises and traumas were his or hers alone" (Interview with Poletti 134). She suggests that "anthropology would be just as useful a word to describe my approach to writing as autobiography or biography" (133–34). Favoring "a more anthropological, sociographic outlook" allows first-person narratives to explore "[h]ow people relate to power, how they move through the setup" (Interview with Heti). Because stories that work within this framework perform characterological studies within "different anthropological setups," writing adopts a mode of transcription: "a transcription of what I see, hear, think, live" (Interview with Heti).

Heti takes up this anthropological method in *How Should a Person Be?* (2010): concerned with creative failure due to dubious talent, the narrator of the novel discards the theater script she has been asked to write in favor of observing her friends' conversations, the transcript of which becomes the novel we end up reading.[1] Aptly, these transcriptions precede the idea of the novel, recording conversations that take place between real-life friends Margaux Williamson (painter), Misha Glouberman (writer), and Sholem Krishtalka (painter). Telling the *Paris Review*, Heti notes that "the conversations were not meant for a book. I was just taping friends. I didn't have a plan for where I was going." Nevertheless, "all the transcribing I was doing was kind of like drinking a glass of water—it was refreshing, like a palate cleanser—a way of getting out of my imagination." Forming a segue between writing *Ticknor*, Heti's first novel, and negotiating the difficulties of writing the play, "[t]aping and transcribing was part of looking around to see what things were really like in my environment. I'd been completely in my room, in my head, not looking at anything" (Interview with La Force).

Transcriptional in literary method, but also in aesthetic mode then: both novels have transcriptional relationships to the failed artworks that haunt the narratives. *I Love Dick* mobilizes transcription through dynamic formal structure. Part 1, "Scenes from a Marriage," is structured with diary entries and letters. Personal forms such as diary entries and letters aren't simply transcribed; they are imbued with agency by transcribing affective experiences, as we see in Part 2's title, "Every Letter Is a Love Letter." *How Should a Person Be?*, too, presents its transcriptional mode in a highly organized fashion. As Kraus noted of the formal frustration of the novel's pretense, "for all of the wildness contained in Heti's account of her struggles, the book is perfectly composed within the classical structure of five-act dramatic narrative" ("What Women Say"); in the struggle to find form, it seems, form emerges. In order to figure out what female conversations *look* like, she records her conversations with Margaux in order to write them down.

Transcription, then, is a way for both writers to butt up against the real, but also a strategy for playing out the failure of things to become real—art forms that fail to realize and ways of being and loving that fail to realize. This echoes what concerned Walter Pater during the 1890s. Noting that "the line between fact and something quite different from external fact" is "hard to draw," he suggests that "in proportion as the writer's aim, consciously or unconsciously, comes to be the transcribing, not of the world, not of mere fact, but of his sense of it, he becomes an artist" (9). By transcribing the world, Heti and Kraus play with authenticity and becoming, both in literary form and in emotional experience. Transcription undertakes the project of writing against the image of life, negotiating failure, in order to build authentic artistic and affective form.

TRANSCRIBING *HOW SHOULD A PERSON BE?*

How Should a Person Be? is a novelistic attempt to formalize be*ing*—the present tense of living. According to Sheila, the novel's playwright-narrator, "[m]ost people live their entire lives with their clothes on, and even if they wanted to, couldn't take them off, then there are those who cannot put them on. They are the ones who live their lives not just as people but as examples of people. They are destined to expose every part of themselves, so the rest of us know what it means to be human" (60). Even with this proposition, Zara Dinnen feels:

> The awkward open-endedness of this question is an unheard final downbeat: How to be . . . what? The novel works through different

versions of the question. How should a person be . . . a good artist, an authentic individual, a social and socially responsible person, famous, known, unknown, a woman, a man, sexual, serious, friends, alone. The novel offers no answer, but is a meditation on the question itself. (82)

To be sure, the novel plays with the ambiguity of first-person narration. Noting that she "just couldn't write a book" with an omniscient narrator "because I wouldn't be interested enough to get to the end" (Interview with Barber), Heti emphasizes that the project is caught up with the dilemma of mediation. So transcribing becomes a way of mediating images of people.

Struggling with her play, Sheila starts recording conversations with Margaux, *the* person—cool, talented, beautiful: "I thought that maybe by talking it over with you—I thought maybe you could help me figure out why it isn't working. Then I can listen to what we say, and think it over at home, and figure out where I'm going wrong" (*How Should a Person Be?* 59). Margaux, on the other hand, is perturbed by her voice being copied:

> MARGAUX
> Why are you looking to me for answers? I don't know anything you don't know?
>
> SHEILA
> I'm not looking to you for answers! Why would you say that? I was just hoping that if I—
>
> MARGAUX
> Don't you know that what I fear most is my words floating separate from my body? You there with that tape recorder is the scariest thing! (59)

Captured, the disembodied voice is a simulacrum of Margaux's voice. And this underpins much of what Margaux fears: the incident that tips their friendship onto the rocks later in the novel—Sheila buying the same yellow dress—too, threatens with the creation of a human simulacrum, a copy, an image of how a person should be.

It is notable that Sheila doesn't choose this mode: "[i]t has long been known to me that certain objects want you as much as you want them" (56). When she happens upon an electronic shop, the discovery of the "silver digital tape recorder" marks a change in Sheila's demeanor:

> I whispered low into the tape recorder's belly. I recorded my voice and played it back. I spoke into it tenderly and heard my tenderness returned. I felt like I was with a new lover—one that would burrow into my deepest recesses, seek out the empty places inside me, and create a warm home for me there. I wanted to touch every part of it, to understand how it worked. I began to learn what turned it on and the things that turned it off. (57)

The following two chapters of the novel introduce its transcriptional mode: a particular kind of contemporary discourse that maps out, spatially and indexically, the way in which mediated conversation works against the discursive narratorial flow typical of novels. The chapter launches immediately into this transcript, the scene framed briefly: "*Later that same week, after buying the tape recorder, Margaux and Sheila sit in the front window of a neighborhood diner. They order a breakfast to share and two coffees. The midday sunlight filters onto Margaux's peroxide hair. They both wear dirty sneakers. They both wear dirty underwear*" (58). Moments of descriptive direction also intersperse the conversation: "*Sheila beckons to the waitress, who comes over*" (58); "*The waitress nods and leaves*" (61); "*Margaux takes some potatoes with a fork. They fall. She eats them with her fingers*" (63; all original emphasis).

Read optimistically, the tonal change between the first of these chapters, "Sheila Wants to Quit," and the second, "Sheila Wants to Live," points to a shift in formal attitude: Sheila wants to quit the play, coming up against creative blocks, but she also wants to quit the novel form, looping the transcript of conversation around a brief moment of interior monologue. Responding to her Jungian therapist, Ann, who suggests that her pathology of quitting speaks to her fear of danger later in Act 2, Sheila is adamant:

> (*defensive*) Wait! I want to cancel the play not because it's *dangerous*, but because life doesn't feel like it's in my stupid play, or with me sitting in a room *typing*. And life wasn't in my marriage anymore, either. Life feels like it's with Margaux—*talking*—which is an equally sincere attempt to get somewhere, just as sincere as writing a play. (82)

"Sheila Wants to Live" signals the earnest prospect of new formal beginnings that continue to shape the rest of the novel: a new artistic direction on the play, but also authentically, metatextually hinting at a new hybrid form that, by transcribing so-called real conversations, gets closer to life.

The transcript prioritizes the formal disruption, fragmentation, and overlapping of Sheila's and Margaux's voices. Typographically creating the effect of a script on the page, with each character or "performer" taking turns to "speak," the section evolves in a carefully balanced tension of slow enrapture. *Slow enrapture* is evoked again by the sometimes accumulative and at other times repetitive patterning of the novel's transcriptions. When the conversation is one-way (an email from Margaux or Israel, Sheila's S-M boyfriend, or a secret recording from Margaux), the phrases are numbered. For the most part, they are numbered sequentially, but occasionally they are divided into separate notes:

1. i am surprised at how much i miss you, like a real teenage girl.
1. hello. i was wondering, if you have red bike lights, could i borrow them tomorrow night? (37)

1. I think I do better with the recordings when you're here. I think what I want to do right now is just record this, then go over to my desk and work. And so to pretend like you're here.
2. The quieter I am in your tape recorder, the more it feels like you're here.

1. (*sighs*) I always had a fantasy of meeting a girl . . . who was as serious as I was. (157)

We aren't supposed to imagine that characters like Margaux and Israel, two characters that don't know one another, number their emails in the exact same way without having ever met; nor are we supposed to think that Margaux records these lines by prefacing her thoughts with numbers. Numbering is *Sheila's* method. When the sequence hits 1 again, time restarts, a breath is taken, and "somehow it all felt possible. It suddenly felt like the simplest thing. Why had I forgotten all the ways that it was natural and easy for me to work?" (157).

Dinnen argues that by marking these out as "graphically distinct from the general narration . . . attend[ing] to the difference of e-mail as a distinct medium within the novel," "[t]he novel is undone by the e-mails and the scripts because they are not within the constraints of the fiction: they attest to Sheila Heti's social life, mediation as becoming-with, and Sheila Heti's work as author" (90). But the novelistic prose is fragmented into numbered email entries that don't *look* like the form of an actual email (as they do in, say, Zadie Smith's *On Beauty*); although the numbering makes the entries distinct from novel form, they are also distinct from email form. The chat, too, does not resemble a chat: in the words of Ben Lerner, another writer who uses e-chats in fiction, "the chat is closer to poetry than prose in so far as the fragmentation of syntax bears an emotional charge" (Interview with Loudis). As we'll see in *I Love Dick*, the inclusion of other forms like emails marks a digression from the conventional novel, but in such a way as to push the form onward, rather than betraying it. By writing against the image of the novel, Heti and Kraus capture the expansive, transcriptional potential of the form.

FABULATION AS PHENOMENOLOGY

The novel form is often happened upon by accident in the self-reflexive texts of the early twenty-first century.[2] Neither Sheila nor Chris (*I Love Dick*'s narrator) intend to write a novel: Sheila is having difficulty writing a play and so tries something closer to life, something that is only shaped into a novel late in the text. Indeed, as Joanna Biggs wrote in a review of the novel for *London Review of Books*, "[m]ost novels which include a character with the name of the author do it as a metafictional game or joke, but when Sheila Heti calls her main character Sheila it is out of exasperation with the novel. *How Should a Person Be?* is the culmination of Heti's attempts to write a novel about life when a novel is written in a room, away from life." Exasperation, a dissonant feeling of novelistic proportions, doesn't actually lead her away from the novel but back to it through another door.

Chris, too, experiments with form and again only happens upon the novel as the only form that truly fits the material. The novel documents Chris's immediate infatuation with cultural theorist Dick after a night of drinking at his house, and her gradual but ascending pain at his aloof rejection prompts her to write him letter after unsent letter. Soon after, her husband (Sylvère Lotringer), prompted by barely concealed grief at his wife's unconcealed obsession with Dick (intellectualized for ameliorating effect) and their unraveling marriage, writes his own letters to Dick. Where previously Chris had "chosen film and theatre, two art forms built entirely on collisions, that only reach their meanings through collisions"—because she "couldn't ever believe in the integrity/supremacy of the 1st person"—her unfamiliar "fragmentary" letter art occasions fraught collisions between herself and the struggles of self-expression (*I Love Dick* 122). Unrequited love becomes the very materials for the experiment Chris and Sylvère develop over months, while art becomes their solace and comfort, however impermanent and transitory the salve: "On December 3, 1994 I started loving you. I still do" (188).

Perhaps it was "the desert wind that went to our heads that night," Sylvère writes, "or maybe the desire to fictionalize life a little bit" (10)—and so it is with desire, which begins the conceptual project that becomes the very text of the novel. In a fax "never sent" to Dick, Chris and Sylvère propose *The Invasion of the Heart Snatchers*, a riff on the 1956 sci-fi horror film *Invasion of the Body Snatchers*: "Basically our idea was to paste the text we've written all over your car, house and cactus garden. We (i.e., Sylvère) would videotape me (i.e., Chris) doing this—probably a wide shot of all the papers flapping in the breeze. Then, if you like, you could enter and discover it" (28). Although they never send the fax, they do suggest the same installation to Dick over the phone. Despite their attempts of actualization, in the end *The Invasion of the Heart Snatchers* exists as concept without form. As Sylvère observes sadly, the form will "never be fulfilled" so long as Dick "never answer[s]" (52)—and indeed, he never is "game" (28) enough to collaborate. And yet, the mere suggestion of the installation enables a vivid imaginary realization—we can see Dick's house set against the Californian desert landscape in Antelope Valley, adorned with the letters that make up the first half of the novel. We can see Chris "past[ing]" page after page to the walls of the house, Dick's "car," and a "cactus garden" (28). The pages might flutter "in the breeze," the sunlight waxing and waning as the mid-December day passes, casting long shadows across the scene. Because "the piece is all about obsession," we can imagine Dick's performed reaction as he "enter[s] and discover[s]" his house, car, and cacti consumed by more than "50 pages" of evidence of unrequited love. And because Sylvère planned to film this installation, with "a wide shot," we can envision viewing the silent performance projected onto the white walls of a gallery space (28). The novel's brief description of Chris

Chris (portrayed by Kathryn Hahn) pasting *The Invasion of the Heart Snatchers* to one of a series of buildings in Marfa at the beginning of episode 6 of *I Love Dick* (2017). Author's screenshot. © Amazon Video, 2017.

and Sylvère's artistic intention simulates the very texture of the artistic enterprise without ever actualizing its atmospheric details in prose.

In Jill Soloway's 2017 Amazon television adaptation of the novel, Chris brings *The Invasion of the Heart Snatchers* to life (fig. 4), but the novel leaves it as a sketched proposal of an art event that never happens. Indeed, the failed installation of the project in the novel intensifies Chris's longing for Dick. So, if the somatic physicality of the installation performed through the body is curbed by the literary form it eventually takes, how can narrative prose foster, rather than subsume, the conceptual emphasis on aesthetic process? Theorizing invention and intellection instead of execution, we find the novel attempting to absorb the essence of *Invasion of the Heart Snatchers*: "what the work of art looks like isn't too important," as Sol LeWitt explained in a famous article for *Artforum* in 1967, "Paragraphs on Conceptual Art," noting that "it is the process of conception" rather than "perception" that holds the artist's attention. And so Sylvère speculates that "these letters seem to open up a new genre, something between cultural criticism and fiction," formulating distance between the emotion of Chris's artistic act and the cool logic of formal methodology; her apprehension about first-person expression is immediately framed by its possible reception, reconfigured as a "kind of confrontational performing art" (27). Exposing the fissures between fictional genres and critical ones—just as the form lends itself to installation and the novelistic—imparts an exegetic air to the novel's descriptive and narratorial impressions of artistic sensibility and desire. Which is to say, the novel encloses upon itself with tailored interpretative methods constructed by its characters' own aesthetic motivations—and the urge to acquiesce is tempting: "if nothing else, you must agree that Chris's letters are some new kind of literary form. They're very powerful" (242).

Mind you, Chris's own reflections on what she is doing expose an artistic sensibility that is explicitly tied to the female psyche. Hers is a new genre but equally a part of what she calls a "Lonely Girl Phenomenology"— something that denotes the way she thinks about making art more than formal method, striking a dissonant chord with external interpretations of her project—tightening the already fluid autobiographical elements of the novel's characters and events. It is not surprising that "Lonely Girl Phenomenology," refracted through a fictionalized version of the author herself, has long been one of Kraus's self-described philosophies of artistic practice. Kraus's second novel, *Aliens & Anorexia* (2000), destabilizes the struggles of self-expression further. When showing her film-art to John Hanhardt, "then the film and video curator at the Whitney," the narrator wonders "why intelligence and courage were considered negative attributes" in her art where "beauty, criticality, and narrative resolution" were valorized (182). As Joan Hawkins argues, "the artistic *problematique* posed by" much of Kraus's writing "is the degree to which narrative and formal convention should dictate 'art.'" This criticality operates, as Chris calls it in *I Love Dick*, at the "Third Remove" (14)—the distance at which the artist can inhabit the art-making process while simultaneously reflecting analytically on the performance of it. For Chris, "art involves reaching through some distance" (*I Love Dick* 14).

Characteristically for Kraus's art, then, the novel traces networks of distance and distances, both formal and affective. Though they eventually settle on the form of novel for the project, Chris and Sylvère's exposé of desire and their pursuit of reciprocation find a vibrant initial model in the conceptual art practices of "Calle Art" (28), named for Sophie Calle's artworks that imitate open books on the wall. What we can locate in *I Love Dick*'s phenomenological approach is the contemporary novel's built-in investment in the critical language and structures used its own interpretation. Just as Chris and Sylvère's project in the novel gathers conceptual momentum, the ambition to merge display and novel form is visually evident in the pages of *I Love Dick* too, with the novel's fragmentary typography arranged as if it were an exhibition. Her textual installations, easily straddling both book and exhibition form, for all their formal experimentations, nevertheless situate art as, in Calle's words, "a way of taking distance" in order to "suffer less." Chris's attempt to "occupy ... the wall" rather than the page, too, seeks to transform the "therapeutic aspects" of ordinary suffering to mobilize the artwork toward something like conceptual love, attaining higher artistic truth as it evacuates the personal (Interview with Neri).

Distance and absence become something of a desirable but unattainable protective shield for Kraus. In an essay on Calle in 2001, Kraus argues that by "[i]nvestigating others through their traces, Calle herself is invisible" (*Video Green* 175). Because "the subject of Calle's investigations is someone she is not particularly interested in"—which in turn "makes the work conceptually clean"—"Calle's work is never considered offensive, objectionable" (177). Though she blurs the line between stalking and documentary in *Suite Venitienne* (1983), her work nonetheless "circles on absence" (175). Moreover, because Calle is not present, nor does she "address us directly," she "does not embarrass us" (175). The tenor of Calle's reception could hardly be further from Kraus's conceptualization of female writing: absence is almost impossible to create in literature because when "[w]riting is too much like talking," "[p]resence is never far away from a demand for recognition: do you see me?" (175). Moreover, although "we are relieved" that Calle, "as absent-investigator," doesn't "explicitly assert [her] presence" (175), for a female writer like Kraus no such relief is possible. Which is why she so vehemently rejects the characterization of *I Love Dick* as confessional: "'Confessional' of what? *Personal* confessions? There's a great line from a book we published by Deleuze: *Life is not personal*. The word 'confessional' is not a good descriptor of my work" (Interview with Frimer). But why not? Today, confessional writing has generated fervent interest in audiences across the world: from Heti to Leslie Jamison to Rachel Cusk to Karl Ove

Knausgård, the most critically lauded of them all.³ *I Love Dick* argues for a new attention to emotional vulnerability that doesn't shelve it naïvely into confession, asking "Why is female vulnerability still only acceptable when it's neuroticized and personal; when it feeds back on itself? Why do people still not get it when we handle vulnerability like philosophy, at some remove?" What seems so repulsive about the term is how it traps female subjectivity within a certain kind of "critical misread[ing] of a certain kind of female art" (191). As we will see, for both Kraus and Heti, the detached restaging of encounters suggests an attempt to bridge this dilemma by curating intimacy via distance.

I/EYE

Contemporary women's writing and female art are both haunted by their own names. Both seek legitimacy through them, while despising their necessity. As Amy Hungerford writes, "Virginia Woolf's view of the situation of women writers as she describes it in *A Room of One's Own*—and Woolf's own contributions to its remedy—remain relevant to women artists nearly a century later" (61). Hustvedt has described her own experience of a reader asking whether her husband, Paul Auster, "had written the sections of [*The Blazing World*] that belong to one of the male characters" (*Living* 350). But if simply by virtue of creating art, the artist imbues it with subjective consciousness, then is not all art personal? As the previous chapter discussed, Siri Hustvedt certainly thinks so, and this is where Kraus's and Hustvedt's perspectives differ: for the latter, art is "enchanted by the artist's intentionality—a force that is prereflective and reflective, one that I engage with as a distinct presence of another human being, albeit the ghost of that other, that absent *you*" (*Living* 342). It is "an embodied *intentionality*" that "necessarily establishes a relation between the artist and imaginary reader, viewer, or listener" because "it is inherently dialogical" (*Living* 342; original emphasis). Art is a conversation between artist, viewer, and the art itself.

So the challenge of female writing now is how to detach the "I" from a personal subjectivity and reorient it within the detached schema of the "a-personal" (Kraus, Interview with Frimer). Chris in *I Love Dick* echoes this sentiment by flipping its form: "If women have failed to make 'universal' art because we're trapped within the 'personal,' why not universalize the 'personal' and make it the subject of our art?" (195). Even when art really is "inherently dialogical," as in Chris's letter writing, the ambition toward universality is paramount: "[w]hat hooks me on our story is our different readings of it," she tells Dick in one letter, "[y]ou think it's personal and private; my neurosis . . . I think our story is performative philosophy" (195). The female "I" as performative philosophy strips the pathology from "this great disgust with female-ness. As if a revelatory female self cannot be anything but compromised and murky" (Interview with Frimer). The female "I" turns the abject into formal possibility.

At stake in the debate about the female "I" in contemporary novels is the uncertainty with which female first-person narration is read. As Leslie Jamison wrote in a review of the novel, "as a reader, Kraus makes me confront my own hunger for autobiographical access; it makes me aware of how much I crave a sense of the true story beneath her written narratives, even as I respect the ways they refuse to deliver any kind of one-to-one correspondence between lived and constructed experience." In an interview in 2016 with Anna Poletti, Kraus grounded the confusion about female performativity by imagining "there's a hard shell around the male narrator and a soft, gelatinous membrane around a female narrator. People love to pick at and prod and pierce this membrane, but they respect the male narrator's shell" (131). In "Emotional Technologies," an essay about S-M from her collection of essays *Video Green*, Kraus describes how the assumption of porousness betrays a naïvety that assumes "speaking in the first person necessarily connotes any kind of truth, sincerity" (103).

Facing this gap between what is personal and what is universal, we find that Chris's epistolary relationship with Dick, both as a version of love and as an art practice, enacts what Lauren Berlant has called "cruel optimism." Explaining that though "all attachments are optimistic," cruel optimism accounts for "the condition of maintaining an attachment to a significantly problematic object" (*Cruel Optimism* 24). Chris's willingness to attach and Dick's unwillingness to reciprocate is not a difficult relation to trace. Chris's attachment to Dick is fundamentally optimistic: "[n]o woman is an island-ess," she writes in her last letter, "[w]e fall in love in hope of anchoring ourselves to someone else, to keep from falling" (*I Love Dick* 114). For her, "in a sense love is like writing: living in such a heightened state that accuracy and awareness are vital" (114). Dick, the object of her desire, is fundamentally cruel. Though his responses of "bemused silence" at each of Chris's letters early on signify small brutalities, when he "confessed how, over the past two years" he'd "stopped reading," as Chris notes, "this broke my heart" (114). And when he writes back at the end of the novel, he refuses to respond to any of her letters, instead replying to Sylvère's letters—Chris gets only a photocopy of Dick's letter to Sylvère. This final act of cruelty, which crushes Chris "under the weight of it," illuminates how Dick is "mostly concerned with salvaging his damaged relationship with Sylvère" (114), rather than giving her the recognition she really wants, as Anne-Christine d'Adesky notes. "When we talk about an object of desire," Berlant explains, "we are really talking about a cluster of promises we wants someone or something to make to us and make possible for us" but "[a] relation of cruel optimism exists when something you desire is actually an obstacle to your flourishing" (*Cruel Optimism* 1). At the close of the novel, Dick breaks these promises by denying Chris his approval for publishing her letters. "I do not share your conviction that my right to privacy has to be sacrificed for the sake of that talent," he tells Sylvère: even though he believes that "Kris has talent as a writer," nothing suits him more than pretending she doesn't exist (244).[4]

One suspects that Kraus would find it unpalatable that Dick's silence and embarrassed opposition would actually obstruct Chris's "flourishing." His lack of response to her letters, after all, sparks rather than spurns her artistic energy. Indeed, her vulnerability and his cruelty are actually productive, bringing her aesthetic and critical projects to fruition. We are told that "through love" Chris is teaching herself "how to think" (116), and later we see how she makes a sideways step into writing art criticism in her letters as a new way of engaging with him: "God what a hoot. I'm moved to talk to you about art because I think you'll understand and I think I understand art more than you" (194). Positioning herself as his "ideal reader"—"one who is in love with the writer & combs the text for clues about that person & how they think"—she also becomes his intellectual foil (194). She praises him—"You write about art so well" (194)—but nevertheless disagrees with his conclusions: "You argue that the frame provides coherence only through repression and exclusion. But the trick is to discover *Everything* within the frame. 'Think Harder' as Richard Foreman used to blast out over the PA in his early plays. Or just Look Closer" (117–18). She writes about Eleanor Antin's *Minetta Lane—A Ghost Story* and a piece on female art called "Monsters." Her piece on R. B. Kitaj, "Kike Art," contains sharp musings on his status in the art world, the recurring criticism of his work ("'abstruse, pretentious'; 'shallow, fake and narcissistic'; 'hermetic, dry and bookish'; 'difficult, obscure, slick and grade f'" [170]), and often poetic observations about four of his paintings. Kitaj's paintings are mostly "studies," in which "[t]hought accelerates to a pitch where it becomes pure feeling" (171). One of her favorites, *The Nice Old Man and the Pretty Girl (with Huskies)*, is "seduced by the frenetic energy and glamour of [the 1960s] while mocking it" (173), as it "draws an outside circle around the giddiness and wit that characterized Pop Art, a movement read by some as the closest thing the art world's come to sophisticate Utopia" (175). In her description of *John Ford on his Deathbed (1983/84)*, we can see Kraus's aversion to delicacy:

> In this painting dissonance's disappeared and been reborn as elevated schtick. It's a grand finale, the production number, where all the show's motifs come back as jokes. And Kitaj-as-Ford delivers, like movies're supposed to do, a dazzling punchline: at the upframe center of Ford's blue wall there's an Ed Ruscha knock-off framed in black that reads
>
> THE
>
> END
>
> and below it, a tiny painting, window opening out from deep blue walls to deep blue sky. There is no road to immortality but there's a porthole to it. In this painting objects, people, dance and move but there's flesh and weight. Transcendence isn't only lightness; it's attained by will. (187–89)

While meditating on Kitaj, this piece is also a work of magical thinking, tracing correspondences between Kitaj's artistic process and Chris's own. One can hear a twinge of self-recognition in how she draws attention to the curatorial task of "mak[ing] this 'difficult' work accessible," which finds its answer in casting "the artist as an admirable freak" (171). Or in how she notes how "[i]t amused me that Kitaj has wrapped himself around the idea of creating 'exegesis' for his art, writing texts to parallel each painting. 'Exegesis': the crazy person's search for proof that they're not crazy. 'Exegesis' is the word I used in trying to explain myself to you" (171). In the midst of this letter, she even breaks off because she "feel[s] so emotional about this writing. Last night I 'replaced' you with an orange candle because I felt you weren't listening anymore. But I still need for you to listen. Because—don't you see?—no one is, I'm completely illegitimate" (175). It seems clear that being struck by the efforts to legitimize Kitaj's art (often wrongly through "fucked-up readings" [172]) occasions a spell of what Kraus so admires in Simone Weil's works: absorbing the conditions of struggle that both Kitaj's path to recognition and subsequent reception take, Chris enacts a state of radical empathy. Questions about her own rocky path to recognition and artistic success distress her: "Did anybody ask me my ideas about Kitaj? Does it matter what they are? It's not like I've been invited, paid to speak. There isn't much that I take seriously and since I'm frivolous and female most people think I'm pretty dumb" (175).

Outside the novel, the critical and aesthetic value of the chapter "Kike Art" is obvious. For Hawkins, "[t]he piece entitled 'Kike Art' is easily the best thing on Kitaj I've ever read, and her meditations on Hannah Wilke and Eleanor Antin are wonderful pieces of art criticism/history." Aptly, Hawkins "particularly like[s] the way she invites us, throughout these essays, to consider who gets 'accepted' into the art world pantheon, who doesn't and why. Again and again she asks us to go back to those moments we consider 'avant garde,' and read through a slightly different lens." The question "Who gets to speak and why?" (175) plagues Chris in this piece on Kitaj, but it also sheds light on Kraus's preference to frame her writing as anthropological. So, if her other novels explore setups such as "the East Village art world, the Parisian intellectual world, and in *Summer of Hate*, the American justice system in the southwest during the Bush era" (Interview with Poletti 134), *I Love Dick* foregrounds Chris's experiences in the artistic and intellectual worlds on both coasts of the United States, but more broadly in outsider art. Her interest in Kitaj denotes her sensitivity to artistic production on the periphery, the politics of the marketplace, and the fraught relationships between the artist and the critic. This, for Kraus, defines not only her "sensibility as a writer" but "the Semiotext(e) sensibility." (134). While her Active Agents series is "no longer exclusively female," as it was for the "first twelve or fourteen titles," "neither does it posit the straight middle-class white male as the ultimate subject" (134). For Kraus now, if not at the time of writing *I Love Dick*, when "[r]eflecting the present ... gender is not the leading card" (135).

SYMMETRY, VACILLATION, FAILURE

Sontag reflected in "The Artist as Exemplary Sufferer," an essay from 1962, that the writer or artist is "the exemplary sufferer because he has found both the deepest level of suffering and also a professional means to sublimate ... his suffering" (*Against Interpretation* 42). By foregrounding artistic failure, Kraus and Heti evince the internal machinations of sufferers: the cruelty inflicted upon them from external sources and the injury conjured up from inside. Given the likelihood of incommensurability, the striving toward the elision of metaphysical and physical feeling is almost always a collapse into a mode of disappointment. But both Sheila and Chris (and Heti and Kraus) find that failure is "sublimated" in transcriptional form.

Reviewers have picked up on these failures. The *Guardian* portrayed *I Love Dick* on its reprint in 2015 as "a screwball tragedy" (Walsh), and when Soloway's adaption was released with Amazon in 2017, Maxine Swann described the show as documenting the rise of the "comic female loser." James Wood for the *New Yorker* considered the central question of *How Should a Person Be?* by couching it in failure: "[o]n the one hand, there is the timeless seriousness of the question, and on the other hand there is the hapless, incoherent present-day chaos of the reply, which takes a whole messy book to fail to answer" ("True Lives"). This "inadequacy of the response," though, "is a kind of contemporary confession, just as Heti intends her book to be a larger portrait of a generation that knows the right questions but struggles to find the right answers" ("True Lives"). The chime of *timeliness* rings across the reception of both novels. "Until recently," according to Elaine Blair, "a comic female antihero was nearly inconceivable. There's nothing funny about failing if you've been overwhelmingly obstructed by sexism and social conventions. If you want to make people laugh, you really have to fail on your own merits" ("Chris Kraus"). The time has come for the female schmuck, whose personal failures might just be outshone by her artistic genius, or whose artistic genius is never quite found because she simply isn't talented enough.

Similar motivations underlie the inclusion of essays on flawed female artists in both *I Love Dick* and Kraus's second novel, *Aliens & Anorexia*:

> And the closer I looked at that, the more interesting it became, and the further it took me away from my own problems and failures and into the lives of others. I became very interested in whatever became of the second-wave feminists, who at that point [in the 1990s] would have been in their fifties and sixties and, you would think, in very visible leadership positions, given the tremendous contributions they made earlier in their lives. But no. They've mostly disappeared. A whole group of women just seemed to have been obliterated. And that became one of the essays/slash/letters in the book, trying to understand the quote-unquote failure of those women, not as a personal failure, but as something that the culture did to them. (Interview with Phillips)

It is for this reason, too, that Kraus considers failure to be "a feminist question" (Interview with Fulton). Despite the sincere intention here, what is notable about both novels' transcriptional responses to their central characters' failures is that they are deliberately *funny*. Though *How Should a Person Be?* is persistently "hideously narcissistic" (in a good way, Wood insists), the novel is aware of its self-absorption: "you get the feeling that the author is making fun of her narrator, or even making fun of her own desire to be an artist, and finds something embarrassing about the earnest and serious questions" ("True Lives"). When *I Love Dick* was first published, critics focused too seriously on the autobiographical elements; now, readers seem to be more attuned to the comedic intentions behind the story than they were in 1997. As Kraus told one interviewer, "I was telling a funny story about an obsessive crush among a triangle of people," not about her own life: "I was trying to describe a moment in the cultural, intellectual world at the end of the 20th century" (Interview with Holton). And another: "People remarked all the time, 'She's so self-hating, she has such a poor self-image.' If a man makes fun of himself, it's a joke. If a woman does, it's a pathology and she needs therapy" (in Blair).

It is somehow ironically fitting, then, that even if the novels make Chris's and Sheila's failures a joke, their transcriptional modes open up space for therapy, for sublimation. With Heti, Kraus recalled the catharsis of writing the letters:

> By the second or third letter, I knew there was a lot I needed to talk about, that had been pent-up for the fifteen years I'd been moving around the art world, which had not come out. It was like something needed to be articulated, and by writing letter after letter after letter, I was not just trying to get Dick's attention—that became the little conceit that made it possible. The real drive was trying to get it right—to talk about all these things that I thought were . . . well, to talk about my own failure. The book was more than anything an attempt to analyze the social conditions surrounding my personal failure. (Interview with Heti)

Kraus's personal failure here refers to the series of films that struggled to "catch on" (Interview with Phillips) in the art and film worlds. "Powerful people said very disparaging things about them. And yet I felt I wasn't stupid; my work was not without merit; and so I decided I wasn't going to make another film until I understood the failure of my films." This is where the novel comes in: an aesthetic mode that transcribed these failures with anthropological attention. Indeed, to do just this she "had to look not just to [herself] and the films, but to the atmosphere in which they were circulating, and the power dynamics of the culture industry and the art world in which they were received" (Interview with Phillips).

Earlier I described how Chris's artistic energy in the novel is spurred on by a structure of cruel optimism. However, Dick's rejection of her is the façade of the true cruelty, one that doesn't see itself enacted in the novel but that haunts it from the first page to the last: artistic rejection. "When I wrote the book," Kraus remarks, "I exaggerated the extent to which she cared about his acceptance or rejection of her. Artistic rejection is much more crushing, and she's trying to escape from that" (Kraus and Gubbins). Dissecting the title, Ruby Gubbins notes in the same conversation that "[t]hough the 'love' part of *I Love Dick* ends in failure, the 'I' part has an adventure that ultimately leads to satisfaction, if not success." Chris's "Dick Adventure" is a distraction from artistic failure; rather than an object of sincere desire, "Dick is a gateway drug to writing." In dealing with artistic crisis, "Chris decides to give up on filmmaking and make herself available to something else" (Kraus and Gubbins), writing her way out of one life and into another.

Gravity & Grace, the film of such notable failure, is the reason the narrator travels to Berlin in *Aliens & Anorexia*. Kraus's second novel, a cerebral sequel to *I Love Dick*, describes the film and plots the attempts to get funding for it, among other projects including recovering female artists and thinkers like Simone Weil from the reject pile of history. *Gravity & Grace*, the novel contextualizes for us, "was an experimental 16mm film about hope, despair, religious feeling and conviction" (*Aliens & Anorexia* 27).[5] "Driven harder by philosophy than plot or character," it constitutes one of the "dense and difficult, unlikeable experimental movies" Chris had been making since 1982, "exhibiting them in clubs and venues where projectors broke and people talked and heckled" (27). The novel begins with Chris "traveling to Germany to attend the European Film Market" because *Gravity & Grace* "had already been rejected twice in all three categories of the Berlin Film Festival" (27).

The scene is set by an atmosphere of resistance: "Diary entry on the plane from Los Angeles to London, January 17, first nine hours of the 20-hour trip: '*I don't want to go to Berlin*'" (27; original emphasis). "There is a symmetry in following a spiral down as far as it will go," Chris tells us, the flat tonal quality of this observation rendering in affective stance her dismaying self-disgust at the film: "*Gravity & Grace* was just so unappealing"; "It was an amateur intellectual's home video expanded to bulimic lengths"; "In the six months following its completion, the film had been rejected by every major festival from Sundance to Australia to Turin" (28). And there's no epiphanic moment, no buried praise or dramatic turnaround. Things keep spiraling down: "The European Film Market was becoming like Room 101 in Orwell's *1984*, a cavalcade of horrors where you confront your deepest fears. And it was so baroque that I was floating just above it, thinking *None of this can hurt me now* . . ." (47). But it does: Chris leaves the market early because "[b]y this time my entire body felt like it was made of glass" (47).

Spirals, grids, mazes: failure takes the linear forms of symmetry. Following this experience, Chris reflects: "There is a tendency among romantic people to see their lives as grids and mazes, unfolding through an erratic but connected set of lines. These randomly occurring series of casualties may be retrospectively observed to *form a pattern*" (51). Though against the romanticization of the self as she is, Chris sees herself as a romantic person; the pattern of her failure in retrospect leads her to the letter-writing practice that, together with essayistic interludes, creates a new form in *I Love Dick*—"if I couldn't make a movie, writing letters was at least something I knew how to do" (41). Chances lead an artist to both failure and success, but in both cases, paraphrasing Deleuze and Guattari, Chris positions "[c]hance as a means of trumping chaos, discovering a more deeply comprehensive *secret* unity in the world" (51). But how to harness chance? "Sadness is the thing I'm moving towards," Chris notes here, suggesting that "sadness is the girl-equivalent to chance" (119). As "a philosophical position" that "connects you instantly to all the suffering in the world," "true sadness" is transcriptional and anthropological: "you are momentarily outside your body because *something else is speaking to you*." By this stage, the novel is positing ways failure could be sublimated by leaving it to chance. But it's not as random as chance usually suggests: forming patterns align chance as ideology to transcription as artistic mode by giving form to what is otherwise spontaneous. "Chance is 'work' and 'work' is always something quantifiable. *Trace the line between two points*..." (119).

If Kraus formalizes artistic and personal failure through linear mapping of chance, from one point to another, Heti traces artistic failure as vacillation—an "everlasting switching" (*How Should a Person Be?* 84)—back and forth between one point and another. An existential pattern that Sheila's therapist, Ann, diagnoses in a transcribed session in Act 2, it signifies a particular kind of danger a particular kind of person lives in. Rather than seeing a plan through its failure, this type of person "will suddenly tell you they have another plan ... the moment things start getting difficult" (84). The novel tracks such moments of 'switching': Sheila leaves her husband when she envisions her marriage as the "brick wall" preventing her completion of her play; she leaves Toronto for New York in order to become An Important Artist when she falls out with her best friend; she comes back to Toronto almost immediately because becoming An Important Artist is too difficult. Attempting to skirt the possibility of failure brings about failure of another kind (of her marriage, of her friendships, of her art); or, as Ann states, "[i]n their quest for a life without failure, suffering, or doubt, that is what they achieve: a life empty of all those things that make a human life meaningful" (84).

The eventual formal switch of the narrative plots—from play to novel—is mirrored by the constant switching between transcriptional modes and conventional realist prose as we read. This switching, though personally destructive, is formally generative; vacillation structures Sheila's experience of failure negatively as formal hesitation and uncertainty, but also meaningfully as conversation. Both *I Love Dick* and *How Should a Person Be?* are dialogic—the dominant mode of transcription—but where for Kraus dialogue fails as unrequited, for Heti the back-and-forth of vacillation denotes an aesthetic idealism in the novel. Grammatically, vacillation works as a narrative mode in which Sheila oscillates between what is and what should be. In her interview with La Force for the *Paris Review*, Heti described how the imperative hidden in the title's question negates the ultimate aim of asking the question in the first place: "it's really hard" to not "live the image of the life which you have in your head." Indeed, it might even be "cheating yourself out of a real engagement with life, which involves surprise, not just you moving through your environment with this pre-determined idea of what you intend to do with it and how it should react to you." As Margaux states to Sheila in the novel, "[b]etter to have your failure right in front of you than the fantasy in your head" (240).

Early in the novel, Sheila desires a genre switch, too, from writing altogether to painting so that she can take part in the Ugly Painting Competition, "secretly" envying her painter-friends, Margaux and Sholem: "*I* wanted to make an ugly painting—pit mine against theirs and see whose would win. What would my painting look like? How would I proceed? I thought it would be a simple, interesting thing to do" (13). The novel's self-help-esque overtones put perfection and beauty as the epitome of *being* and *creating*, but those characters who aim for beauty are completely undone when they create anything less. The "reluctant" Sholem "didn't see the point"; "[t]he premise turned him off so much—that one should *intentionally* make something ugly" (13). And when he does make his ugly painting, this betrayal of aesthetics results in crisis. He found the painting "so revolting that he had to get it out of his studio"; he goes out to buy groceries, feeling "nauseous" "the entire time," and "[f]rom there, the day just got worst. Making the painting had set off a train of really depressing and terrible thoughts, so that by the time evening came, he was fully plunged in despair" (14).

Sheila's despair at her play also hinges on a revulsion at anything less than beautiful: "I had spent so much time trying to make the play I was writing—and my life, and my self—into an object of beauty. It was exhausting and all that I knew" (13). As Heti noted to La Force, "Sholem's approach to making an ugly painting is like Sheila's attempt to construct a beautiful life—thinking she ought to marry and whatnot; follow the rules of how she thinks she should be, just as Sholem has rules about what's beautiful and what's ugly and tries to follow them in his painting." Where Sholem and Sheila's flawed rule books set them up for affective dissolve, Margaux, a technically perfect painter with "distinctive brushstrokes," is unfazed, because "*beautiful*" is "a word she claimed not to understand" (17).

Though the paintings are discussed in detail in the final pages of the novel, we never know whether the winner of the competition was "the person who made the uglier painting" or "the person who, though trying just as hard, made a painting that was inadvertently beautiful" (304). Unable to decide, Margaux and Sholem compete in a squash game to resolve the question. But rather than resolving it, the game pushes the novel further into ambiguous vacillation. Watching the game from above with two other friends, "none of [them] could hear anything from below except for explosions of laughter, moans, and cursing, and Sholem saying, 'Fuck! I hate this fucking game!'" (306). As one of them mused, "I don't think they even know the rules. I think they're just slamming the ball around."

The squash game is on one level a transparent metaphor for the unguided way Sheila feels she experiences life, but aesthetically, it produces a lack of narrative closure. The ending's insistence on vacillation—the everlasting switching—becomes inertia, a form of inactivity through action that also demonstrates another connotation from its Latin root: "want of art or skill." The lack of skill and unartfulness that Kraus and Heti position as crucial aesthetic catalysts for diegetic failure and formal innovation make both projects what Sheila calls an "experiment of being contemporary" (Interview with Barber). By writing against the image of reality, against the image of the ideal, Heti's vacillation and Kraus's spontaneous patterns use transcription to designate new aesthetic categories for the struggles of living aesthetically today.

FIVE

SUSPENSION

In the summer of 2015, the Contemporaries section of the website of the Post45 collective launched a series of reading experiments called "Slow Burn." Inspired by the opportunity to pleasurably languish over books afforded by the long summer months away from teaching schedules and deadlines, the experiment was born from the question "can we stretch this time out?" Instigated by Sarah Chihaya, the project resists quick-paced, deadline-induced, utilitarian reading-writing practices, and was envisioned as a safe haven for like-minded leisure-reading seekers who wanted to "luxuriate in the unique pleasures of leisurely writing, of savoring a text, of conversing more deeply"; those who wanted to partake in "'slow-form criticism': readings that happen on the back burner while your mind is mostly elsewhere, that, in their extended simmering, develop a different richness and depth over time from a quick-fired review" (Chihaya). It is also a project that sought to mirror its subject: the first volume took on Elena Ferrante's Neapolitan novels, the second basked in Karl Ove Knausgård's *My Struggle*, the third savored *Twin Peaks*, and the fourth relished *Sex and the City*, a series that percolates a lifetime of reading, viewing, writing, and conversation. Aesthetic experiences like reading are often purported to escape quotidian chronology or stretch out time, but the deliberate action of reading slowly enforces a further ideological insistence on dilation. Performing slowness is both a political and an aesthetic act.[1]

In a contemporary world where speed, efficiency, and instantaneity are de rigueur, slowness is increasingly figured as a desirable strategy for dealing with the various environmental stresses that contemporary life produces. The Slow Movement—from the original slow food movement of the 1960s to contemporary slow fashion, slow cinema, and slow reading—seeks to decelerate the systems of daily experience, often illuminating the ethical priorities responsible citizens ought to possess. Yet despite the eponymous insistence on *slow*, as Jesse Matz has acknowledged, such "movements do not simply choose a slower pace or a longer present over those allowed in contemporary life" but instead "try for 'balance'" ("Art of Time" 286). For Carl Honoré, this means to privilege "what musicians call the tempo giusto—the right speed" which means to "[b]e fast when it makes sense to be fast, and be slow when slowness is called for" but to never rush (15). Lutz Koepnick has recently mapped slowness as a distinct aesthetic of the contemporary, arguing that it is precisely the ephemeral nature of the present—constantly historicizing the future—that not only pulls us to stillness but allows us greater comfort in multifaceted uncertainty. "[T]o go slow," he claims, "means to open up to the opulence and manifoldness of the present; to unfetter this present from the burdens of mindless visions of automatic progress and nostalgic recollections of the past and to produce presence beyond existing templates of meaning" (4).

Such an approach, he continues, reflects disciplinary practices of periodization, where the idea of the contemporary has itself "come to describe pluralistic forms of artistic practice" resistant to historicizing the affective "pleasures of newness" that the contemporary epitomizes (5). The contemporary, Koepnick argues, celebrates both facets of this aesthetic of slowness: the ability slowness gives us to perceive the multiplicity of the unfolding present and the consolations that slowing down the moment of perception affords us. Returning to the dialectic of the moment that spans Romantic poetry (stilled moment), modernist documentary photography (*instant decisif*), and postmodern artistic production (reproduced moment), it negates the twentieth century fascination with speed. Modernity exalted speed as "a panacea for modern culture's logic of disenchantment," to borrow Koepnick's phrasing (248). While in part it "liberated the body from its stubborn biological pulses and measures, and it thereby disengaged the clocks of human mortality" (Koepnick 250), it also evinced an aspirational, "reflexive wish" to recreate the Romantic aesthetic time as "human time" (Matz, "Aesthetic/Prosthetic" 227). In both schools of thought, speed was "envisage[d] . . . as a kind of drug, an intensifier, an *excitant moderne*" of modern experience (Schnapp 31). But where modernity's aesthetics of speed intensified experience, Fredric Jameson famously characterized postmodernism by "the waning of affect" (*Postmodernism* 14) induced by the privileging of speed for speed's sake over felt experience. Speed, for postmodernists, had "less to do with kinetic energy" as it often did for the modernists, and more to do "with all kinds of new reproductive processes" that speed entails, as the velocity of these processes made "very different demands on our capacity for aesthetic representation than did the relatively mimetic idolatry of the older machinery of the futurist moment" (36). Artistically, this speed entailed the end "of style, in the sense of the unique and the personal, the end of the distinctive individual brush stroke," the death of artistic practice à la Monet in favor of the birth of Andy Warhol "as symbolized by the emergent primacy of mechanical reproduction" (14).

Being able to experience time aesthetically in order to slow it down involves a complex mix of phenomenological and narratological techniques. Reading across a range of contemporary writing, we find that this desire for slowness or pausing daily life hasn't dissipated. But rather than focusing on the singular intensity of the present moment, contemporary novelistic practices recast the instant of aesthetic experience as possessing longer narrative duration. Although realist novels traditionally compel us to believe time passes by filling narrative space with plot details that push time onward, recent novels have drawn on slowness to flip this formula: filling time with space, we can luxuriate in the lengthened aesthetic moment. The suspension that comes with close examination of one's feelings during encounters with art thus becomes a vital strategy for mediating experience. But even if not to the extreme Proustian dilation that Knausgård takes it in the six-part *My Struggle*, this strategy "plays a long, meticulous game" in creating the effect of experience: as Adam reflects in Ben Lerner's debut novel *Leaving the Atocha Station* (2011), "I came to realize that far more important to me than any plot or conventional sense was the sheer directionality I felt while reading prose, the texture of time as it passed, life's white machine . . . the sweep of predication was more compelling than the predicated" (19–20). Indeed, as Lerner remarks in a review of the third part of Knausgård's series, "lengthy digression and extremely . . . detailed description" make quotation difficult: "one would have to excerpt pages and pages, not a sentence or paragraph, to give an accurate sense of the effect" ("Each Cornflake"). Or as Zadie Smith remarked about Tom McCarthy's *Remainder* (2006), regardless of whether the novels are "filled with pretty quotes," they operate "by accumulation and repetition, closing in on its subject in ever-decreasing revolutions" ("Two Directions" 95).

The slowness of accumulation and repetition works as a suspensive mode. As experiential detail builds and repeats itself, the present and the recently overlapped orbit the shifting categories of the real and the replicated. The preoccupation with experience as *absorptive* that we find at the heart of Lerner's second novel, *10:04* (2014), and as *debris* that we find in Rachel Kushner's novel *The Flamethrowers* (2013) orbits this same preoccupation with the real and the artifice. As both are concerned with de-mediating aesthetic experience, this chapter will explore the textual claims toward immediacy and will continue the work of the last chapter in exploring the contemporary collapse of art and life. It will also construct a poetics for slow reading of the contemporary intermedial novel. Not only theorizing strategies for experiencing the aesthetic and the political in terms of immediacy, the writers make these strategies take place on the page. Lerner's and Kushner's experiential constellation of intermedial, mediacy, and immediacy exerts its own aesthetic and affective mode I call *suspension*. This critical methodology reflects a novelistic turn toward interrogating experience that works on the level of plot (affective immersion) and form (the experiential immersion of the reading process), both brought on by *suspensive* time. Tracing the aesthetic affinities between Lerner and Kushner, suspended together, I telegraph the velocity of aesthetic experience as these aesthetics intersect with formal attempts to capture the pause through intermedial efforts.

RESEMBLE, REASSEMBLE

The suspensive time of aesthetic possibility is in full force in *10:04*—a novel suspended in a single point of time—but even more so when the narrator, Ben, sits down to view Chris Marclay's *The Clock* (2010). Rather than helping to measure time, as clocks are meant to do, the installation establishes a clear divide between experiential time and clock time. Jimena Canales has noted recently that although "[w]e usually think of clocks as instruments that help us count and divide days, roughly defined as intervals between one sunrise and the next," clock time "measure[s] universal or 'real' time only imperfectly" (114). And yet, when Ben sits in a darkened gallery room at the Lincoln Center in New York, the temporality of *The Clock* operates in paradox: the clock keeps going in real time, but so-called "real" clock time is suspended when it is experienced. Ben experiences this gap between the time of the work and temporal perception as palpable:

> I'd heard *The Clock* described as the ultimate collapse of fictional time into real time, a work designed to obliterate the distance between art and life, fantasy and reality. But part of why I looked at my phone was because that distance hadn't been collapsed for me at all; while the duration of a real minute and *The Clock*'s minute were mathematically indistinguishable, they were nevertheless minutes from different worlds. I watched time in *The Clock*, but wasn't in it, or I was experiencing time as such, not just having experiences through it as a medium. As I made and unmade a variety of overlapping narratives out of its found footage, I felt acutely how many different days could be built out of a day, felt more possibility than determinism, the utopian glimmer of fiction. When I looked at my watch to see a unit of measure identical to the one displayed on the screen, I was indicating that a distance remained between art and the mundane. (54)

Ben describes himself as suspended outside of the clock time created by Marclay's work, experiencing not the linearity of time as it ticked by but a more expansive aesthetic time that expanded with every narrative "possibility." As this book has argued, this is the suspension and delay of aesthetic experience, or as Matz describes, "the temporality of aesthetic engagement or art's ontological time" ("Aesthetic/Prosthetic" 227). Aesthetic mediation of time, such as Marclay's, or indeed the mediation of experiences of Marclay's work such as Lerner's, also "asserts the further possibility that art makes time meaningful" (227); it adds space to time.

Just as art does, the threat of two storms causes the suspension of everyday time and activity within 10:04. The similarities of temporal perception are oddly resonant: while the eye of the storm is experienced as suspended from the chaos of the surrounding atmospheric disruption, so too is the wait for hurricanes such as Irene and Sandy to hit and then pass. Storms slow both individual and commercial routine and cause us to enter an almost equally familiar practice of retreating into our homes and waiting. The practice casts an odd light on even our most regular habits—as Ben observes, "the approaching storm was estranging the routine of shopping just enough to make me viscerally aware of both the miracle and insanity of the mundane economy" (19). In the case of the first storm of the novel, Hurricane Irene, in the suspension of normal experience a previously unseen "physical intimacy . . . opened up between" Ben and his friend Alex, only to "dissolve . . . with the storm" (24). The second hurricane, during which the novel ends, causes simple capitalist functions to come to a halt: even taxis refuse to take Ben and Alex from Manhattan to Brooklyn. Waiting for the storm to hit this time causes Ben to remark that he "felt equidistant from all my memories as my sense of time collapsed" (236). It is in this collapse that narrative time both stops and speeds up time: time is resuscitated as the narrative is projected into the future, the present tense overtaken by future constructions. Indeed, "[t]he storm irresistibly propels him into the future to which his back is turned" (25). This line from Walter Benjamin's "Theses on the Philosophy of History" captions a reproduction of Paul Klee's monoprint "Angelus Novus" (1920), which depicts a human figure constructed by intersecting lines that occurs in the narrative just after the Hurricane Irene fails to hit New York.[2] Both this allusion to Benjamin and the novel's overt references to *Back to the Future* engage in "retrofuturism," what Elias describes as "a twenty-first-century historical perspective on the near past, a looking back upon these futuristic production of the past that sees them as quaint utopian hopes of a future tha[t] never arrived" ("Past/Future" 39). Not coincidentally, it is at 10:04 that "the lightning strike[s] the courthouse clock tower in *Back to the Future* that allows Marty to return to 1985" (52).

The recombinatory aesthetics of contemporary artists like Marclay, who dissect artworks to recombine into new works of art, and collaboratives like the Institute of Totaled Art we see later in the novel, which create new artistic and economic value in destroyed artworks, illuminates Lerner's own formal project of fragmentation. In *10:04* we see a development of the recombinatory aesthetics that were already so evident in his first novel, *Leaving the Atocha Station*, to say nothing of interviews and essays, to embody what one reviewer has called "a neon Rubik's Cube" (Maughan). It also attempts to reimagine the mediacy of experience that preoccupied the narrator of *Leaving the Atocha Station* (chemical, aesthetic, and political) in sincere terms. What arises in such a discussion around the "disconnect between the virtual and the actual" in the arts is the question of how and what the novel persuades the reader is a virtual experience (Interview with Console). Adam, the narrator of *Atocha*, experiences the Madrid train bombings, for example, in a way that intensifies his perception of mediation. Although he "feels he is having—or should be having—a firsthand experience of this tragic historical event," he is also "acutely aware of how mediated his experience is, despite his literal proximity: mediated by his foreignness, and mediated by the mass media, the inevitable spectacularization of the tragedy into a 'media'" (Interview with Console). But where Adam had a "long worr[y] that I was incapable of having a profound experience of art" (*Atocha* 8), viewing art in *10:04* becomes a collective experience—Ben and his best friend were closest "in the galleries," where "our gazes were parallel, directed in front of us at a canvas and not at each other, a condition of our most intimate exchanges," and in doing so, "we coconstructed the literal view before us" (*10:04* 8).

Affective and formal distance, proximity, and fragmentation all hover in the vicinity of Lerner's fixation on what he calls the potential of the novel to "absorb and constellate other forms" (Interview with Rogers 228). Constructing a remarkable vision of novel form as "curatorial" across several interviews between 2011 and 2015, he reflects that he had "been thinking of the novel a lot as a kind of curation" because it tracks the way fiction "can stage encounters with works of art" (Interview with Smith): the "ability of the novel to absorb other genres is . . . a wonderful potential of the form" (Interview with Rogers 229), a "porous" process that allows not just forms, but "language and concepts [to] migrate from one genre to the other" (Interview with Derbyshire). But the absorptive potential of the novel isn't just formal: curation as a strategy "lets you embed artworks (like the poems or images . . .) in various artificial environments" specifically "in order to test how one's response is altered" (Interview with Rogers 228). Suggesting that, ultimately, all feeling is screened, Lerner has argued that while "the power of the arts is the way they model—and so give one the opportunity to explore—the mediacy that is generally characteristic of our experience in an era of spectacle," fiction also bridges distance to "let us experience" this "mediacy immediately" (Interview with Console). Affective suspension seems to be Lerner's poetic key, where distance and disconnect from feeling the work of art measure not an absence of profundity but its intensification. So, too, with his sense of poetry: "I tended to find lines of poetry beautiful only when I encountered them quoted in prose" (*Atocha* 8). Beauty arises in the ephemeral impression structured by citation, "where the line breaks were replaced with slashes, so that what was communicated was less a particular poem than the echo of poetic possibility" (8). In privileging aesthetic distance, Adam's impressionist sensibilities stitch together a compelling contemporary mode ventriloquizing Lerner's broader curatorial strategy: challenging us to view literature as "function[ing] as a laboratory in which we test responses to unrealized or unrealizable art works, or in which we embed real works in imagined conditions in order to track their effects" ("Actual World"). As Lerner himself remarks, the radical politics of Adam's position here constitutes both an "embarrassing confession of poetic fraudulence, but [also] a statement in support of prose's ability to incorporate other modes of writing in a manner that retains or even amplifies their power" (Interview with Hodgkinson).

Recalling Virginia Woolf's description of the novel as cannibal art, both 10:04 and Lerner's debut novel are remarkable for their collective practice of embedding—the latter's acknowledgments outline no less than six accounts of collage, while the novel itself possesses seven photographs and two poems; the former embeds twelve photographs, two poems, and two short stories. Rather than "mocking fiction's inability to make contact with anything outside of itself," Lerner has been aiming for an elevated virtual mode: "how we live fictions, how fictions have real effects, become facts in that sense, and how our experience of the world changes depending on its arrangement into one narrative or another" (Interview with Bollen). This ontology manifests as an intrinsic interrogation of realism, or what Lerner describes as "the oldest novelistic question," concerning "what counts as an authentic aesthetic experience" (Interview with Bollen). In an interview with Tao Lin following the publication of his second novel, he pondered what the limits of "lived experience" are. His novels self-consciously gesture toward this epistemological boundary, and indeed within this framework such a collage of genre is where "[t]he edge of fiction flickers." Emphasizing a key aesthetic difference in the conceptualizations of each of his novels, he claims that while his first was predominately about fraudulence—"the way Adam Gordon approached truth through its opposite"—his second "has an explicit relation to that one, in part tracking how that fiction became a fact in my life, but it's primarily a relation of difference—the second narrates a moving away from the first" (Interview with Lin). Indeed, his novels aim for a fiction that questions its own authenticity; not necessarily in counterpoint to reality, but in order to amplify a texture of the "real" literary experience. Or, in other words, they advance the case for a reinvestment in fiction, and embody what David James has called the "attempt to make formal integrity viable again" ("Integrity" 494). Here, I argue that while, for Lerner, writing a novel is suspensive in the sense that it can be an "echo chamber" of multiple sources and forms, curation also becomes a byword for affective suspension, a way of building a mediacy into form that short-circuits binary distinctions between the fictive and the real.

Like "how readymades work in visual art," existent artworks curated by novels become so "obviously changed by being placed in the novel" that "in a sense they're no longer the works that preceded the novel" (Interview with Lin). They instead move forward, onward, outward: "they're recontextualized by the novel or the museum and, while they're materially identical—every word is the same—they're utterly transformed" (Interview with Lin). These interartistic, hybrid spaces, although about the *art* of writing and the *writing* of art, question the fictional conditions for artistic practice: the transposition of "fact into fiction" (Interview with Lin) applies also to the visual image and poem. Lerner's poetics suggest an interminable interest in the ontology of the work of art: how do we engage with an imaginary poem? His use of collage thus articulates an important turn to contemporary poetics in emergent literature—indeed to suggest how novels and poems can, and even must, become conversant. The composition of Lerner's novel poems becomes not the registration of Lerner's efforts, but the creation of his narrators: while blurring the lines between fictional and nonfictional elements, the fictionalizing of the poem's composition sheds light on the epiphenomena of contemporary poetic practice. How can we account for the pressures these artworks place on literary description and narration? In addressing these questions, Lerner's novelistic style adheres closely to his conception of poetry, as one that is, as Ben from *10:04* states, "neither fiction nor nonfiction, but a flickering between them" (194). Indeed, as Ben continues, "part of what I loved about poetry was how the distinction between fiction and nonfiction didn't obtain, how the correspondence between text and world was less important than the intensities of the poem itself, what possibilities of feeling were opened up in the present tense of reading" (170–71).

But these we find equally in the present tense of contemporary viewing. Joel Burges and Amy J. Elias suggest that "[n]o recent artwork addresses this notion of the multiplicity of present time—the present as times that take time together—more than Christian Marclay's 2010 installation *The Clock*" (4). The "multiplicity of present time" is precisely what Ben experiences when he and a friend first view the installation at the Lincoln Center in New York, and on subsequent viewings he came "to love how, as you spend time with the video, you develop a sense of something like the circadian clock of genre.... Marclay had formed a supragenre that made visible our collective, unconscious sense of the rhythms of the day—when we expect to kill or fall in love or clean ourselves or eat or fuck or check our watch and yawn" (53). Layering the binaries of fictional/nonfictional time and clock/actual present time is achieved not by a single linear narrative but through collage of edited scenes from hundreds of films—different fictions absorbed into the representation of one twenty-four-hour period, as "fictional time [is] synchronized with nonfictional duration" (53). As Burges and Elias note, *The Clock* dramatizes how time in the present is both a multiplicity and yet also a "singularity": it both "pluralizes each minute of the day with many moments," as well as situates "contemporary time" as "a singular simultaneity" (8). Nevertheless, because of the work's recontextualizing assemblage, viewing the work as constructing "an overarching narrative" is made effortless: for Ben, "it was a greater challenge . . . to resist the will to integration than to combine the various scenes into coherent and compelling fiction" (54).

Ben's comments echo metatextually with the construction of Lerner's enclosing novel, as gazes, voices, selves, and forms layer to expose a lyric parsing of self-referentiality and a concerted nod to the readymades of twentieth-century literary collage. As Ellen Levy notes of a particularly twentieth-century American tradition, artists and poets like Marianne Moore, Joseph Cornell, and John Ashbery "all conceive[d] of themselves as collectors and link[ed] the practice of collecting cognate ways to the practice of their respective arts" (xxiv). Extending our gaze further back, Robin Walz and Elza Adamowicz both emphasize the prominence of surrealist collage in establishing the disruptive textual aesthetics of the twentieth century. Instead, the surrealists used it as a strategy of dislocating material from a rational structure, and emphasizing "surreal" connections between words and images—heightening their virtual or latent relationships—without rendering them as a coherent, linear whole, with fixed relationships. Such an impulse is manifested in Ashbery's reappropriation of movie titles and suggests why the surrealists developed collage as a technique: it offered a strategy for the reconfiguration of neglected or disregarded material into new aesthetic forms. Thus, critics like Adamowicz tend to "focus" on the "mechanisms of collage production or the 'cut-and-paste' technique" of Burroughs, because it suggests the surrealists' predilection for "cut-out materials which are trivial or outmoded, marginal or ephemeral" (24). Yet as an aesthetic practice collage is "a process rather than a product, an experimental mode of textual and pictorial production more than a fixed genre, a disruptive activity, not a static form" (25). Unlike the collage aesthetic of twentieth century examples, however, twenty-first century poets and writers are less interested in the questions of class, high and low art, and formal dexterity that the collection of demotic materials suggests, but focus their interests in a lyrical and aesthetic reanimation of everyday experience in the very manner of contemporary reading practices: porous and resistant to formal isolation.

The fictional composition of the central poem curated in the novel mirrors its actual composition: both narrator and author wrote it during a poetry residency in Marfa. Indeed, according to Lerner, "the novel was, in part, formed" around this poem (Interview with Reines). "The dark threw patches down upon me also," as described by Ben in the novel, is "a weird meditative lyric in which I was sometimes Whitman, and in which the strangeness of the residency itself was the theme" (170). But what happens to art that is saturated with different methods of mediation? Is there a point at which it, as in translation, does not resemble the original anymore? Does its artfulness subtract from or intensify the reading experience? The end of the poem—inserted several pages later at the end of Ben's residency—is concerned with precisely this problem of lyric readership, as emphasized by the nature of the collage:

> I've been worse than unfair, although he was
> asking for it, is still asking for it, I can hear
> him asking for it through me when I speak,
> despite myself, to a people that isn't there,
> or think of art as leisure that is work
> in houses the undocumented build, repair.
> It's among the greatest poems and fails
> because it wants to become real and can
> only become prose, founding mistake
> of the book from which we've been expelled. (194)

Fending off a kind of *realpoesie* is of course a hypothetical ideal possible only in literature itself. If Lerner's work is not overtly a defense of the literary arts, it certainly is on closer inspection. And so, while collage traditionally makes overtures to political realities and injustices, Lerner's does not. If thinking formally, we find this particularly clear: the novel's prose quotes the beginning of the poem, rather than incorporating the poem through a cut-and-paste technique, to draw attention to everyday life's actualities. In doing so, it suggests a praxis motivated by more than just formal innovation: "'I am alien here with a residency, light/ alien to me, true hawks starting from the trees/ at my footfall on gravel, sun-burnt from reading/ *Specimen Days* on the small porch across/ the street from where another poet died/ or began dying'" (171). With virgules delineating each line break, Lerner's treatment of the poem recalls Adam's belief in the "poetic possibility" of the quotation in *Leaving the Atocha Station*, where the novel becomes a space for modulating the texture of poetic language and form: from prose narrative to poetry quoted in prose to the form of the poem itself. Adam's position establishes the virgule as an important visual symbol that designates the delineation between possibilities (as in either/or). Even the final line of *10:04* reinforces how the very form of the novel has started to turn inward on itself, or turn toward, turn into, poetry, gesturing to a future of prose that may tip, if only briefly, into poetry, moving from the first-person reflection, "I will begin to remember," to the third, "our walk in the third person," to the second, "I am looking back at the totaled city in the second person plural," to the virguled line, "I know it's hard to understand/ I am with you, and I know how it is" (240). The novel ends in the present, the past, and the future: the slowing down of narrative prose to poetic form allows the multiplicity of aesthetic time to be occupied all at once.

ON THE PERENNIAL VERGE

Just as ecological and aesthetic time exists on the precipice in *10:04*, at the level of form, the novel too occurs in suspensive time. And although art and ecology find consolation in slowing time—climate change or melting of glaciers for instance—Ben finds solace in the propulsion into a utopic vision by slowing down the perceptual experience of finding spaces of connection. As Elaine Blair notes in a review of *10:04*, Lerner's poet-narrators "mark a closeness between narrator and author that we don't usually see," in which "their ruminations on matters of art are an important vein of sincerity in his novels," rather than the "lyrical flights" of "the everyman" narrator that readers sometimes find "distracting and artificial." Indeed for Lerner, the novel needed "a first person that is intensely felt to move across the levels of fiction. There's no way for me to do it without inviting that conflation of fact and fiction" (Blair, "So This Is How It Works"). To free the novel from the limiting requirements of these categories also requires a poetic re-envisioning of the second person: where the novel is also ostensibly "*to* the second person plural on the perennial verge of existence" (Interview with Reines). In an interview with poet and performance artist Ariana Reines, Lerner remarks that writing is all "about exercising the faculty of address in the abstract." The narrator, Ben, often addresses a vacant "you," particularly when thinking about universal experiences like mourning:

> Have you seen people pause in revolving doors like divers decompressing, transitioning slowly so as to prevent nitrogen bubbles from forming in the blood, or noticed the puzzled look that many people wear—I found a bench across Fifth Avenue and sat and watched—when they step onto the sidewalk, as if they've suddenly forgotten something important, but aren't sure what: their keys, their phone, the particulars of their loss? (43)

Or in "The Golden Vanity"—a short story initially published in the *New Yorker* and embedded in the novel as a piece written by Ben—where this kind of question pervades even the author's own compositions:

> Would you know what he meant if the author said he never really saw her face, that faces were fictions he increasingly could not read, a reductive way of bundling features in the memory, even if that memory was then projected into the present, onto the area between the forehead and chin? (68)

Apostrophes that address the second person prompt aesthetic questions of audience—and are more likely to be found in discussions of poetry or theater performances than in the novel. In effect, this suggests how the second person is defined by a state of ineffability and elusiveness as an imagined construct; no attempt is made to produce an audience. Indeed, 10:04 aims to provide an answer to the perennial question of who is the lyric addressee that the "you" embodies, and how it can be embodied. This voice switch lies in the ability of fiction to capture a "*process* of characterization and re-characterization instead of offering up a few stable, easily summarized individuals," the movement of "reading bodies and behaviors (and skies and skylines or whatever), constructing brief and shifting coherences" (Lerner, Interview with Lin; my emphasis).

While "never realized," this lyric dream nonetheless "remains live" for Lerner in a way that it doesn't for Smith, Heti, or Kraus, unfurling reflexively in both his poetry and his novels. Indeed, he considers the voice of the self and the ear of the other "as an invitation to a certain kind of participation on the reader: Think about these things with me. Can you see this?" (Interview with Bollen). The problem, however, lies in the question of response—who is to respond, can they respond, and is there an expectation of response?

Lerner suggests that despite "the sense that the reader is invited to imagine herself as the 'I' and 'You' simultaneously," such an invocation necessarily prescribes "total failure" (Interview with Reines). Yet this issue of intimacy is nevertheless subject to its own wavering coherencies—the address must be absorbed, in the form of listening, or reflected back, as response. In *10:04*, Lerner offers a strategic solution to overcome this semi-flickering absence of the second person, or recipient of poetic address, through the parallel gaze, the site of Ben and his best friend Alex's "most intimate exchanges" (8), as if simultaneously experiencing a profound work of art or gazing at the stars. What makes *10:04* a particularly innovative example of how writers are attempting to overcome a dislike of poetry is precisely the fact that Lerner poeticizes simple acts, like waving, to explore such an abstracted long-standing problem with failed address. Poetically, waving signifies a physical act of reciprocation, but as a rhetorical strategy, it can also embody its abject failure. As Lerner noted:

> I have a line in a newer poem about the phenomenon of waving to somebody who in fact was waving behind you. Or someone waves and you can't decide if they mean you. That to me seems to be a great figure in all kinds of ways for the embarrassment of receiving or performing poetic address. Poetry as overheard, in the traditional formulation. It can be hard to know if you're being hailed, whom you're hailing. And there's also delay and an awkwardness and a sociality to it. It's both a breach in communication and a way of imagining, albeit accidentally, a second person plural. (Interview with Reines)

Poetically, then, waving can be the ideal signifier of reciprocation. It is a mirrored action of directed intimacy, a conscious acknowledgment of the other—"having hesitated and knowing I'd been seen, even in the dark, I felt a pressured to turn around and signal some kind of greeting to the other nocturnal resident ... he raised his arm and I raised mine" (*10:04* 167)—and when Ben encounters the unnamed Polish poet across the road from his Marfa residence; it is also an unreciprocated expression of goodbye to Alena, Ben's occasional lover (210). Functioning similarly to unfulfilled reciprocity in love poetry, where one can "think about the 'I' and 'you' as sites for love poems," the unrequited, Lerner claims, has the "[o]ne advantage ... that it provides a fictional support for apostrophe—the recipient of address isn't responding, isn't there, because of her coldness or superiority, not because she's been objectified, or because she's a personified abstraction, or whatever" (Interview with Kunin). While Lerner's latest collection of poetry, *Mean Free Path* (2010), for example, "has many moments of address . . . their failure to be reciprocal is understood as a limitation of the speaker or his medium, not some attribute of the beloved (perfection, indifference, death)" (Interview with Kunin). The kind of poetic address *10:04* is trying to achieve "is also just about opening a channel, about making a space for the possibility of address more than communicating any particular thing" (Interview with Kunin). So, while the lyric inherently acknowledges both the realism of the first person and the vivacity of the imaginary second, it also accepts the failure of the latter to materialize; as the narrator says to himself, "You have failed to reconcile the realism of my body with the ethereality of the trees" (*10:04* 31–32).

Talking poetry in *10:04* of course requires a mention of Walt Whitman, just as *Leaving the Atocha Station* invokes an obvious aesthetic debt to Ashbery. Lerner's interest in the lyric, the second person, and address is informed substantially by the legacy of Whitman's attempts at democratizing the poet. Obsessed with Whitman's *Specimen Days*, Ben begins to inhabit "a Whitman of the vulnerable grid" (4): just as Whitman "has to be nobody in particular in order to be a democratic everyman, has to empty himself out so that his poetry can be a textual commons for the future into which he projects himself" (168), so too does Ben. As Lerner has noted, through an "emptying" of the "self," the novel form can be "imagine[d] . . . as a space of transpersonal imagination," while the self needs to behave less as a singularity and more "as a multitude" (Interview with Bollen). The "you," at least for Lerner, occupies "a collective person who didn't yet exist, a still-uninhabited second person plural to whom all the arts, even in their most intimate registers, were nevertheless addressed" (108). For Lerner, the failure of Whitman's project lies in his "dream of corporate personhood," the mode in which "you can dissolve yourself through art into collective possibility," in which "[w]e can all fit in his 'I' and we can all be addressed by his 'you'" (Interview with Lin). This dissolve is placed into effect by "democratiz[ing] pronouns" (*Hatred* 65). The interest in the democratization of the self brings us back to Lerner's perennial concern of the actual effects of poetry in social and political spheres. Yet, as Wai Chee

Dimock argues, "the problem with Whitman" is located in "a conflict between the opposing claims of universality and particularity in the definition of personhood, and between the opposing domains of human experience to which each corresponds. How can we reconcile the categorical conception of the self in democratic theory with our experiential sense of the self in human attachments?" (71) While for William Waters, poetic address enacts "a form of contact" (1), Dimock sees this conflict as fundamentally flawed, unable to fully reconcile personal "affective preferences" (70) with "democratic politics" (72). My sense is that this is what also troubles Lerner about the political inefficacy of poetry. Yet in revitalizing lyric address in novel form, whether also democratic or not, Lerner imagines a literature still capable of crossing the void.

> One angel holds her head in her hands. Joan appears to stagger toward the viewer, reaching her left arm out, maybe for support, in the swoon of being called. Instead of grasping branches or leaves, her hand, which is carefully positioned on the sight line of one of the other angels, seems to dissolve. The museum placard says that Bastien-Lepage was attacked for his failure to reconcile the ethereality of the angels with the realism of the future saint's body, but that "failure" is what makes it one of my favorite paintings. It's as if the tension between the metaphysical and physical worlds, between two orders of temporality, produces a glitch in the pictorial matrix; the background swallows her fingers. (10:04 9)

In the early pages of the novel, Ben stands in the Metropolitan Museum of Art in New York in front of Jules Bastien-Lepage's 1879 painting, *Joan of Arc*. Here, Joan's outstretched arm is a visual representation of the struggle between personal introspection and need of the other in poetry, where the reflective meditation of art allows for more than self-enclosure. Resisting the inward turn of postmodern literary contraption, Lerner's constellatory poetics envisions a literary mode unconcerned with borders of time and space that comprehends its own struggle while redefining the parameters for its reconciliation within the poetics of experience. Indeed, Ben is hopeful: "it is a presence, not an absence, that eats away at her hand: she's being pulled into the future" (9). Formally speaking, so are we.

BLANKS

When Rachel Kushner began writing *The Flamethrowers*, she began "with images" ("Flamethrowers"). Although noting in an interview that this is her standard practice—"I begin a book with imagery, more than I do with an idea or a character. Some kind of poetic image" (Interview with Barron)—it was a visual image that sparked the inspiration for her second novel's aesthetic and affective key. As Kushner explained in a reflexive piece for the *Paris Review* in 2012 on the images that inspired her as she wrote the prize-winning novel, for this novel she "wanted to conjure New York as an environment of energies, sounds, sensations" and "[n]ot as a backdrop, a place that could resolve into history and sociology and urbanism" ("Flamethrowers"). When she "looked at a lot of photographs and other evidentiary traces of downtown New York and art of the mid-1970s," all she "kept finding were nude women and guns." The process of writing the novel then became a matter of facing "the pleasure and headache of somehow stitching together the pistols and the nude women as defining features of a fictional realm," in such a fashion as to attend to how "the female narrator, who has the last word, and technically all words, is nevertheless continually overrun, effaced, and silenced by the very masculine world of the novel she inhabits." Kushner cultivated a mode of working "*contra*-diction . . . to merge what were by nature static and iconic images into a stream of life, real narrative life" (my emphasis).

In a way that echoes Chris Kraus's aesthetics of chance, "the first image" Kushner "pinned up to spark inspiration for what would eventually be . . . *The Flamethrowers*" is visually attuned to this particular affective and linguistic resistance. An image that also donned the cover of the first US edition, it features "a woman with tape over her mouth":

> She floated above my desk with a grave, almost murderous look, war paint on her cheeks, blonde braids framing her face, the braids a frolicsome countertone to her intensity. The paint on her cheeks, not frolicsome. The streaks of it, dripping down, were cold, white shards, as if her face were faceted in icicles. I didn't think much about the tape over her mouth (which is actually Band-Aids over the photograph, and not over her lips themselves). . . . A creature of language, silenced. ("Flamethrowers")

Also published in this same issue of the *Paris Review* was the short story "Blanks," the novel's fourth chapter, which traces a snapshot of the narrator's first interception with the art world she moved to New York to be a part of. A *blank* refers to absence: the narrator recalls disappearances of people she had known (Lisa—the girl Reno was in a McDonald's commercial with when Reno was a child—and Chris Kelly, a fellow University of Nevada, Reno graduate and budding artist "who'd gone to the South of France to find Nina Simone, only to be shot at with a gun she'd lifted from the pocket of her robe" [*Flamethrowers* 55]); the blanks that artists Thurman and Nadine shoot each other with, which induce a metallic tang of violent threat; and the casual mysteries about the artists: "you weren't supposed to ask basic questions," Reno tells us, "[n]ot even 'What is your name?' You pretended you knew, or didn't need to know. Asking an obvious question, even if there were no obvious answer, was a way of indicating to them that they should jettison you as soon as they could" (58). Playing with the epistemological blankness of misnaming or the absence of names—a mysterious man she sleeps with, who we later learn is Ronnie Fontaine, "started calling me Reno" because she "was from Nevada" (57); she later professes that she did not "want to know his name. I didn't think much about it" (69)—Reno is a particular kind of experiential creature who "want[s] to pass over names and go right to the deeper thing" (71). Kushner presents this "deeper thing" as something that courts enchantment through a paradoxical yearning "to want something and also to know, somewhere inside yourself, not an obvious place, that you aren't going to get it" (71). Blankness conflates desire with reticence.

When writing about the image of the rebellious woman with plasters over her mouth, Kushner reflected also on how "[a]n appeal to images is a demand for love"—a form of love in which one demands "something more than just their mute glory. We want them to give up a clue, a key, a way to cut open a space, cut into a register, locate a tone, without which the novelist is lost" ("Flamethrowers"). Indeed, this image clues us into the novel's aesthetic aspiration to telegraph what is blank or vacant or void—salt flats, ski fields, snow, China girls, and unblemished white skin before it is bruised.[3] This blankness enacts a double twist when it comes to the narrator's mute passivity. "Three or four drinks in," Reno reflects in a scene in "Blanks," "still they hadn't asked me anything. But what interesting thing did I have to tell?" (*Flamethrowers* 51). Although the way Reno is restricted by her questions of belonging in such interactions in the novel have irritated some reviewers, for whom the suspensive passivity of her observational narratorial style has contributed to the novel's affective "malaise," Matthew Hart and Alexandra Rocca have noted that "Kushner's refusal to name her narrator-protagonist relates to that character's attractively unfinished, almost liquid, quality" (Interview with Hart and Rocca 197).[4] For Kushner, "the fact that she has no name was somehow important" (Interview with Hart and Rocca 200), as she "wanted a narrator who could convey a tone that was like thought" rather than "a spoken account or historical testimony or a confession or a performance of any kind" (201). Detaching the first and last names that "a close third- but especially a first-person narrator would identify themselves with"—and the attendant "set of relations and joys and traumas and, most importantly, desires"—created an opportunity to interrogate the "false" "way subjectivity is treated in the novel" (203). As "a first-person narrator who expresses herself like thought, in a neutral and interior way," Reno is able to "report . . . on her experience from inside . . . so that the book can have compression and forward motion"—while "[n]ames come from outside," Reno's experiences come from the inside route (201).

Reno's blankness draws on the 1975 film *Anna*, directed by Alberto Grifi; indeed, the novel is dedicated to the eponymous character, "whose last name no one seems to remember, or possibly they never knew it to begin with—never mind the fact that she is the point of absolute gravity and star of this nearly four-hour film" in which the actress "plays only herself" (Kushner, "Women in Revolt"). In an essay for *Artforum* in 2012, Kushner meditated on how "the electrifying presence of filmed beauty and the obsessive gaze itself form a vivid and mysterious historical record: of 'stars' who exist purely as stars, leaving no trace of lives continued offscreen, outside their moment of celluloid fame. Their only record is their record on film" ("Women in Revolt"). Though not a star herself, Reno leaves a trace on the screen in a more disposable fashion as a China girl. By evoking Anna in Reno's role as a China girl, Kushner traces the image of a woman playing herself, connecting the technology of film and speed of the reel with the postmodern figure of the disposable actress who enjoys a brilliant moment and then disappears from life, like "certain of Warhol's subjects we never heard from again" ("Women in Revolt"). As Kushner remarked elsewhere, "[i]f the projectionist loaded the film correctly, you didn't see the China girl. And if you did see her, she flashed by so quickly she was only a quick blur. They were ubiquitous and yet invisible, a thing in the margin that was central to each film, these nameless women that, as legend has it, were traded among film technicians and projectionists like baseball cards" ("Flamethrowers").

Far from an absence, being a blank slate works as its own aesthetic mode produced in the self-reflexive relation between making and experiencing. It allows an artist to shape-shift—to "merge into an environment" without an audience, in such a way to "understand your subject" that filming it won't (*Flamethrowers* 88). This is the approach that Reno's friend Giddle takes, who was "performing, as a real but not *actual* waitress" (89). She acts as if she were "living inside a film about a lonely woman who threw her life away to work at a diner" (90), and the longer her performance, the more "authentic" her role becomes. Though Giddle epitomizes what Lerner calls "the evolving (or devolving) avant-garde dream of dissolving the art/life distinction" ("Trace of a Trace") by *joining* so as to avoid creating distance between art and life, Reno's passivity paradoxically de-mediates experience; in other words, although Reno's narratorial style records the experiences of others, her passiveness allows us direct access to real experience. Rachel Greenwald Smith argues that this "tendency to sit back and let experiences happen to her is what allows the novel to achieve its blend between realism and the insistence on artifice that it maintains through its metafictional reflections on art, its incorporation of documentary photographs, and its fictionalization of historical events" ("Six Propositions" 182). Unlike Lerner's work, where the narrator's dissociative posture reinforces the novel's mediacy, *The Flamethrowers* "can be read without much concern with the questions of mediation and artificiality that it might otherwise highlight, because Reno seems like a reliable and neutral vehicle for the registration of a larger social landscape" ("Six Propositions" 182).

Oddly, it is the novel's representation of experience as propelled from the interior that motivates Reno's self-reflexive acknowledgment that she is not simply "trying to survive" as Nadine is, but is "shopping for experience" (*Flamethrowers* 313). This largely detached, discerning attitude locates Reno on the outside of experience, a position that allows her to deposit conversations and images into her memory that others can't. When encountering Nadine later in the novel, Reno observes her unnoticed "as she drank the entire thing in one quick and continuous series of gulps, then wiped her mouth with the back of her hand, looked around nervously like a hungry animal eating some other animal's food, and refilled the cup" (312). Why would Nadine remember her, when it was "I who remembered her and everything she had said to me, and that was enough. It was enough that I remembered her" (313). Critics have tended to ignore the fact that Reno's mode of experience relies on not an affective *blankness*—we know that Reno feels—but the kind of blankness that Kushner argues is "how people actually are" (Interview with Hart and Rocca 204). The novel doesn't account for conventional artistic and personal development, but plots the "profound introversion" that represents "what it means to be young" (204)—the temptation to map the outside world onto an internal sense of being. While the novel might gesture in its early pages to fulfill the generic expectations of a coming-of-age novel, the novel ends at Mont Blanc—a "border territory" (213)—in a state of ambiguity. Waiting endlessly in Chamonix for Gianni, who was supposed to be traversing a "no-man's-land of snow, wind, steeps" (*Flamethrowers* 380) from Italy to find exile in France, Reno faced Mont Blanc, "a monolith of doubt" (383). Reno's reflection that "[y]ou can think and think a question, the purpose of waiting, the question of whether there is any purpose, any *person* meant to appear, but if the person doesn't come, there is no one and nothing to answer you" voices the narrative mode of suspension the novel ends with (383). The final lines signal a future point for Reno "inside the spell of waiting" to find "the open absence" to "tear myself away" and "[l]eave with no answer" (383). As Reno steels herself for agency, the novel steels us for the inevitability of moving "on to the next question," threatening to propel us out of the blankness (383).

SALTERN STUDIES

The Flamethrowers's portrayal of the need to live art treats art as experience rather than object. The novel doesn't shy away from the gender politics hinted at in this configuration: young women are often self-styled as aesthetic objects—Reno "wanted to be looked at" (83) as an "object of universal attraction" (93), while Sandro also advises her that she doesn't "have to immediately become an artist," because as a "young woman is a conduit" for experience, "[a]ll she has to do is *exist*" (30). Reno reflects that to "[b]e a conduit," to "pass through time in patience, waiting for something to come," and to "[p]repare for its arrival" rather than "rush[ing] to meet it" might sound to some like "passivity," but she "considered it living" (30). Indeed, this urge to be a medium for experience spurs her to ride a motorcycle across the Bonneville Salt Flats, a project that moves the aesthetic event into the absolute present. While Marclay's *The Clock* encapsulates this same aesthetic immanence, Reno's involves "going as fast as you possibly could" and experiencing its temporality, unmediated, by accessing only "*[t]he time it took*" (28; original emphasis).

So, the pure time of experience collapses the distance between art and life. For many of the novel's artists, art "had to involve risk, some genuine risk" (10)—and in order to truly risk anything, this often means risking the real body. For Reno, it is speed that allows access to this risk as "a causeway between life and death" (13). Hurtling across the salt flats is only the first step in Reno's art project; the second is photographing the trace, the debris of experience, left behind. She reinforces the aesthetic intention of *experiencing* "the experience of speed" first and foremost as something that is *felt*, but she acknowledges how the photographs "might fail entirely to capture what I hoped for" (30). Speed appears as an overdetermined, stimulating category outside the normal register of experience. Although speed can be recorded, as Enda Duffy has noted, "[a]s with any pleasure, speed's thrill is polymorphous and resists being pinned down" (5). Reno's photographs can't capture her experience of speed, only the trace of this experience. Even though the narrator is situated in the seventies, where cultural images of speed such as those of her childhood hero and former land-speed world record holder Flip Farmer were abundant and car ownership was widespread, speed manages to retain an element of the brilliance of the new. This is emphasized by how the noted musings are interspersed in narrative time: they interrupt the straightforward descriptions of the handling of the bike and the movement from one place to another. Their enigmatic and open texture has, paradoxically, the effect of slowing the narrative down—enacting, in a way, speed's extraordinariness, while failing to represent it.

This rhetoric of speed neatly aligns with what Duffy has called the emergence of "a wholly new experience" at the turn of the twentieth century, in which people, for the first time, "were allowed to feel modernity in their bones: to feel its power as a physical sensation" (4). Modernist experience was "rerouted" away from experiences of speed by schedules, clocks, and the accelerating industrial regimentation of the working day. Instead, the body came to be the site where this experience could be felt as "directly physical rather than intellectual or aesthetic" (5). The defamiliarizing modernist shock of the new became visceral; it is felt in the body, and increasingly it was made available to all through the emergence of new technologies such as the automobile. Yet it did not become identical with these objects: the vehicle is the precondition of speed, but speed is an experience "outside the realm of the illusory fetish of the commodity" (8). Because of the way it is constructed, speed in modernity comes to evade the possibility of being situated on a commodity or—more relevantly for *The Flamethrowers*—in the work of art. This observation allows one to establish the outline of speed as what Kushner has called the "phantom link" between the separate time periods represented in the novel: speed is sensuous and more closely tied to the bodily and the experiential than to representation or commodities (Interview with Barron).

The narrative of T. P. Valera—the patriarch of the Valera family and industrial empire—tracks similar sensations to those that speed generates in Reno some fifty years later. As Marie, the woman he lusts after early in the novel, is taken away on a motorcycle by an unknown lover in early twentieth-century Egyptian Alexandria, Valera suddenly experiences "the need to enter the space of air, too as that machine had, as that man had, taking Marie with him, man and bike and Marie making an obscene double-humped centaur's profile" (37). The odd imagery is jarring, but it demonstrates how the "encounter with the new" that "is merged with his lust for a young woman" (Interview with Hart and Rocca 202) produces a new experiential subject: futurists such as F. T. Marinetti write of themselves as being "about to see the Centaur's birth" (Marinetti) in the coming of the figure of the driver that attaches them to machines. The image of this sensuous centaur in *The Flamethrowers* is initially "obscene" to Valera, but he is soon fully integrated into a futurist lifestyle. He partakes in the general call of futurists to "metalize themselves" (75), and a few years later realizes that he "moved at a different velocity," giving him a virility that would in time get him "ready for Marie's daughter" (79). For Valera and the futurists, re-creating the body was tied to the "defamiliarizing shocks" brought on by new experiences of speed that were "directly physical rather than intellectual or aesthetic" (Duffy 5).

The Flamethrowers grants this embodiment to novel form as well. Andrew Strombeck has isolated the motorcycle as "in some sense, the novel's form" (454), arguing that "the motorcycle, as object performs unifying work: it simultaneously fulfils the elder Valera's artistic ambitions, fuels the postwar Italian recovery . . . and serves as an icon of Fordist progress" (456). Tracking the post-Fordist condition of postmodernity, the novel undoes the motorcycle as a symbol of Fordist integration; its mixture of "art, personal desire, and even national destiny" becomes, in the seventies, "a trace—a thing not signifying history, but merely a physical thing" (471). While the motorcycle can be used to track discontinuity and change across time, speed is a more suitable candidate for performing the novel's "unifying work": it is an experience inaugurated in modernity that persists in postmodernity, demanding different engagements with it across time. To read the work of Reno's art—and the ways the novel frames this practice—from the standpoint of the experience of velocity highlights that at stake in the novel are categories that gain their boundaries from the primacy of bodily and sensuous experience. Attentiveness to speed performs a critical task that, unlike that of the motorcycle, does not vanish when the action in the novel reaches the postmodern age.

Treating speed as sensuous reinforces the "visceral" "machine shocks" Reno feels when crashing her Moto Valera motorcycle. As she speeds across the flat, buffeted by "wind gusts" "threatening to rip [her] helmet off," she narrates the slightest alterations to sensation: "I seemed to be moving around a lot, as if I were riding on ice, and yet I had traction, a slightly loose traction that had to be taken on faith" (*Flamethrowers* 29). Accelerating to 125 miles per hour, "I felt alert to every granule of time. Each granule *was* time, the single pertinent image, the other moment-images, before and after, lost, unconsidered" (29; original emphasis); soon "I was going 145 miles an hour. Then 148. I was in an acute case of present time," a speed at which "[n]othing mattered" but "the milliseconds of life" (30). Narrative time echoes the temporal suspension of speeding across the flats, but also the speed of the eighty-mile-an-hour gust of wind that slams into her from the side that breaks this suspensive velocity: "the bike skipped end over end"; Reno "skidded and tumbled" (31). The narrative tumble reinforces Reno's reflection on the "false idea that accidents happen in slow motion." Instead, "[w]hat happens slowly carries in each part the possibility of returning to what came before. In an accident everything is simultaneous, sudden, irreversible. It means this: no going back" (31).

The crash does something odd to time. Reno's immediate recovery takes place in the midst of a "slowdown" in the Valera team "in solidarity with the [factory] workers back in Milan" (122). *Crashing* runs the aesthetic labor, which blurs the role of motorcyclist and artist, into the mechanical labor. The artistic act of speeding across the salt flats, which draws "the time it took" or the experience of speed "in a fast and almost traceless way" (28), catapults her into a way of "time stretching" (119). Playing on photography as *writing with light*, this act recalls Reno's earlier obsession with skiing as "drawing *in time*":

> When I was little, skiing in the Sierras, I felt that I was drawing on the mountain's face, making big sweeping graceful lines. That was how I had started to draw, I'd told Sandro, as a little girl, five, six years old, on skis. Later, when drawing became a habit, a way of being, of marking time, I always thought of skiing. When I began ski racing, slalom and giant slalom, it was as if I were tracing lines that were already drawn, and the technical challenge that showed the primary one, to finish with a competitive time, was to stay perfectly in the lines, to stay early through the gates, to leave no trace, because the harder you set your skis' metal edges, the bigger wedge of evidence you left, the more you slowed down. You wanted no snow spraying out behind you. You wanted to be traceless. (9)

But in order "to photograph my tracks as an art project," Reno needed to form traces—the dramatic kind that the crash produced. "What seemed like endless perfect white on white was only a very thin crust of salt. Where the crust had been broken by the force of impact, mud seeped up," a contrast of color that etched out "a Rorschach of my crash" (114). Capturing the trace of experience is the closest Reno gets to pinching together the phenomenological gap between art and life, with its magic and unreality heightened by the photographic medium. Analog photography, as Margaret Iverson notes, is associated "with a kind of attentive *exposure* to things in the world marked by chance, age, and accident" (35; original emphasis). With coincidental phrasing, she also argues that "[a]n analogue record of an object bearing traces of wear or age doubles the indexicality of the image, making the image a trace of a trace, and thereby drawing attention to an aspect of the medium within the image" (35).

In theory, Reno's photographs had the potential for doing just that, but as she predicts, "the photographs were nothing but a trace. A trace of a trace" that held no aesthetic value (30). Having developed them after returning to New York, she discovers that "[t]hey weren't at all spectacular. They were detritus of an experience, ambiguous marks in the white expanse of the salt flats" (138). Although in his review of the novel Lerner points out that "[w]hen Reno slams headfirst into the salt, she is colliding with the legacy and limits of some of modernity's most persistent and dangerous dreams: the obliteration of the boundary between art and life, the aestheticization of force and speed" ("Trace of a Trace"), she is also colliding with the edge of two modes of temporality previously held in suspension: speed and slow. And thus, the crash becomes the ultimate aesthetic event, because the marks of the collision with the salt and bike appear on her skin as a sensuous trace of the experience of speed. By marking her skin, the crash negates the narrative of blankness Reno otherwise occupies. When Reno returns to the China girl studio after the crash, her employers Marvin and Eric were "annoyed" with her, as most China girls "don't suggest trauma"; the "problem with the bruises is they make you not anonymous," and a China girl is "not supposed to evoke real life. Just the hermetic world of a smiling woman holding the color chart" (140). No longer a blank image that anyone could project anything on, *she* becomes real. Indeed, because "the photographs by themselves were too ephemeral" (139), tracing the residue of experience isn't enough, nor is performing the role of motorcyclist. The only thing left to do is actually become one, not as enactment or "infiltration" (139), but to live it. "Maybe women were meant to speed past," Reno reflects in a feminist reversal of the predominantly male postmodernist obsession with speed: "just a blur. Like China girls. Flash and then gone" (297).

IMAGE RHYTHM

Unlike the image of a China girl, the images in the novels are not only meant to be seen but meant to be pored over, as one would a series of contact prints. Though we don't do this with a magnifier, novel images require us to stop and really look. Sometimes this means pausing when we come across them, mining them for narrative resonance and aesthetic secrets; other times this means flicking over them on the first reading to return to them once we finish the novel. We've already seen how Jennifer Egan imagines the image musically as a novelistic pause, Zadie Smith imagines zooming in on the image, and Teju Cole attributes the medium specificity of photography as "bringing slowness to everything I do" ("Pitch Forward"). Reading across the contemporary novel's intermedial investments, we can identify a new mode of reading influenced by this image rhythm, a stop-start tempo that imbues the time of reading with what Louise Hornby has called the "pace of stillness" (108).

In talks and interviews, Kushner has described "visual passages" in *The Flamethrowers* in similar terms. Images would act as "pauses, or counterpoints," to the narrative "that would complicate, function in a relation" to it in a non-"obvious" way (Interview with Cotton). Appearing on the page opposite the beginning of a new chapter, the images in *The Flamethrowers* all frame what comes next. But by immediately preceding the chapter, the images, though naturally falling into the gap between chapters which themselves jump between different times, nevertheless perform a radical cut to the narrative rhythm. Kushner's larger aesthetic project imbues this image pause with the language of film. As Jesse Barron describes, Kushner's "strategy of interrupting scenes with long dashes in the middle of lines of dialogue" is "like crosscutting." Kushner agrees: it was a deliberate notational technique that bisected narrative rhythm with a "radical cut," but which also demonstrates on the level of plot "a deep continuity with film narrative, and the way that characters bloom on the screen and disappear from our lives, in terms of filmic time and energy" (Interview with Hart and Rocca 213). Not interested in the "fadeout" or "soft echo," the images also perform a quick shock to narrative time in order to slow down the time of our reading.

When we slow down to take in the images Kushner selected to go into the novel, we notice a serialization in the oblique gaze that is mediated through reflective surfaces like mirrors and glass. Adding to this narrative continuity are the titles of the proceeding chapter that act as oblique captions. The film still from *Wanda* (1970), which shows a forlorn woman behind a counter and glass screen, is followed by the chapter title "Imitation of Life"; the clipped title "Faces" shadows a photograph by Richard Prince of a woman's made-up eye reflected in the mirror of a pressed powder compact; "The March on Rome" echoes the photograph by Aldo Bonasia of riot police tear-gassing rioters in Italy.

Playing to the difference between what Jacques Rancière calls "the form (artistic/pictorial)" and "the anecdote (empiricist/photographic)" ("Notes on the Photographic Image" 9), the contemporary novel's use of photocopied and heavily reproducible photographs "activates" what Lerner calls "the relationship between reading and looking within fiction" (Interview with Derbyshire), while also accentuating "the relationship between seeing and writing" (Interview with Console). In so doing, both *The Flamethrowers* and *10:04* intersect, to various degrees, with the neorealist novel's claims to indexicality. "Rather than use the ontological status of the photograph as a complex, syllogistic demonstration of art's necessary autonomy from the world," Lee Konstantinou argues, neorealists "have used enigmatic, usually uncaptioned photographs . . . as devices for suggesting that writing itself might do more than represent a world," that "[w]riting might also give us direct access to reality" (120). Aligning such aesthetics with the autofictional collapse "between 'who I appear to be' and 'who I am'" that *10:04* dramatically stages and Reno likewise maps in *The Flamethrowers*, Konstantinou suggests that "a systematic conflation or confusion of the normative (fictional) and the ontological (fakeness) . . . has fueled the most interesting work by a range of writers during the first two decades of the twenty-first century." Both novelists draw images into a proximal antagonism with their prose.

Though neither Kushner nor Lerner "want[ed] anything that would illustrate the narrative" (Kushner, Interview with Cotton), their images do appear at different places in the novel—and though *The Flamethrowers* doesn't have conventional captions, Lerner's novels do, crumpling the texts onto themselves. In *Leaving the Atocha Station*, the system goes something like this: the caption, as a quote from another section in the novel, suggests an affinity between the section of quoted prose and the section in which the photograph occurs. For example, the third image is Esther Singleton's photograph of the Alhambra, inserted into the section during which the narrator ups his dosage of "white pills," spiraling after he realizes "how much I was invested in the idea that Isabel and Teresa were invested in me" (101). The photograph is captioned thus: "*The relationship I might have had in the flattering light of the subjunctive*" (103; original emphasis). This line, taken from an earlier scene in which he first questions what he thought about his relationship with erstwhile girlfriend Teresa (88), inflects the latter passage with equal uncertainty.

If the photographs in *The Flamethrowers* require us to pause, Lerner's intermedial practice produces a double take. In both novels, "[t]he author gratefully acknowledges the object world," to borrow a line from one of his *Lichtenberg Figures* poems (47); the inclusion of seven images in *Leaving the Atocha Station* and twelve in *10:04* responds to what Mieke Bal describes as an "attempt to *object*ify experience," which produces a "rhetoric" that creates "an effect of the real" as well as one of reification (8). Perplexed by the lack of "interesting talk among novelists about how fiction has had to reassess its priorities in light of cheaply reproducible photographs" (Interview with Lin), Lerner describes how "their presence" in novels and the "ambiguity" they create "links up with the conversation about mediation" and "spectacle" (Interview with Console). To Lerner's eye, a suspensive form dramatizes the experience of novelistic realism: "[e]ven grainy photographs are more optically realistic than the most realistic novelistic prose" (Interview with Derbyshire), subsequently making "the difference between reading and looking . . . more acutely felt" (Interview with Console). Indeed, by holding art works in tension with the surrounding literary prose, visual art sheds its actual conditions and becomes part of the subjunctive mode, the imagination, of the prose. While the novel explores this idea through both the inclusion of actual images and ekphrastic description, the aesthetic achieved by this combination creates something more akin to a virtual gallery, where the reader must reject a passive role for that of a perusing observer who too *experiences* art. By arguing that "[w]e're often told that the figure within the work was replaced with the viewer standing before it," Lerner suggests that "[e]jecting the virtual from the object increased the former's power: now it could reabsorb the object along with [its] viewer" ("Actual World").

For Lerner, the relationship between text and image "is crucial to the contemporary novel as a form" (Interview with Console). Proposing that the "text-image relationship in the novel raises and sustains" not only "the question of the degree to which either prose or the image have a purchase on the real," but whether "the extent to which the meaning of one is stabilized or undercut by the other," *10:04*'s "brand of absorptive aesthetics resists the conventions of literary realism" (Interview with Console). Because "[t]he thickest novelistic description is less *optically* realistic than any conventional photograph . . . including photographs both subtracts and adds pressure to the prose: it relieves it of the burden of stimulating the optical if only because it reminds us how narrative prose just isn't as good at that as the camera" (Interview with Lin). Lerner's use of images thus creates a formal suspense by calling attention to what is absent or failed about what his characters experience. He notes that although "there are passages of very thick or realistic description," "there is also a lot of physical detail left out or withheld," leaving images to instead take their place (Interview with Lin). Rather than simply illustrative, the photographs nevertheless "always contain the promise of the illustrative" (Interview with Fitzgerald). So, the photograph of the Alhambra details a place that Adam lies about having been to in the novel, and the cropped image of a woman's face from the film *The Passenger* (1975) is intended to overlay the absence of, or "withheld," physical descriptions of Teresa. Indeed, Lerner couches his claims about the captions in terms of failure: they are intended to "inflect how we view the images, so that they end up illustrating the problematic nature of the illustrative as much as actually anchoring the prose in a visually intelligible world." *10:04*'s images develop this practice but do so in order to sharpen our perception in relation to the subjective: what we would have seen or might see that fades out because of an alteration to the future that erases the past. The photograph of Benjamin's and Klee's angel of time and the vertical diptych of the fading hands of Joan of Arc in Jules Bastien-Lepage's 1879 painting and Michael J. Fox in *Back to the Future* visually demarcate the things and experiences "retrospectively erased" (figs. 5 and 6): "[b]ecause those moments had been enabled by a future that had never arrived, they could not be remembered from this future that, at and as the present, had obtained; they'd faded from the photograph" (24).

Lerner imaging the "presence" and "absence of the future" in *10:04*. Detail from Jules Bastien-Lepage's *Joan of Arc* (1879). Metropolitan Museum of Art Open Access.

Film still, Michael J. Fox in *Back to the Future* (1985). © Universal Pictures, 1985.

SUSPENSION 165

To my eye, the slow reading of such contemporary intermedial novels functions as relational art. Though authors rarely have the capacity to dictate time spent in their books, the formal rhythm of the images—as they echo and reverberate off the aesthetic, affective, and political velocity of their narrators' art practices—positions contemporary reading practices as close to unmediated as possible. Just as the novels plot the experience of making art, the images—as found object and as readymade—rewrite novel form as made, assembled, and serialized. And although in doing so the authors write into the form the very mediated experience that both novels attempt to overwrite, by swinging the lens around to focus *our* time of reading such a technique seems to offer us an aesthetic experience that continues to ask us to take our time. Indeed, although Lerner has lamented that "the contemporary is characterized by the anxiety that . . . the only kind of aesthetic experience left" is a suspended, "second-order aesthetic experience" (Interview with Rogers 229), we might take inspiration from the forms both *10:04* and *The Flamethrowers* actually create—to relish suspending time as we read and experience the simple, unmediated *time it takes*.

AFTERWORD
Politics of Aesthetic Experience Now

The modes of against that underpin this book might have been compelled to conform to the insistent structure of mutual exclusion: an antagonistic relation that means that as we turn to one thing we necessarily turn away from another. Indeed, the tricky territory of against recurs in two long-standing critical and colloquial tendencies: first, to pit visual art and the literary against one another, and, second, to pit life and art against one another. Semantically, this insistence on a mode of against is visualized by the trope of "this vs. that"—of the kind that has recently informed the essays "MFA vs. NYC" (Harbach) and "MFA vs. POC" (Díaz). As with these examples, the structure of Art vs. Literature and Art vs. Life is deeply hostile, but unlike that of the MFA's opponents, the hostility is unwarranted. For all of the literary examples in this book, such arbitrary delineation is old news, as if to ask "seriously, guys, are we still talking about this?"—but popular reviews seem to have a hankering for it all the same.[1] Many of the interviews with writers and reviews of the novels this book considers had "art vs. writing" in their titles, as if this is one of the persistent battles that will keep the more encompassing defense of the arts on fresh soil. But while formal developments since the 1970s like intermediality have largely taken the art/literature *either/or* to task, even as I write this sentence another opinion piece about the state of the contemporary novel has appeared in my Twitter feed, bemoaning not just the fact but the performative necessity of the question of why contemporary novelists—so-called *fiction* writers—are drawing "on life" instead of "making things up" (Clark).

In all these texts, the threat of incommensurability occurs in another dialectic: aesthetic experience vs. political experience. This secondary mode of mutual exclusion organizes the colloquial worry about the point of aesthetic experience now, by asking, in the context of global terror events, migrant crises, global warming, and political precarity—what Ruth Cruikshank terms *"fin de millénaire* aesthetics of crisis" (4)—how and whether art should help. As Cruikshank argues, "aesthetics cannot be separated from questions of ethics and ideology—not in the mid-twentieth-century sense of political commitment—but rather in the sense that language (and therefore literature) is always already inscribed in the system it may seek to transcend or criticize" (5). Through this attention to how aesthetic experience is mediated in and through novelistic prose, such writers attempt to find ways to engage with the limits of their own practice, and of the efficacy of language itself in representing both kinds of experience. Placing novelistic prose in direct conversation with the actual visual images or poems included in the text, as well as narratives of experiencing them, highlights precisely this problem of the inability of language to express. In doing so, it exposes the ineffability shared by accounts of aesthetic and traumatic experience.

What unites these novels is a suspicion of this implied exclusion. Even though writers like Cole have maintained that searching for subtlety today is a form of political resistance, the demands of linear political experience are often perceived to negate aesthetic experience, as if they cancel each other out. Many of the novels discussed in this book gesture to political events, usually in passing by referring to what's on TV, but few deeply engage with the affective repercussions of such traumas. The deliberate negation of active political engagement in these novels, however, reinforces rather than refutes political experience. As Greil Marcus puts it, "negation is always political," no matter the territory (9).

The ethics of viewing rather than directly experiencing events such as 9/11 captures the essence of this aesthetic problem. The ending of Ottessa Moshfegh's *My Year of Rest and Relaxation* (2018) details such transgressive aesthetic experience. The narrator, having come out of a yearlong period of hibernation—tranquilizing herself with pharmaceuticals prescribed by her hack psychiatrist—lost her best friend, Reva, in the towers. Finally repairing her broken VCR, she videotapes the footage of the planes flying into the towers, watching it "over and over to soothe myself" not only "that day" but repeatedly:

> I continue to watch it, usually on a lonely afternoon, or any other time, I doubt that life is worth living, or when I need courage, or when I'm bored. Each time I see the woman leaping off the Seventy-eighth floor of the North tower—one high-heeled shoe slipping off and hovering up over her, the other stuck on her foot as though it were too small, her blouse untucked, hair flailing, limbs stiff as she plummets down, one arm raised, like a dive into a summer lake—I am overcome by awe, not because she looks like Reva, and I think it's her, almost exactly like her, and not because Reva and I had been friends, or because I'll never see her again, but because she's beautiful. There she is, a human being, diving into the unknown, and she is wide awake. (289)

This isn't supposed to be beautiful or comforting or encouraging or entertaining; in other words, it's not supposed to hold all the qualities associated with aesthetic experiences. Of course, in some ways, this final scene fits the darkly comic tone of Moshfegh's novel, but it also echoes a host of twenty-first-century American novels that are concerned with how hard it is to reconcile formal and aesthetic dilemmas in the face of increasingly troubling world events. According to Peggy Brand, amid a bombardment of images in the twenty-first century, the aesthetic "must compete with the horrors of the world as well as the images we are not allowed to see," asking how we can "see and process world events, such as the quiet and unremarkable return of a woman to her home devastated by war," and reconcile these with ideas of beauty (1). But it is precisely this overload of images that also leads to pervasive feelings of ubiquity in the face of the aesthetic, so that beauty seems either "relegated to the scrap heap or insistently, perhaps even unintentionally, ever-present" (1). This is reminiscent of W. J. T. Mitchell's claim in 2004 that when "living in a time of the plague of the fantasies"—like now—"perhaps the best cure that artists can offer is to unleash the images, in order to see where they lead us, how they go before us. A certain tactile irresponsibility with image might just be the right sort of homeopathic medicine for what plagues us" (*What Do Pictures Want?* 335). By offering a capacious mode of aesthetic experience that encompasses a broad spectrum of negative feelings, the contemporary novel doesn't attempt to reconcile the anxiety and banality of contemporary living.

If anyone needs the kind of solace art purports to impart, it's *My Year of Rest and Relaxation*'s narrator. Her year of sleep is brought on by a persistent sense of ennui; she aimed to reduce the amount of "excruciating" time she spent "coming out of that sleep," in which "[m]y entire life flashed before my eyes in the worst way possible, my mind refilling itself with all my lame memories, every little thing that had brought me to where I was" (40). Asleep, she felt "awake," "[a]lmost happy" (40); "nothing else could ever bring me such pleasure, such freedom, the power to feel and move and think and imagine, safe from the miseries of my waking consciousness" (46). The final stage of her sleep becomes a conceptual art work by the "star artist" Ping Xi, represented by the gallery the narrator worked at before being fired at the beginning of the novel. But where the narrator's ambition for this project was "to clear my mind, purge my associations, refresh and renew the cells in my brain, my eyes, my nerves, my heart" (263), Ping Xi "just wanted to shock people. And he wanted people to love and despise him for it. His audience, of course, would never truly be shocked. People were only delighted at his concepts. He was an art-world hack. But he was successful. He knew how to operate" (262–63). At the end of the novel, the narrator wakes up—"My sleep had worked. I was soft and calm and felt things"—but the art world was still asleep: it "was all just canned counterculture crap, 'punk, but with money,' nothing to inspire more than a trip around the corner to buy an unflattering outfit from Comme des Garçons" (36).

To be sure, the novel suggests that the encounter with "true" art might simulate a form of existential dizziness. Standing "too close to [a] painting" (286) in the Met once she is properly awake, the narrator comes to cognitive clarity:

> The notion of my future suddenly snapped into focus: it didn't exist yet. I was making it, standing there, breathing, fixing the air around my body with stillness, trying to capture something—a thought, I guess—as though such a thing were possible, as though I believed in the delusion described in those paintings—that time could be contained, held captive. I didn't know what was true. So I did not step back. Instead, I put my hand out. I touched the frame of the painting. And then I placed my whole palm on the dry, rumbling surface of the canvas, simply to prove to myself that there was no God stalking my soul. Time was not immemorial. Things were just *things*. (286–87)

Pulled to the side by the guard, this realization was enough: "That was it. I was free" (287).

Although by rejecting the consoling or transformative power of art by asserting that "things were just things," such novels might seem nihilistic about the importance of aesthetic experience, this isn't the case. Making aesthetic experience ordinary instead detaches it from the realm of high culture, insisting upon its social, democratic importance in everyday life. One of the major contentions of this book has been that echoing this same shift in our own critical practices—moving from critical detachment to affective attachment, from suspicious to sympathetic—allows us to view works of art not as fixed coordinates of political importance but as shifting constellations of feeling now. We might do well to lean forward, ignore the guard yelling "Stand back!," and reassess what our own aesthetic experiences mean to us. At a time where we are often pushed into being "pro-this" and "anti-that," defending our corners without the opportunity to feel complexly about a situation, art that continues to challenge standardized modes of feeling makes space for a subtler but no less powerful mode of political resistance. What this multioperational, multidirectional mode of against charts, then, is a route that not only helps us evade the imminent reversal of the contemporary period's many aesthetic, formal, and political mutual exclusions, but that encompasses a multifaceted way of feeling that many of us have felt but haven't put into words yet. Aesthetic categories that emerge from telescoping between text and author, art and literature, aesthetics and politics, show how fertile the spaces are between what we expect to know and feel, and what we actually do.

NOTES

PREFACE

1. As James argued,

    [T]he analogy between the art of the painter and the art of the novelist is, so far as I am able to see, complete. Their inspiration is the same, their process (allowing for the different quality of the vehicle) is the same, their success is the same. They may learn from each other, they may explain and sustain each other. Their cause is the same, and the honour of one is the honour of another. Peculiarities of manner, of execution, that correspond on either side, exist in each of them and contribute to their development. (167)

2. Adam Kelly has called this sensibility "The New Sincerity," and Lee Konstantinou has distinguished contemporary writing as "postironic." "If nothing else," Konstantinou argues, comments by contemporary writers in the last ten years or so "signal that the term *postmodernism* and its cognates have, at some unspecified time, achieved a newly historical status. Whatever it once was, *postmodernism* no longer designates anything like the cutting edge of ambitious aesthetic and theoretical production" (3). In part this comes down to the resistance to irony that defines much of postmil-

lennial fiction, critical work, and theory: "postironists want to move beyond postmodern irony partly because irony has lost its critical power or because irony's mode of critique no longer adequately addresses contemporary reality. They seek to imagine what shape a postironic, rather than uncritically earnest or naïvely nostalgic literary practice, might take" (8).

3. It is significant that the novelists in this book are seen to push formal boundaries even while entertaining immense popularity and cultural prestige. All have been employed by universities in literature or creative writing programs; Zadie Smith, Rachel Kushner, Sheila Heti, and Teju Cole have written or edited columns for magazines and newspapers (*Harper's, Artforum, The Believer,* and *The New York Times*); several have benefited from prestigious institutional grants (Cole won the Windham-Campbell Literature Prize; Lerner received the MacArthur "Genius Grant"; Kushner was a Guggenheim Fellow). Most have won or been short-listed for major prizes: Cole's *Open City* received the 2012 Hemingway Foundation/PEN Award; Hustvedt's *The Blazing World* was awarded the Los Angeles Times Book Prize for Fiction in 2015; Lerner was celebrated as one of Granta's Best Young American Novelists in 2017; Smith received the Langston Hughes Medal in 2017; and *The Blazing World,* Smith's *On Beauty and Being Just* and *Swing Time,* and Kushner's *The Mars Room* were short-listed for the Man Booker Prize in 2015, 2005, 2017, and 2018, respectively. All these authors have topped annual best books and bestsellers lists. All reflect volubly in interviews on everything from their writing habits to the thematic, theoretical, and conceptual territory of their own works to contemporary literary culture.

4. Interviews, as Rebecca Roach writes, have been "[d]eployed as a promotional tactic since the late nineteenth century" but have in the last twenty years or so have "become entrenched in the cultural imagination following New Journalistic deployment and as the book industry and wider media ecology has undergone a series of structural transformations" (199). For writers and critics alike, "the interview, with its promise of objective truth and personal expressivity, offers one of the most engaging forms and practices through which to think about the work of fiction and the creative process" (231).

INTRODUCTION

1. See Balzer, *Curationism;* O'Neill, *Culture of Curating;* and Terry Smith, *Thinking Contemporary Curating.*

2. This scene occurs in episode 4 of season 2 of *Killing Eve*.
3. Recent books that explore negative feelings include Heather Love, *Feeling Backward* (2009); Sara Ahmed, *The Promise of Happiness* (2010); Lauren Berlant, *Cruel Optimism* (2011); C. Namwali Serpell, *Seven Modes of Uncertainty* (2014); Eugenie Brinkema, *The Forms of the Affects* (2014); and David James, *Discrepant Solace* (2019).
4. Or graduate from MFA programs, in which this theoretical knowledge is institutionally obligatory. See McGurl's *The Program Era* (2009), along with *After the Program Era* (2017), edited by Loren Glass.
5. This is not to say that modernity is past: among others, metamodernism and altermodernism continue the project of modernity today. See David James's *Modernist Futures* (2012).
6. Except for Chris Kraus's *I Love Dick* (1997). In true proleptic fashion, many critics have noted how *I Love Dick* was published too soon, into a cultural world that wasn't ready. Its reprint, and first British release, in 2016 propelled the novel out of the art world milieu to mainstream readership.
7. The same has been said for "[u]ntrustworthy" but nevertheless "deeply illuminating" ekphrastic novels, to borrow Mark Ledbury's formulation (xi), which might mislead us or attempt to hoodwink us when we least expect it. Surely being hoodwinked is not just a peril, but a pleasure, of criticism.

CHAPTER 1

1. It is a paradox of the discipline of aesthetics, too, which, as Jacques Rancière asserts, "refers to a specific regime for identifying and reflecting on the arts: a mode of articulation between ways of doing and making, their corresponding forms of visibility, and possible ways of thinking about their relationships" (*Politics of Aesthetics* 10).
2. Jerry Dantzic's son, Grayson Dantzic, compiled these photographs, many of which were published before, for this collection. Jerry Dantzic died in 2006.
3. Although authorship is attributed to Claire Malcolm in the novel, it was actually authored by poet Nick Laird, Smith's husband.

CHAPTER 2

1. See Silverman, *The Miracle of Analogy*.
2. Available at open.spotify.com/user/tejucole as of April 2019.

3. "The problem is not one of too many unsettling images," Cole argues, "but of too few" (*Known and Strange Things* 216).
4. Available at op-cit.tumblr.com.
5. #_blindspot has since been removed from Cole's Instagram account. Thank you to Teju Cole for allowing me to screenshot two images before it was archived. The book was first published in Italian, under the title *Punto d'ombra*, which means "shadow point." This is not Cole's first solo exhibition of photography. His first took place in Goa, India, in 2011, with another at Ithaca College in New York in 2012. Again, these photographs had textual mirrors, again lyrical. But this time, they were written by Amitava Kumar on Cole's artistic influences in each image. Incidentally, the title, "Who's Got the Address?," is a line from Tranströmer's poem "The Scattered Congregation."
6. Available at open.spotify.com/user/tejucole/playlist/2rz7L9AVK1Z20FksrL gYIL?si=dyvsx5L-Tcm0oiQKb_XMXQ as of April 2019.

CHAPTER 3

1. See "Louise Bourgeois," "Kiki Smith," and "Annette Messager: Hers and Mine," in Hustvedt, *Living*, and "My Louise Bourgeois," in Hustvedt, *A Woman Looking*.
2. Hustvedt has also written extensively on Goya, dedicating two essays in *Mysteries of the Rectangle* to contemplation of his works: "Narrative in the Body: Goya's *Los Caprichos*" and "More Goya: There Are No Rules in Painting." In *What I Loved*, Leo, too, turns to Goya for spiritual distraction and new paths forward: "While Goya didn't feed my gloom, his savage paintings gave new license to my thoughts—permission to open doors that in my former life I had left closed" (166).
3. Goya flickers in the background of these comments too, as his black paintings reference her comments about cannibalism: the first black painting is titled *Saturn Devouring His Son* (1819–23).
4. In the words of Judith Butler's early work, Harry intends her gender to be "a *corporeal style*" (521)—"both intentional and performative, where 'performative' itself carries the double-meaning of 'dramatic' and 'non-referential'" (523). Queering the "corporeal style" of the self is performance art. Indeed, *The Blazing World* enacts Ashley Sheldon's formulation that "[c]ontemporary writers find queerness potentially anywhere: where expectations are thwarted, where organization becomes disarticulated, where multiplicity disturbs and makes impossible unity" (2).

CHAPTER 4

1. Heti has reflected on how the novel engages with her sense of creative failure:

   So much of the book is about the anxiety of failure—the failure of the play and the failure of the divorce and the failure of not feeling like a good person. Those feelings in the book came out of real feelings I was having about all of those things. So, if there hadn't been a very recent artistic failure, and, I felt, a failure as a person—because I had made a contract with the people at the theater—a commitment—and I failed to fulfill it . . . I'm just happy that the book happened the way it did, and now the play's even happening. It feels like nothing was lost, whereas when I canceled the play, it felt like everything was lost. (Interview with Schwiegershausen)

2. Lerner's novels, *Leaving the Atocha Station* (2011) and *10:04* (2014), follow this same denial of novel-writing until the end of each of the books.
3. They even all have adjoining legal scandals around their writing that echo Dick's response in the novel, in addition to the "real" Dick's (cultural critic Dick Hebdige's) reception of the novel in 1997.
4. Yes, Dick misspells Chris's name as Kris. Anne-Christine d'Adesky writes that this represents "a breathtaking act of humiliation, an unambiguous Fuck You" (30).
5. *Gravity and Grace* is also the title of the volume of Simone Weil's unpublished writing, compiled and published in 1952 after her death.

CHAPTER 5

1. Pedagogically, this even offers practical value. According to Jesse Matz, "texts that imply they should be read pragmatically for their forms of temporal engagement occupy a pedagogical position in relation to the public they would serve, whether or not they participate in the larger context of contemporary time work, and that position raises questions not only about their cultural status but about their ideological implications" ("Art of Time" 287).
2. Benjamin's full response to Klee's monoprint, which he owned, is as follows:

   A Klee painting named "Angelus Novus" shows an angel looking as though he is about to move away from something he is fixedly contemplating. His eyes are staring, his mouth is open, his wings are spread. This is how one pictures the angel of history. His face is turned toward the past. Where we perceive a chain of events, he sees one single catastrophe which keeps piling wreckage upon wreckage and hurls it in front of his feet. The angel would like to stay, awaken the dead, and make whole what has been smashed. But a storm is blowing from Paradise; it has got caught in his wings with such violence that the angel can no longer close them. This storm irresistibly propels him into the future to which his back is turned, while the pile of debris before him grows skyward. This storm is what we call progress. (257–58)

3. A China girl is an image of a woman, usually made up to look like a doll, used in filmmaking to help calibrate skin color in the film. Kushner refers to the models as China girls in the novel.
4. For Cristina Garcia, the clincher for this "malaise" was the fact that "the aspiring, even reckless Reno we glimpse in the early pages of the book bears little resemblance to the Reno who forgoes much of her own agency to stand by her man and be carried along by events, however dramatic, instead of pursuing her own agenda."

AFTERWORD

1. Such is the not-so-subtle undertone of this comment by Rachel Kushner in an interview with Eben Shapiro for *The Wall Street Journal*:

There are lots of writers who love to talk about the novelist's decline, the novelist's race against visual culture, television, YouTube, blablabla, I don't know, I just don't think about writing as being eclipsed by other forms. I think what's impacted our society most is the marketplace, greed, disparities between rich and poor, the influx of cheap and disposable and essentially useless goods from China that are produced under near-slave-like conditions and sold by nonunion labor to people trying to get some shred of meaning from stuff and stuff yields no meaning.

WORKS CITED

Adamowicz, Elza. *Surrealist Collage in Text and Image: Dissecting the Exquisite Corpse.* Cambridge UP, 1998.
Adichie, Chimamanda Ngozi. *Americanah.* Fourth Estate, 2013.
Ahmed, Sara. *The Promise of Happiness.* Duke UP, 2010.
———. *Strange Encounters: Embodied Others in Post-Coloniality.* Routledge, 2000.
Altieri, Charles. *The Particulars of Rapture: An Aesthetics of the Affects.* Cornell UP, 2003.
Anker, Elizabeth S., and Rita Felski, editors. *Critique and Postcritique.* Duke UP, 2017.
Arendt, Hannah. *The Human Condition.* U of Chicago P, 1958.
Armstrong, Isobel. *The Radical Aesthetic.* Blackwell, 2000.
Armstrong, Nancy. "The Affective Turn in Contemporary Literature." *Contemporary Literature,* vol. 55, no. 3, Fall 2014, pp. 441–65.
Bal, Mieke. "Visual Essentialism and the Object of Visual Culture." *Journal of Visual Culture,* vol. 2, no. 5, 2003, pp. 5–32.
Baldwin, James, and Sol Stein. *Native Sons.* Ballantine Books, 2004.
Balzer, David. *Curationism: How Curating Took Over the Art World and Everything Else.* Pluto Press, 2015.

Barthes, Roland. *Camera Lucida*. Hill and Wang, 1981.

Bauman, Zygmunt. *Liquid Times: Living in an Age of Uncertainty*. Polity, 2007.

Beckman, Karen, and Liliane Weissberg. Introduction. *On Writing with Photography*, edited by Beckman and Weissberg, U of Minnesota P, 2013, pp. ix–xviii.

Beeston, Alix. *In and Out of Sight: Modernist Writing and the Photographic Unseen*. Oxford UP, 2018.

Benjamin, Walter. *One Way Street*. Translated by Edmund Jephcott and Kingsley Shorter, NLB, 1979.

Bergson, Henri. *Matter and Memory*. Translated by Nancy Margaret Paul and W. Scott Palmer, Dover, 2004.

Berlant, Lauren. *Cruel Optimism*. Duke UP, 2011.

———. "Structures of Unfeeling: *Mysterious Skin*." *International Journal of Politics, Culture, and Society*, vol. 28, no. 3, 2015, pp. 191–213.

Best, Stephen. *None Like Us: Blackness, Belonging, and Aesthetic Life*. Duke UP, 2018.

Bewes, Timothy. "Reading with the Grain: A New World in Literary Criticism." *differences*, vol. 21, no. 3, 2010, pp. 1–33.

Beyoncé and Jay-Z. "Apes**t - The Carters." *YouTube*, uploaded by Beyoncé, 16 June 2018, www.youtube.com/watch?v=kbMqWXnpXcA.

Biggs, Joanna. "It Could Be Me." *London Review of Books*, vol. 34, no. 2, 24 Jan. 2013, www.lrb.co.uk/v35/n02/joanna-biggs/it-could-be-me.

Blair, Elaine. "Chris Kraus, Female Antihero." *New Yorker*, 21 Nov. 2016, www.newyorker.com/magazine/2016/11/21/chris-kraus-female-antihero.

———. "So This Is How It Works." *London Review of Books*, vol. 37, no. 4, 2015, www.lrb.co.uk/v37/n04/elaine-blair/so-this-is-how-it-works.

Bourriaud, Nicolas. *Relational Aesthetics*. Les Presses Du Reel, 1998.

Brand, Peggy Zeglin. *Beauty Unlimited*. Indiana UP, 2012.

Brinkema, Eugenie. *The Forms of the Affects*. Duke UP, 2014.

Burges, Joel, and Amy J. Elias. "Introduction: Time Studies Today." *Time: A Vocabulary of the Present*, edited by Burges and Elias, New York UP, 2016, pp. 1–32.

Burke, Edmund. *A Philosophical Enquiry into the Origin of Our Ideas of the Sublime and Beautiful: With an Introductory Discourse Concerning Taste; and Several Other Additions*. Cambridge UP, 2014.

Butler, Judith. "Performative Acts and Gender Constitution: An Essay in Phenomenology and Feminist Theory." *Theatre Journal*, vol. 40, no. 4, 1988, pp. 519–31.

Calle, Sophie. Interview with Louise Neri. *Interview*, 7 Mar. 2009, www.interviewmagazine.com/art/sophie-calle.

———. *Suite Venitienne*. Siglio, 2015.

Canales, Jimena. "Clock/Lived." *Time: A Vocabulary of the Present*, edited by Joel Burges and Amy J. Elias, New York UP, 2016, pp. 113–28.

Cartier-Bresson, Henri. "Introduction to *The Decisive Moment*." *Photographers on Photography*, edited by N. Lyons, Prentice Hall, 1966, pp. 41–51.

Cavendish, Margaret. *Observations upon Experimental Philosophy*, edited by Eileen O'Neill, Cambridge UP, 2001.

Chihaya, Sarah. "Slow Burn 1: A Summer of Elena Ferrante's Neapolitan Novels." *Post45*, 22 Jun. 2015, post45.research.yale.edu/2015/06/the-slow-burn-an-introduction/.

Clark, Alex. "Drawn from Life: Why Have Novelists Stopped Making Things Up?" *Guardian*, 23 June 2018, www.theguardian.com/books/2018/jun/23/drawn-from-life-why-have-novelists-stopped-making-things-up.

Clune, Michael. "Make It Vanish." *Postmodern/Postwar—and After: Rethinking American Literature*, edited by Jason Gladstone, Andrew Hoberek, and Daniel Worden, U of Iowa P, 2016, pp. 241–50.

———. *Writing Against Time*. Stanford UP, 2013.

Cohen, Jonathan. "Synesthetic Perception as Continuous with Ordinary Perception, Or, We're all Synesthetes Now." *Sensory Blending: On Synaesthesia and Related Phenomena*, edited by Ophelia Delroy, Oxford UP, 2017.

Cole, Teju. *Blind Spot*. Faber and Faber, 2017.

———. "The Consummate Mahlerian." *Radio Open Source*, 24 Apr. 2014. http://radioopensource.org/teju-cole-the-consummate-mahlerian/.

———. "Disappearing Shanghai." *New Inquiry*, 30 Sep. 2012, thenewinquiry.com/blog/disappearing-shanghai/.

———. *Every Day Is for the Thief*. Random House, 2014.

———. "Google's Macchia." *New Inquiry*, 29 May 2013, thenewinquiry.com/blog/googles-macchia/.

———. Interview with Aaron Bady. *Post45*, 19 Jan. 2015, post45.research.yale.edu/2015/01/interview-teju-cole/.

———. Interview with Charl Blignaut. "Teju Cole: Even Breathing Is a Political Act." *City Press*, 19 Sep. 2013, www.news24.com/Archives/City-Press/Teju-Cole-Even-breathing-is-a-political-act-20150430.

———. Interview with Christopher Bollen. *Interview Magazine*, 21 Mar. 2014, www.interviewmagazine.com/culture/teju-cole/.

———. Interview with Emma Brockes. "Teju Cole: 'Two Drafts of a Tweet?

Insufferable. But When I Tweet I'm Still a Writer.'" *Guardian*, 21 June 2014, www.theguardian.com/culture/2014/jun/21/teju-cole-every-day-thief-interview.

———. Interview with Zack Hatfield. *Artforum*, 12 June 2017, www.artforum.com/interviews/teju-cole-discusses-his-new-book-and-project-68843.

———. Interview with Aleksandar Hemon. *Bomb Magazine*, no. 127, 2014, bombmagazine.org/article/10023/teju-cole.

———. Interview with Max Liu. "Palimpsest City." *3:AM Magazine*, 16 Aug. 2011, www.3ammagazine.com/3am/palimpsest-city/.

———. Interview with Patrick Marschke. "Exploring the 'Irrepressibly Subjective' with Teju Cole." *Liquid Music*, 29 May 2018, www.liquidmusic.org/blog/exploring-the-irrepressibly-subjective-with-teju-cole.

———. Interview with Chelsea Matiash. "Life in Lagos, as Shown in Teju Cole's 'Every Day Is for the Thief.'" *Wall Street Journal*, 30 Apr. 2014, blogs.wsj.com/photojournal/2014/04/30/life-in-lagos-as-shown-in-teju-coles-every-day-is-for-the-thief/.

———. Interview with Paul Morton. "You Can't Avert Your Eyes." *The Millions*, 24 Apr. 2014, www.themillions.com/2014/04/you-cant-avert-your-eyes-the-millions-interviews-teju-cole.html.

———. Interview with Supriya Nair. "Teju Cole: The Voice of the Mind." *Livemint.com*, 30 Dec. 2011, www.livemint.com/Leisure/B1Fzos9jUiB3EI31eocl5O/Teju-Cole--The-voice-of-the-mind.html.

———. Interview with Guy Somerset. *Listener*, 1 June 2012, www.listener.co.nz/culture/books/teju-cole-interview-the-long-version/.

———. Interview with Anderson Tepper. *Tin House*. 26 Jan. 2011, https://tinhouse.com/a-conversation-with-teju-cole/.

———. Interview with Kishwer Vikaas. "Teju Cole: A Good Photograph Is Like a Pinprick." *Aerogram* 11 Mar. 2013, theaerogram.com/teju-cole-on-photography/.

———. *Known and Strange Things*. Faber and Faber, 2016.

———. "Known and Strange Songs." *Spotify*, open.spotify.com/user/tejucole/playlist/2rz7L9AVK1Z2oFksrLgYIL?si=dyvsx5L-TcmooiQKb_XMXQ. Accessed 26 Apr. 2019. Playlist.

———. *Open City*. 2010–11, op-cit.tumblr.com.

———. *Open City*. Random House, 2011.

———. "Pitch Forward." *Guernica*, 15 Mar. 2013, www.guernicamag.com/pitch-forward/.

———. "Public Playlists." *Spotify*, open.spotify.com/user/tejucole. Accessed 24 Apr. 2019.

———. "Serious Play." *New York Times Magazine*, 9 Dec. 2015, www.nytimes.com/2015/12/13/magazine/serious-play.html.

Conrad, Peter. Review of *Changing My Mind*, by Zadie Smith. *Guardian*, 15 Nov. 2009, www.theguardian.com/books/2009/nov/15/changing-my-mind-zadie-smith-review.

Cruikshank, Ruth. *Fin de Millénaire French Fiction: The Aesthetics of Crisis*. Oxford UP, 2009.

Culler, Jonathan. *Theory of the Lyric*. Harvard UP, 2015.

d'Adesky, Anne-Christine. Review of *I Love Dick*, by Chris Kraus. *Nation*, 1 June 1998.

Dames, Nicolas. "The Theory Generation." *n+1*, no. 14, Summer 2012, nplusonemag.com/issue-14/reviews/the-theory-generation/.

de Bolla, Peter. *Art Matters*. Harvard UP, 2001.

Deleuze, Gilles, and Félix Guattari. *A Thousand Plateaus: Capitalism and Schizophrenia*. Translated by Brian Masumi, U of Minnesota P, 1987.

Derrida, Jacques. *On Touching—Jean Luc Nancy*. Translated by Christine Irizarry, Stanford UP, 2005.

Dewey, John. *Art as Experience*. 1934. Penguin, 2005.

Díaz, Junot. "MFA vs. POC." *New Yorker*, 30 Apr. 2014, www.newyorker.com/books/page-turner/mfa-vs-poc.

Dickinson, Emily. *Complete Poems*. Faber and Faber, 2016.

Didion, Joan. Interview with Linda Kuehl. *Paris Review*, 74, Fall–Winter 1978, www.theparisreview.org/interviews/3439/the-art-of-fiction-no-71-joan-didion.

Dimock, Wai Chee. *Residues of Justice: Literature, Law, Philosophy*. U of California P, 1996.

Dinnen, Zara. *The Digital Banal: New Media and American Literature and Culture*. Columbia UP, 2018.

Donougho, Martin. "Stages of the Sublime in North America." *MLN*, vol. 115, no. 5, 2000, pp. 904–40.

Duffy, Enda. *The Speed Handbook*. Duke UP, 2009.

Egan, Jennifer. Interview with Zara Dinnen in 2014. "'This Is All Artificial.'" *Post45*, 20 May 2016, post45.research.yale.edu/2016/05/this-is-all-artificial-an-interview-with-jennifer-egan/.

———. *A Visit from the Goon Squad*. Corsair, 2011.

Elias, Amy J. "The Dialogical Avant-Garde: Relational Aesthetics and Time Ecologies in *Only Revolutions* and *TOC*." *Contemporary Literature*, vol. 53, no. 4, 2012, pp. 738–78.

———. "Past/Future." *Time: A Vocabulary of the Present*, edited by Joel Burges and Amy J. Elias, New York UP, 2016, pp. 35–50.

———. "Postmodern Metafiction." *Cambridge Companion to American Fiction after 1945*, edited by John N. Duvall, Cambridge UP, 2011, pp. 13–29.

Elkins, James. *The Object Stares Back: On the Nature of Seeing*. Simon and Schuster, 1996.

Elsner, Jaś. "Art History as Ekphrasis." *Art History*, vol. 33, no. 1, 2010, pp. 10–27.

Felski, Rita. "The Invention of Everyday Life." *New Formations*, no. 39, 1999, pp. 13–31.

———. *The Limits of Critique*. U of Chicago P, 2015.

Forster, E. M. *Howard's End*. Penguin, 2012.

Foster, Hal. *Design and Crime: And Other Diatribes*. Verso, 2002.

Fuentes, Carlos. Introduction. *Henri Cartier-Bresson: Mexican Notebooks*. Thames and Hudson, 1996, pp. 1–11.

Garber, Marjorie. *Academic Instincts*. Princeton UP, 2001.

Garcia, Cristina. "Revolutions Per Minute." Review of *The Flamethrowers*, by Rachel Kushner. *New York Times*, 26 Apr. 2013, www.nytimes.com/2013/04/28/books/review/rachel-kushners-flamethrowers.html.

Gasiorek, Andrzej, and David James. "Introduction: Fiction since 2000: Postmillennial Commitments." *Contemporary Literature*, vol. 53, no. 4, 2012, pp. 609–27.

Glass, Loren, editor. *After the Program Era*. U of Iowa P, 2017.

Goldman, Alvin I. "Two Routes to Empathy: Insights from Cognitive Neuroscience." *Empathy: Philosophical and Psychological Perspectives*, edited by Amy Coplan and Peter Goldie. Oxford UP, 2011, pp. 31–44.

Gould, Emily. "I Love Dick: The Book about Relationships Everyone Should Read." *Guardian*, 2 Nov. 2015, www.theguardian.com/lifeandstyle/2015/nov/02/i-love-dick-sex-chris-kraus-men-women-book.

Greenwald Smith, Rachel. *Affect in the Age of Neoliberalism*, Cambridge UP, 2015.

———. "Six Propositions on Compromise Aesthetics." *Postmodern/Postwar—and After: Rethinking American Literature*, edited by Jason Gladstone, Andrew Hoberek, and Daniel Worden, U of Iowa P, 2016, pp. 181–98.

Grethlein, Jonas. "Aesthetic Experiences, Ancient and Modern." *New Literary History*, vol. 46, no. 2, 2015, pp. 309–33.

Grifi, Alberto, director. *Anna*. 1975.

Gumbrecht, Hans Ulrich. "Aesthetic Experience in Everyday Worlds:

Reclaiming an Unredeemed Utopian Motif." *New Literary History*, vol. 37, no. 2, Spring 2006, pp. 299–318.

Haidu, Rachel. "Transmission/Influence." *Time: A Vocabulary of the Present*, edited by Joel Burgess and Amy J. Elias, New York UP, 2016, pp. 323–36.

Hale, Dorothy. "Aesthetics and the New Ethics: Theorizing the Novel in the Twenty-First Century." *PMLA*, vol. 124, no. 3, 2009, pp. 896–905.

———. "*On Beauty* as Beautiful? The Problem of Novelistic Aesthetics by Way of Zadie Smith." *Contemporary Literature*, vol. 53, no. 4, 2012, pp. 814–44.

Harbach, Chad. "MFA vs. NYC." *n+1*, no. 10, Fall 2010, nplusonemag.com/issue-10/the-intellectual-situation/mfa-vs-nyc/.

Hawkins, Joan. "Smart Art and Theoretical Fictions." *CTheory*, 20 Feb. 2001, journals.uvic.ca/index.php/ctheory/article/view/14880/5775.

Heti, Sheila. *How Should a Person Be?* Vintage, 2010.

———. Interview with John Barber. "How Should a Novel Be? Don't Ask Sheila Heti." *Globe and Mail*, 13 Apr. 2013, www.theglobeandmail.com/arts/books-and-media/book-reviews/how-should-a-novel-be-dont-ask-sheila-heti/article11134050/.

———. Interview with Thessaly La Force. "Sheila Heti on *How Should a Person Be?*" *Paris Review*, 18 June 2018, www.theparisreview.org/blog/2012/06/18/sheila-heti-on-how-should-a-person-be/.

———. Interview with Erica Schwiegershausen. "Sheila Heti on Bringing Her Play Back from the Dead." *The Cut*, 20 Feb. 2015, www.thecut.com/2015/02/sheila-heti-brought-her-play-back-from-the-dead.html.

———. *Ticknor*. Picador, 2007.

Higgins, Dick. *Horizons*. Ubu Editions, 2007.

Hoberek, Andrew, et al. "Postmodern, Postwar, Contemporary: A Dialogue on the Field." *Postmodern/Postwar—and After: Rethinking American Literature*, edited by Jason Gladstone, Hoberek, and Daniel Worden, U of Iowa P, 2016, pp. 28–56.

Honoré, Carl. *In Praise of Slow: How a Worldwide Movement Is Challenging the Cult of Speed*. Orion, 2005.

Hornby, Louise. *Still Modernism: Photography, Literature, Film*. Oxford UP, 2017.

Huehls, Mitchum. "The Post-Theory Theory Novel." *Contemporary Literature*, vol. 56, no. 2, 2015, pp. 280–310.

Hume, David. "Of the Standard of Taste." *Essays: Moral, Political, and Literary*. Cosimo Classics, 2007, pp. 231–57.

Hungerford, Amy. *Making Literature Now*. Stanford UP, 2016.

Hustvedt, Siri. *The Blazing World*. Sceptre, 2014.

———. Foreword. *Blind Spot*, by Teju Cole, Faber, 2017, pp. ix–xvi.
———. *Living, Thinking, Looking*. Sceptre, 2012.
———. *Mysteries of the Rectangle*. Princeton Architectural Press, 2005.
———. *What I Loved*. Sceptre, 2003.
———. *A Woman Looking at Men Looking at Women: Essays on Art, Sex, and the Mind*. Sceptre, 2016.
Iverson, Margaret. "Analogue: On Zoe Leonard and Tacita Dean." *Critical Inquiry*, vol. 38, no. 4, 2012, pp. 796–818.
Iyer, Pico. Afterword. *Violet Isle*, by Alex Webb and Rebecca Norris Webb, Radius, 2009.
Jackson, Sarah. *Tactile Poetics: Touch and Contemporary Writing*. Edinburgh UP, 2015.
James, David. *Discrepant Solace*. Oxford UP, 2019.
———. "In Defense of Lyrical Realism." *Diacritics*, vol. 45, no. 4, 2017, pp. 68–91.
———. "Integrity after Metafiction." *Twentieth-Century Literature*, vol. 57, nos. 3–4, Fall/Winter 2011, pp. 492–515.
———. *Modernist Futures: Innovation and Inheritance in the Contemporary Novel*. Cambridge UP, 2012.
———. "A Renaissance for the Crystalline Novel?" *Contemporary Literature*, vol. 53, no. 4, 2012, pp. 845–74.
James, Henry. *The Art of Criticism: Henry James on the Theory and the Practice of Fiction*, edited by William Veeder and Susan M. Griffin, U of Chicago P, 1986.
———. "The Art of Fiction." *Partial Portraits*. London: Macmillan, 1894, pp. 378–408. Originally published in 1884.
James, William. *Essays in Radical Empiricism*. Dover, 2003.
———. "Habit." *The Heart of William James*. Harvard UP, 2003, pp. 101–12.
Jameson, Fredric. "The Aesthetics of Singularity." *New Left Review*, vol. 92, 2015, pp. 101–32.
———. *Postmodernism, or, The Cultural Logic of Late Capitalism*. Duke UP, 1991.
———. *A Singular Modernity: Essay on the Ontology of the Present*. Verso, 2002.
Jamison, Leslie. "This Female Consciousness: On Chris Kraus." *New Yorker*, 9 Apr. 2015, www.newyorker.com/culture/cultural-comment/this-female-consciousness-on-chris-kraus.
Jay, Martin. "Drifting into Dangerous Waters: The Separation of Aesthetic Experience from the Work of Art." *Aesthetic Subjects*, edited by Pamela R. Matthews and David McWhirter, U of Minnesota P, 2003, pp. 3–27.

Joyce, James. *A Portrait of the Artist as a Young Man*. Oxford UP, 2000.

Keen, Suzanne. *Empathy and the Novel*. Oxford UP, 2007.

Kelly, Adam. "Formally Conventional Fiction." *American Literature in Transition: 2000–2010*, edited by Rachel Greenwald Smith, Cambridge UP, 2017, pp. 46–60.

———. "The New Sincerity." *Postmodern/Postwar—and After: Rethinking American Literature*, edited by Jason Gladstone, Andrew Hoberek, and Daniel Worden, U of Iowa P, 2016, pp. 197–208.

Killing Eve. HBO, 2018–19.

Knausgård, Karl Ove. *A Death in the Family*, translated by Don Bartlett, Vintage, 2012.

———. Interview with Steven Gale. *Sydney Writers Festival*, July 22, 2013.

———. Interview with James Wood. "Writing *My Struggle*." *Paris Review*, vol. 211, 2014, pp. 73–86.

Koepnick, Lutz. *On Slowness: Toward an Aesthetics of the Contemporary*. Columbia UP, 2014.

Konstantinou, Lee. *Cool Characters: Irony and American Fiction*. Harvard UP, 2016.

Kraus, Chris. *Aliens & Anorexia*. Semiotext(e), 2000.

———. *I Love Dick*. 1997. Serpent's Tail, 2016.

———. Interview with Denise Frimer. *Brooklyn Rail*, 10 Apr. 2006, brooklynrail.org/2006/04/art/chris-kraus-in-conversation-with-denise-frimer.

———. Interview with Jeni Fulton. *Sleek*, no. 53, 5 May 2017, www.sleek-mag.com/2017/05/05/chris-kraus-interview-i-love-dick/.

———. Interview with Sheila Heti. *Believer*, no. 101, 1 Sept. 2013, believermag.com/an-interview-with-chris-kraus/.

———. Interview with Emma Holton. "Chris Kraus Interview: Changing Lives." Aug. 2013. *YouTube*, uploaded by Louisiana Channel, 13 Sep. 2017, www.youtube.com/watch?v=pa-pG9UCTyI.

———. Interview with Julie Phillips. "The Art of Losing: A Talk with Chris Kraus." *Julie Phillips*, 15 Jul. 2016, www.julie-phillips.com/wp/?p=879.

———. Interview with Anna Poletti. *Contemporary Women's Writing*, vol. 10, no. 1, 2016, pp. 123–35.

———. *Video Green: Los Angeles Art and the Triumph of Nothingness*. Semiotext(e), 2004.

———. "What Women Say to One Another: Sheila Heti's 'How Should a Person Be?'" *LA Review of Books*, 18 June 2012, lareviewofbooks.org/article/

what-women-say-to-one-another-sheila-hetis-how-should-a-person-be/.
Kraus, Chris, and Sarah Gubbins. "Infatuation Is a Gateway Drug to Writing." Interview with Ruby Brunton. *Hazlitt*, 11 May 2017, hazlitt.net/feature/infatuation-gateway-drug-writing-interview-chris-kraus-and-sarah-gubbins.
Kushner, Rachel. "The Flamethrowers." *Paris Review*, no. 203, Winter 2012, www.theparisreview.org/art-photography/6197/the-flamethrowers-rachel-kushner.
———. *The Flamethrowers*. Vintage, 2013.
———. Interview with Jesse Barron. "Insurrection." *Paris Review*, 3 Apr. 2013, www.theparisreview.org/blog/2013/04/03/insurrection-an-interview-with-rachel-kushner/.
———. Interview with Jess Cotton. "Voiceless Voices." *Quietus*, 3 Feb. 2014, thequietus.com/articles/14407-rachel-kushner-the-flamethrowers-interview.
———. Interview with Matthew Hart and Alexandra Rocca. *Contemporary Literature*, vol. 56, no. 2, 2015, pp. 192–215.
———. Interview with Eben Shapiro. "Rachel Kushner on Art vs. Writing." *Wall Street Journal*, 18 May 2014, www.wsj.com/articles/rachel-kushner-on-art-vs-writing-1401295445.
———. *The Mars Room*. Jonathan Cape, 2018.
———. "Women in Revolt: Alberto Grifi and Massimo Sarchielli's *Anna*." *Artforum*, Nov. 2012, www.artforum.com/print/201209/woman-in-revolt-alberto-grifi-and-massimo-sarchielli-s-anna-36151.
Lebrecht, Norman. *Why Mahler?* Faber and Faber, 2011.
Ledbury, Mark. "Introduction: Compelling Fictions." *Fictions of Art History*, edited by Mark Ledbury, Sterling and Francine Clark Art Institute, 2013.
Lee, Vernon. *The Beautiful: An Introduction to Psychological Aesthetics*. Cambridge UP, 1913.
Leighton, Angela. "Lyric and the Lyrical." *The Cambridge History of Victorian Literature*, edited by Kate Flint, Cambridge UP, 2012, pp. 149–71.
———. *On Form: Poetry, Aestheticism, and the Legacy of a Word*. Oxford UP, 2007.
Lerner, Ben. "Actual World." *Frieze Magazine*, no. 156, June 2013, www.frieze.com/issue/article/actual-world/.
———. "Each Cornflake." Review of *My Struggle*, vol. 3, *Boyhood Island*, by Karl Ove Knausgaard, translated by Don Bartlett. *London Review of Books*, May 2014, www.lrb.co.uk/v36/n10/ben-lerner/each-cornflake.
———. "The Golden Vanity," *New Yorker*, 18 June 2012, www.newyorker.com/magazine/2012/06/18/the-golden-vanity.

———. *The Hatred of Poetry*. FSG, 2016.

———. Interview with Christopher Bollen. *Interview Magazine*, 4 Sep. 2014, www.interviewmagazine.com/culture/ben-lerner.

———. Interview with Cyrus Console. "A Portrait of the Artist as a Young Man in the Age of Spectacle." *Molossus*, 2 Sep. 2011, www.molossus.co/prose/fiction/a-portrait-of-the-artist-as-a-young-man-in-the-age-of-spectacle-ben-lerner-in-conversation-with-cyrus-console/. Accessed 1 Feb. 2013.

———. Interview with Jonathan Derbyshire. "The Books Interview." *New Statesman*, 8 Aug. 2012, www.newstatesman.com/culture/culture/2012/08/books-interview-ben-lerner.

———. Interview with Adam Fitzgerald. *Bomb Magazine*, Sep. 2011. bombsite.com/issues/999/articles/6081. Accessed in 2012.

———. Interview with Ted Hodgkinson. *Granta*, no. 120, 9 Jul. 2012, granta.com/interview-ben-lerner/.

———. Interview with Aaron Kunin. *Jacket Magazine*, no. 37, 2009, jacketmagazine.com/37/iv-kunin-ivb-lerner.shtml.

———. Interview with Tao Lin. *Believer Magazine*, 1 Sep. 2012, believermag.com/an-interview-with-ben-lerner/.

———. Interview with Jessica Loudis. *Book Forum*, 15 Sep. 2011, www.bookforum.com/interview/8321.

———. Interview with Ariana Reines. *Bomb Magazine*, no. 129, 1 Oct. 2014, bombmagazine.org/article/10101/ben-lerner-ariana-reines.

———. Interview with Gayle Rogers. *Contemporary Literature*, vol. 54, no. 2, 2013, pp. 219–38.

———. Interview with Karl Smith. "Time Is a Flat Circle." *Quietus*, 8 Feb. 2015, thequietus.com/articles/17190-ben-lerner-interview-1004-leaving-atocha-station-poetry-time-knausgaard.

———. *Leaving the Atocha Station*. Coffee House Press, 2011.

———. *The Lichtenberg Figures*. Copper Canyon Press, 2004.

———. *Mean Free Path*. Copper Canyon Press, 2010.

———. *10:04*. Faber and Faber, 2014.

———. "A Trace of a Trace: The Framing of Art and Life in Rachel Kushner's *The Flamethrowers*." *Frieze*, 18 Oct. 2013, frieze.com/article/trace-trace.

Levasseur, Jennifer. "Image, Identity, and Sex." *Sydney Morning Herald*, 15 Mar. 2014, www.smh.com.au/entertainment/books/image-identity-and-sex-20140313-34nal.html.

Levine, Caroline. *Forms: Whole, Rhythm, Hierarchy, Network*. Princeton UP, 2017.

———. "'The Strange Familiar': Structure, Infrastructure, and Adichie's *Americanah*." *MFS*, vol. 61, no. 4, Winter 2015, pp. 587–605.

Levinson, Jerrold. *Contemplating Art*. Oxford UP, 2006.

Levy, Ellen. *Criminal Ingenuity: Moore, Cornell, Ashbery, and the Struggle between the Arts*. Oxford UP, 2011.

LeWitt, Sol. "Paragraphs on Conceptual Art." *Artforum*, vol. 5, no. 10, 1967, www.artforum.com/print/196706/paragraphs-on-conceptual-art-36719.

Lorenz, Taylor. "The Instagram Aesthetic is Over." *Atlantic*, 23 Apr. 2019, www.theatlantic.com/technology/archive/2019/04/influencers-are-abandoning-instagram-look/587803/.

Love, Heather. *Feeling Backward*. Harvard UP, 2009.

———. "Truth and Consequences: On Paranoid Reading and Reparative Reading." *Criticism*, vol. 52, no. 2, 2010, pp. 234–41.

Maclagan, David. *Psychological Aesthetics: Painting, Feeling, and Making Sense*. Jessica Kingsley Publishers, 2001.

Marcus, Greil. *Lipstick Traces: A Secret History of the Twentieth Century*. Harvard UP, 1990.

Marinetti, F. T. "The Founding and Manifesto of Futurism," translated by R. W. Flint. *Documents of 20th Century Art: Futurist Manifestos*, edited by Umbro Apollonio, Viking, 1973.

Marks, Lawrence E. "Synesthesia, Then and Now." *Sensory Blending: On Synaesthesia and Related Phenomena*, edited by Ophelia Deroy, Oxford UP, 2017, pp. 9–39.

Massumi, Brian. *Parables for the Virtual: Movement, Affect, Sensation*. Duke UP, 2002.

Matz, Jesse. "Aesthetic/Prosthetic." *Time: A Vocabulary of the Present*, edited by Joel Burges and Amy J. Elias, New York UP, 2016, pp. 225–39.

———. "The Art of Time, Theory to Practice." *Narrative*, vol. 19, no. 3, 2011, pp. 273–94.

Maughan, Philip. "A Neon Rubik's Cube of a Novel, Designed for Our Economic Age: *10:04* by Ben Lerner." *New Statesman*, 15 May 2015, www.newstatesman.com/culture/2015/01/neon-rubik-s-cube-novel-designed-our-economic-age-1004-ben-lerner.

McCarthy, Tom. Interview with Matthew Hart, Aaron Jaffe, and Jonathan Eburne. *Contemporary Literature*, vol. 54, no. 4, 2013, pp. 656–82.

———. *Satin Island*. Knopf, 2015.

———. *Transmission and the Individual Remix: How Literature Works*. Vintage Digital, 2012. Kindle edition.

———. "Writing Machines: Tom McCarthy on Realism and the Real." *London Review of Books*, vol. 36. no. 24, 18 Dec. 2014, www.lrb.co.uk/v36/n24/tom-mccarthy/writing-machines.

McGurl, Mark. *The Novel Art: Elevations of American Fiction after Henry James*. Princeton UP, 2001.

———. "The Novel's Forking Path." *Public Books*, 1 Apr. 2015, www.publicbooks.org/the-novels-forking-path/.

———. *The Program Era*. Harvard UP, 2009.

Michaels, Walter Benn. *The Beauty of a Social Problem: Photography, Autonomy, Economy*. U of Chicago P, 2015.

———. "On Photography and Politics." *Nonsite*, no. 2, 12 June 2011, nonsite.org/issues/issue-2/interview-with-walter-benn-michaels-on-photography-and-politics.

Mishra, Pankaj. "Modernity's Undoing." Review of *A Visit from the Goon Squad*, by Jennifer Egan. *London Review of Books*, vol. 33, no. 7, 2011, www.lrb.co.uk/v33/n07/pankaj-mishra/modernitys-undoing.

Mitchell, W. J. T. *Image Science: Iconology, Visual Culture and Media Aesthetics*. U of Chicago P, 2015.

———. *Picture Theory: Essays on Verbal and Visual Representation*. U of Chicago P, 1994.

———. *What Do Pictures Want?* Princeton UP, 2004.

Moshfegh, Ottessa. *My Year of Rest and Relaxation*. Jonathan Cape, 2018.

Muhammad, Ismail. "Second Sight." Review of *Blind Spot*, by Teju Cole. *Slate*, 15 June 2017, www.slate.com/articles/arts/books/2017/06/teju_cole_s_blind_spot_reviewed.html.

Nehamas, Alexander. *Only a Promise of Happiness: The Place of Beauty in a World of Art*. Princeton UP, 2010.

Nemerov, Alexander. "Coda." *Panorama*, vol. 1, no. 1, 2015, editions.lib.umn.edu/panorama/wp-content/uploads/sites/14/2015/01/Nemerov_Coda.pdf.

Nelson, Maggie. Interview with Brandon Stosuy. *Creative Independent*, 29 Dec. 2016, thecreativeindependent.com/people/interview-maggie-nelson/.

Ngai, Sianne. Interview with Adam Jasper. *Cabinet*, no. 43, Fall 2011, www.cabinetmagazine.org/issues/43/jasper_ngai.php.

———. *Our Aesthetic Categories: Zany, Cute, Interesting*. Harvard UP, 2012.

———. *Ugly Feelings*. Harvard UP, 2005.

Norris Webb, Rebecca, and Alex Webb. Interview with Teju Cole. "Slant Rhymes." *New Yorker*, 11 Aug. 2014, www.newyorker.com/culture/photo-booth/slant-rhymes-alex-webb-rebecca-norris-webb-memory-city.

———. *Slant Rhymes*. Fabrica, 2017.

Nusbaum, Emily, and Paul J. Silvia. "Unusual Aesthetic States." *Cambridge Handbook of the Psychology of Aesthetics and the Arts*, edited by Pablo P. L. Tinio and Jeffrey K. Smith, Cambridge UP, 2014.

O'Connell, Mark. "Escaping the Novel." *Slate*, 6 Apr. 2014, www.slate.com/articles/arts/books/2014/04/teju_cole_s_every_day_is_for_the_thief_reviewed.html.

Olin, Margaret. *Touching Photographs*. U of Chicago P, 2011.

O'Neill, Paul. *The Culture of Curating and the Curating of Culture(s)*. MIT Press, 2012.

Otter, Samuel. "An Aesthetics in All Things." *Representations*, vol. 104, no. 1, 2008, pp. 116–25.

Pater, Walter. *Appreciations with an Essay on Style*. Macmillan, 1895.

Pressman, Jessica. *Digital Modernism: Making It New in New Media*. Oxford UP, 2014.

Prinz, Jesse. "Emotion and Aesthetic Value." *The Aesthetic Mind*, edited by Elisabeth Schellekens and Peter Goldie, Oxford UP, 2011, pp. 71–88.

Rancière, Jacques. *Aesthetics and Its Discontents*. Translated by Steven Corcoran, Polity, 2009.

———. *Dissensus: On Politics and Aesthetics*. Translated by Steven Corcoran, Continuum, 2010.

———. "Notes on the Photographic Image." Translated by Darian Meacham, *Radical Philosophy*, vol. 156, 2009, pp. 8–15.

———. *Politics of Aesthetics*. Translated by Gabriel Rockhill, Continuum, 2005.

Roach, Rebecca. *Literature and the Rise of the Interview*. Oxford UP, 2018.

Ryan, Judith. *The Novel After Theory*. Columbia UP, 2014.

Scarry, Elaine. *Dreaming by the Book*. Princeton UP, 2001.

———. *On Beauty and Being Just*. Gerald Duckworth, 2006.

Schnapp, Jeffrey T. "Crash (Speed as Engine of Individuation)." *Modernism/modernity*, vol. 6, no. 1, 1999, pp. 1–38.

Sebald, W. G. Interview with Christian Scholz. "But the Written Word Is Not a True Document." *Searching for Sebald: Photography after W.G. Sebald*, edited by Lisa Patt and Chris Dillbohner, ICI Press, 2007, pp. 104–09.

Sedgwick, Eve Kosofsky. *Novel Gazing: Queer Readings in Fiction*. Duke UP, 1997.

Serpell, C. Namwali. *Seven Modes of Uncertainty*. Harvard UP, 2014.

Shaw, Philip. *The Sublime*. Routledge, 2006.

Sheldon, Ashley. *Unmaking Love: The Contemporary Novel and the Impossibility of*

Union. Columbia UP, 2017.

Shklovsky, Viktor. "Art as Device." Translated by Alexandra Berlina. *Poetics Today*, vol. 36, no. 3, 2015, pp. 151–74.

———. *Theory of Prose*. Translated by Benjamin Sher, Dalkey Archive Press, 1990.

Silverman, Kaja. *The Miracle of Analogy, or the History of Photography, Part 1*. Stanford UP, 2015.

"Slow Burn." *Post45*. 2015–18, post45.research.yale.edu/sections/contemporaries/slowburn/.

Smith, Adam. *The Theory of Moral Sentiments*. London, 1759. Accessed in Eighteenth Century Collections Online.

Smith, Terry. *Thinking Contemporary Curating*. Independent Curators International, 2012.

Smith, Zadie. "Crazy They Call Me." *Jerry Dantzic: Billie Holiday at Sugar Hill*, edited by Grayson Dantzic, Thames and Hudson, 2017, pp. 7–12.

———. "Fail Better." *Guardian*, 13 Jan. 2007, faculty.sunydutchess.edu/oneill/failbetter.htm. Accessed 1 Feb. 2013.

———. *Feel Free*. Hamish Hamilton, 2018.

———. "I Have a Very Chaotic Mind." *Guardian*, 21 Jan. 2018, www.theguardian.com/books/2018/jan/21/zadie-smith-you-ask-the-questions-self-doubt.

———. Interview with Cressida Leyshon. "This Week in Fiction: Zadie Smith on Inhabiting the World of Billie Holiday." *New Yorker*, 27 Feb. 2017, www.newyorker.com/books/page-turner/fiction-this-week-zadie-smith-2017-03-06.

———. "Love, Actually." *Guardian*, 31 Oct. 2003, www.theguardian.com/books/2003/nov/01/classics.zadiesmith.

———. *NW*. Hamish Hamilton, 2012.

———. *On Beauty*. Hamish Hamilton, 2005.

———. "Read Better." *Guardian*, 20 Jan. 2007. www.sissevres.org/en/the-limits-of-fiction-part-2.html.

———. *Swing Time*. Penguin, 2016.

———. "Two Directions for the Novel." *Changing My Mind*, Penguin, 2011, pp. 71–96.

———. "Two Paths for the Novel." *New York Review of Books*, 20 Nov. 2008, www.nybooks.com/articles/2008/11/20/two-paths-for-the-novel/.

Soloway, Jill, director. *I Love Dick*. Amazon, 2017.

Sontag, Susan. *Against Interpretation*. Penguin, 2009.

———. *On Photography*. Penguin, 1979.

———. *Regarding the Pain of Others*. Picador, 2003.

Stewart, Susan. "Rhyme and Freedom." *The Sound of Poetry / The Poetry of Sound*, edited by Marjorie Perloff and Craig Dworkin, U of Chicago P, 2009, pp. 29–48.

Strombeck, Andrew. "The Post-Fordist Motorcycle: Rachel Kushner's *The Flamethrowers* and the 1970s Crisis in Fordist Capitalism." *Contemporary Literature*, vol. 56, no. 3, 2015, pp. 450–75.

Swann, Maxine. "I Love Dick on Television Marks the Rise of the Female Loser." *Guardian*, 11 May 2017, www.theguardian.com/tv-and-radio/2017/may/11/i-love-dick-amazon-tv-chris-kraus-kathryn-hahn.

Titlestad, Michael. "Jazz Bodies: In Process, on Trial and Instrumental." *Journal of Literary Studies*, vol. 16, no. 2, 2000, pp. 1–22.

Turner, Jenny. "Thanks for Being Called Dick." *London Review of Books*, vol. 37, no. 24, 2015, pp. 35–38.

Walls, Seth Colter. "Blindspot by Vijay Iyer and Teju Cole—Evoking an Ugly America." *Guardian*, 14 Mar. 2016, www.theguardian.com/music/2016/mar/14/blindspot-vijay-iyer-teju-cole-review-ugly-america.

Walsh, Joanna. "A Cult Feminist Classic Makes Its UK Debut." Review of *I Love Dick*, by Chris Kraus, *Guardian*, 11 Nov. 2015, www.theguardian.com/books/2015/nov/11/i-love-dick-chris-kraus-review.

Walz, Robin. *Pulp Surrealism*. U of California P, 2000.

Waters, William. *Poetry's Touch: On Lyric Address*. Cornell UP, 2003.

Weil, Simone. *Gravity and Grace*. Routledge, 2002.

Wolff, Janet. *The Aesthetics of Uncertainty*. Columbia UP, 2008.

Wood, James. "Human, All Too Inhuman." *New Republic*, 24 July 2000, newrepublic.com/article/61361/human-inhuman.

———. "True Lives." Review of *How Should a Person Be?*, by Sheila Heti. *New Yorker*, 25 June 2012, www.newyorker.com/magazine/2012/06/25/true-lives-2.

Wood, Michael. *Literature and the Taste of Knowledge*. Cambridge UP, 2009.

Wu, Yung-Hsing. "Doing Things with Ethics: *Beloved*, *Sula*, and the Reading of Judgment." *Modern Fiction Studies*, vol. 49, no. 4, 2003, pp. 780–805.

INDEX

9/11, 42, 71, 169–170
10:04 (Lerner), 137–150, 164–166; and fragmentation, 140–146; and images, 162–166; and the lyric, 146–150; and mediacy, 141–144; and time, 138–139, 143

Acker, Kathy, 110–111
Adams, Robert, 58
Adichie, Chimamanda Ngozi, 43–44
aesthetic experience, 3–4, 8, 22, 29; and affect, 37; and anxiety, 166; and crying, 10, 47, 53, 101; demediation of, 137; democratization of, 52–54; and description, 40; and ethics, 17, 18, 20–21; as exhaustion, 3–4, 32, 42, 44; and form, 13–17; and literary style, 17, 20; and music, 8–9, 13–16, 78–84; as negative, 5–8; and the political, 17, 18, 168–171; and speechlessness, 31–33, 56; and time, 5–6, 65. *See also* aestheticization; beauty; sublime, the
aesthetic subject, 3–4, 19, 29, 55, 65
aestheticization, xv, 1–3, 5, 8, 17, 21, 74, 160; literary, 18, 42
affect, 6, 21, 23, 29–30; absence of, 71–75; and aesthetic experience, 37, 46–50; and estrangement, 52; and perception, 32; touch and, 93–94, 101–105
afterimage, 12, 36, 56, 109; as reading, 109
Aliens & Anorexia (Kraus), 8–9, 120, 128; and failure, 130–131
Altieri, Charles, 20
ambivalence, 7, 26, 35, 90

Americanah (Adichie), 43–44
The Anatomy Lesson of Dr. Nicolaes Tulp (Rembrandt), 37–38
anti-sublimity, 110
"Apeshit" (Beyoncé and Jay-Z), 1–2
Arendt, Hannah, xiii, 5, 19
Aristotle, 49
art novel, xii, xv, 21–22, 29
aura, 4, 86
autocritique, 23–24
autofiction, 111, 146, 162

Baldwin, James, 1, 61
Barthes, Roland, 66–69
beautiful, the: aesthetic judgement of, 41–42, 56, 63, 69, 70, 84, 133, 141; and photography, 70, 88
beautiful/sublime index, 3–5
beauty: and art, 120; experience of, 5, 10–12, 141; and the novel, 44–45; and politics, 70, 169; the pursuit of, 6, 132–133
Benjamin, Walter, 4, 66–67, 139, 164
Bergson, Henri, 36–38
Beyoncé and Jay-Z, 1–2, 4
The Blazing World, (Hustvedt), 19, 94–100, 122
Blind Spot (Cole), 59, 86–88
boredom, xiv, 33, 52–53, 110
born-digital, the, 85–90
Bosch, Hieronymus, 21
Bourgeois, Louise, 95–96
Brewster, John, 65–66, 76

Calle, Sophie, 121
Cartier-Bresson, Henri, 66–67
Cavendish, Margaret, 99
Chardin, Jean-Baptiste-Siméon, 101–103

The Clock (Marclay), 138–140, 143, 156
Cole, Teju, 18, 26, 57–90, 93, 100, 161, 168; and collaboration, 58–59; and Dutch Enlightenment, 62–63; and ethics, 60–62, 88; Instagram practice, 85–90; and the lyric, 58, 63; as performance artist, 58; and photography, 58–59, 63, 69–71; and reading, 64; and theory, 22–23. See also *Blind Spot*; *Every Day is for the Thief*; *Open City*
consolation, 38, 41–42; in art, 118; and music, 79, 81–84
contemporary fiction: and aesthetic boredom, xiv; and anxiety, xiv; and authenticity, xiv; and convention, xiv; and literary culture, xiii–xiv
contemporary women's writing, 122
critique, 23, 25–26, 46; and empathy, 52; with love, 49–50. See also postcritique
curation, 2, 17, 31, 58, 65; and form, 19, 140–142, 144; as practice, 122, 125, 141; as sensibility, 75, 88
curator: figure of, 2
Cusk, Rachel, 121

de Bolla, Peter, 5, 11, 31–32, 77
A Death in the Family (Knausgård), 9–13
Deleuze, Gilles and Félix Guattari, 24, 131
desensitization, 33, 35
Dewey, John, 5
Dickinson, Emily, 66
Didion, Joan, 18
dilation, 135–136
disenchantment, 136

Egan, Jennifer, 13–17, 161. See also *A Visit from the Goon Squad*
ekphrasis, 19, 32, 44–45, 51, 54–56; and ineffability, 32
enchantment, 5, 18, 27, 32, 42, 122, 152
enrapture, 116
enstrangement, 29–30, 31–56; and affect, 52; and art, 33; as "artistic immortality," 55; and the automatic, 38–39; and order, 31; and repetition, 38; as seeing again, 40, 45–46; and writing, 52
"erotics of art" (Sontag), 105
ethics: and aesthetic experience, 17–21; literary, 17–18, 33, 40–46, 60–62, 69–72, 74–76; of viewership, 67–68, 93, 169
Every Day is for the Thief (Cole), 59, 86

failure: as artistic, 127–131; as symmetry, 130–131; as vacillation, 131–133
Feel Free (Smith), 28–50
Felski, Rita, 5–6, 25–27, 106
The Flamethrowers (Kushner), 62, 137, 151–163, 166; art as lived in, 154–156; and blankness, 152–155; and China girls, 153–154, 160; crashing in, 159–160; and images, 161–163; and photography, 151, 156, 159–160; and speed, 156–160; and time, 158–163
Foster, Hal, 2
Frieze Magazine, xi, 22

Gumbrecht, Hans Ulrich, 3–5, 42, 53

habit, 34–35; and aesthetic experience, 37–38; and literary style, 33, 41, 52; as repetition, 33–35, 37–39
Hendrickje Bathing (Rembrandt), 35–36, 55
Heti, Sheila, 18, 109–117, 127–133, 147. See also *How Should a Person Be?*
Hippolyte, Hector, 21; *Maîtresse Erzulie*, 48–49
Hopper, Edward, 21
How Should a Person Be? (Heti), 110; and failure, 128, 131–133; and form, 112–117; reception of, 128
Hume, David, 4
Hustvedt, Siri, 18, 91–108, 122; and art criticism, 105–108; and theory, 22–23. See also *The Blazing World*, *What I Loved*

I Love Dick (Kraus), 109–113, 117–132; and confession, 121–122; and cruelty, 123; and distance, 120; and failure, 127–130; letters in, 117–121, 124, 129; and love, 117–124, 126; reception of, 110–111, 127–128
I Love Dick (Soloway), 119
ineffability, xv, 9, 17, 18, 31–33, 147, 168
inexhaustibility, 9, 12
Instagram, 2–3, 58–59, 85–90
intentionalism, 26–28
intermediality, 16–17, 29, 62, 89, 122, 137, 168; and ethics, 60
Iyer, Vijay, 58

Jacob Wrestling the Angel (Rembrandt), 46–47
James, David, 8, 20, 25, 27, 42
James, Henry, xii

James, William, 34, 54, 82
Jameson, Fredric, 2, 6, 136
Jamison, Leslie, 121, 123
Joyce, James, 32

Knausgård, Karl Ove, 9–13, 121–122, 134, 136–137. See also *A Death in the Family*
Kondo, Marie, 2, 4–5
Kraus, Chris, 18, 109–113, 117–133, 147, 151; and art criticism, 123–127; and theory, 22–23. See also *Aliens & Anorexia*; *I Love Dick*
Kushner, Rachel, 18, 62, 137, 151–163, 166; as art critic, 153–154. See also *The Flamethrowers*

Leaving the Atocha Station (Lerner), 21, 110, 137; images in, 163–164; and mediation, 140
Lerner, Ben, 18, 27, 63, 110, 117, 137–150, 162–166; and theory, 22–23. See also *10:04*; *Leaving the Atocha Station*
LeWitt, Sol, 119
literary style: and cliché, 33–34; and ethics, 42–44; and familiarity, 41, 44–45; as lyrical, 20. See also aesthetic experience; lyrical realism
lyrical address, 144, 147
lyrical realism, 41–44, 63; and aestheticization, 42; and ethics, 42–44; and familiarization, 41, 44
lyrical subject, 63, 65, 144

Mahler, Gustav, 22, 79–84
Maîtresse Erzulie (Hippolyte), 48–49

Marclay, Christian, 22, 138–140, 143, 156
Massumi, Brian, 94
McCarthy, Tom, 28, 137; *Remainder*, 41
McGurl, Mark, xiii, 41
memoir, 111–113
memory-image, 36–37
Merleau-Ponty, Maurice, 93
Mitchell, W. J. T., 59–60
Morrison, Toni, 28
Moshfegh, Ottessa, 169–171. See also *My Year of Rest and Relaxation*
Mozart, Wolfgang, 22, 52–53
Munkácsi, Martin, 66–68
mutual exclusion, xii, 30; art and literature as, 167–68, 171
My Year of Rest and Relaxation (Moshfegh), 169–171; art as things in, 171; images in, 169; and sleep, 170

Nelson, Maggie, xiii
Netherland (O'Neill), 41–42
Ngai, Sianne, 3–4, 6–7, 34–35
Norris Webb Rebecca and Alex Webb, 57–58

Observations upon Experimental Philosophy (Cavendish), 99
On Beauty (Smith), 21, 22, 31–40, 42, 44–50, 52–56; and art history, 32, 47–49; and familiarity, 37–40; and habit, 35; and love, 35–36, 48–50; and music, 52–54; and perspectivalism, 45–46, 56; and sentimentality, 39, 46–50; and speechlessness, 31–32, 56; and uncertainty, 53–54

O'Neill, Joseph, 41–42
Open City (Cole), 19, 22, 59, 64–68, 71–84, 86; and blackness, 76–78; and the digital, 86; and empathy, 75; and ethics, 60–62, 67–72, 74–76; and flat affect, 71–75; and music, 78–84; and photographic aesthetics, 61; and photography, 65–68; and rape, 71–74; and rereading, 73–75; and silence, 65, 72–75; and time, 64–65

perception, 35–36, 39–40; aesthetics of, 45; and affect, 32; as "attentive," 36; decomposition of, 38; and familiarity, 33–34; and form, 13, 16–17; and habit, 33; as a mode of experience, 19–20; and politics, 88; and reading, xv, 19, 27; as reflexive, 36; as repair, 49–50; and synesthesia, 100; and time, 37, 139
photograph, the: as analogy, 57; in crisis, 88; as fragment, 59
photography: and aesthetics of speed, 62; and ethics, 67–71; and indexicality, 57, 62, 70, 160, 162; and the lyrical, 86–88; as negation, 61; and stillness, 62, 67; and time, 64–65
postcritique, 23, 26. See also critique
Pound, Ezra, 40

Rancière, Jacques, 2, 4, 8, 162
reflexive reading, 23–30
Rembrandt van Rijn, 21, 35–38, 45–46
Requiem (Mozart), 52–53
rereading, 73–75

The Sampling Officials of the Drapers' Guild (Rembrandt), 39–40
Seated Nude (Rembrandt), 47
Sebald, W. G., 45, 61, 90
Sedgwick, Eve Kosofsky, 107–108
self-reflexivity, xiv, 8, 23, 27
Shklovsky, Viktor, 33, 37, 55
slant rhyme, 29–30, 57–90; as chiasmus, 57, 60; as echo, 57; as formal relation, 59, 89; as interartistic mode, 57–90; as negation, 60–61
slow reading, 134–137, 161
slowness: as contemporary time, 135–137; as repetition, 137
Smith, Adam, 92
Smith, Kiki, 95
Smith, Zadie, 18, 28, 63, 90, 117, 137, 161; and Billie Holiday, 50–51; and essays, 22, 33, 51–52; and failure, 33, 43; and music, 50–51; and photography, 50; and style, 33–34, 41–44. See also Feel Free; On Beauty; "Two Directions for the Novel"
Sontag, Susan, 68–70, 105–107, 127
speed: aesthetics of, 135–136, 156–160; and modernity, 136; and postmodernity, 136, 158
sublimation, 127, 129, 131
sublime, the: and aesthetic experience, xv, 8–9, 28–29, 34; exhaustion of, 4; and ineffability, 32, 55; and music, 5, 9, 14, 53, 79–81, 83–84; and narration, 110; and the novel, 8–9, 12, 14, 20. See also aesthetic experience
suspension, 29–30, 134–160; as formal rhythm, 161–166

INDEX 199

synesthesia, 29–30, 93–108; as aesthetic mode, 93; as chiasmus, 100–105; as mixing, 94–100; as repair, 105–108

The Theory of Moral Sentiments (A. Smith), 92
thinglyness, xi–xii
touch: and affect, 93–94; and empathy, 92–93; erotics of, 91–93; and mourning, 101–105
transcription, 29–30, 109–133; as aesthetic mode, 112–113; as literary method, 112–117; as form, 116–177, 127
Twitter, 85, 89
"Two Directions for the Novel" (Smith), 18, 41–44

van der Weyden, Rogier, 21
virtuality, xi–xii, 74, 94, 140–141, 144, 163
A Visit from the Goon Squad (Egan), 13–17

Wallace, David Foster, 52
What I Loved (Hustvedt), 21, 91–93, 100–105; and erotics, 91–93, 105; and mourning, 94–95, 101–105; and touch, 91–93
Whitman, Walt, 149–150
Wood, James, xiv, 52, 127
writer-critics, xiii, 52
writing as performance, 111–112, 116, 120, 123, 135

THE NEW AMERICAN CANON

Half a Million Strong: Crowds and Power from Woodstock to Coachella
by Gina Arnold

Violet America: Regional Cosmopolitanism in U.S. Fiction since the Great Depression
by Jason Arthur

The Meanings of J. Robert Oppenheimer
by Lindsey Michael Banco

Neocolonial Fictions of the Global Cold War
edited by Steven Belletto
and Joseph Keith

Workshops of Empire: Stegner, Engle, and American Creative Writing during the Cold War
by Eric Bennett

Places in the Making: A Cultural Geography of American Poetry
by Jim Cocola

The Legacy of David Foster Wallace
edited by Samuel Cohen
and Lee Konstantinou

Race Sounds: The Art of Listening in African American Literature
by Nicole Brittingham Furlonge

Postmodern/Postwar—and After: Rethinking American Literature
edited by Jason Gladstone, Andrew Hoberek, and Daniel Worden

After the Program Era: The Past, Present, and Future of Creative Writing in the University
edited by Loren Glass

Hope Isn't Stupid: Utopian Affects in Contemporary American Literature
by Sean Austin Grattan

It's Just the Normal Noises: Marcus, Guralnick, No Depression, *and the Mystery of Americana Music*
by Timothy Gray

Contemporary Novelists and the Aesthetics of Twenty-First Century American Life
by Alexandra Kingston-Reese

American Unexceptionalism: The Everyman and the Suburban Novel after 9/11
by Kathy Knapp

Visible Dissent: Latin American Writers, Small U.S. Presses, and Progressive Social Change
by Teresa V. Longo

Pynchon's California
edited by Scott McClintock and John Miller

Richard Ford and the Ends of Realism
by Ian McGuire

Poems of the American Empire: The Lyric Form in the Long Twentieth Century
by Jen Hedler Phillis

Reading Capitalist Realism
edited by Alison Shonkwiler and Leigh Claire La Berge

Technomodern Poetics: The American Literary Avant-Garde at the Start of the Information Age
by Todd F. Tietchen

How to Revise a True War Story: Tim O'Brien's Process of Textual Production
by John K. Young